CUTTING EDGE

a practical approach to task-based learning

INTERMEDIATE

STUDENTS' BOOK

LONGMAN

peter moor

Part A Language

Module	Language focus	Vocabulary	Speaking
Module 1 About you **page 6**	1) **Questions and answers** (auxiliary verbs) *Pronunciation:* stressed and weak forms in questions and answers 2) **Present Simple and Continuous**	People around you (*best friend, acquaintance, classmate*, etc.) **Wordspot:** *have* (and *have got*)	**Mini-task:** find five things you have in common with a partner Talk about the changing state of the family
Module 2 Memories **page 17**	1) **Past Simple and Continuous** *Pronunciation:* -ed forms / weak forms of *was, were* 2) **Comparing past and present** (*used to, still, not ... any more / longer*)	Remembering and forgetting (*remember, learn, remind, forget, recognise, lose*) **Wordspot:** *time*	Talk about ways of remembering **Mini-task:** describe an important meeting in your life
Module 3 Around the world **page 26**	1) **Comparatives and superlatives** (*slightly higher than, one of the biggest ... in the world*, etc.) 2) **Comparing things in different ways** (*not as ... as, fewer / less than, similar to*, etc.) *Pronunciation:* /ə/ in comparative phrases	**Wordspot:** *place* Describing towns and cities	Do a geography quiz **Mini-task:** describe similarities and differences between two countries
Module 4 Life stories **page 36**	1) **Present Perfect Simple (and Past Simple)** *Pronunciation:* strong and weak forms of *have* 2) *for, since* and *ago* (and Present Perfect Continuous) *Pronunciation:* weak form of *been* /bɪn/	Life experiences (*leave home, start work, move house*, etc.) **Wordspot:** *get*	**Mini-task:** find three things that you and a partner have both done

Consolidation Modules 1–4 (pages 46–47)

Module	Language focus	Vocabulary	Speaking
Module 5 Making plans **page 48**	1) **Future plans and intentions** (Present Continuous, *will, going to, intend to, due to*, etc.) *Pronunciation:* future forms and phrases 2) **Future clauses with *if, when*,** etc.	**Wordspot:** *work* Training and work (*well-paid, challenging, stressful*, etc.)	Discuss how organised you / people you know are **Mini-task:** talk about the plans and ambitions of friends / family
Module 6 News and media **page 59**	1) **-ing / -ed adjectives** 2) **Passive forms** *Pronunciation:* was /wəz/ and were /wə/ in passive sentences	Television (*advertisements, sports coverage, thrillers*, etc.) **Wordspot:** *by*	**Mini-task:** talk about stories in the news

Part B Task

Reading / Listening	Task	After the task
Reading: *A quiet revoloution?* (the changing state of the family)	**Preparation for task:** listen to people meeting for the first time **Task:** interview another student using a pie-chart (extended speaking)	**Task link:** how you spend your time (*I absolutely love ..., I'm not very good at ...,* etc.) **Real life:** writing an informal letter Do you remember?
Reading: *All in the memory*	**Preparation for task:** listen to two descriptions of childhood memories **Task:** describe a childhood memory (extended speaking and writing)	**Task link:** short questions *Pronunciation:* using intonation to show interest Do you remember?
Listening: geography quiz **Reading:** *Amazing cities!*	**Preparation for task:** listen to recommendations for a tour of Ireland **Task:** plan a tour of your country or region (extended speaking and writing)	**Task link:** recommending and advising *Pronunciation:* intonation for giving recommendations Do you remember?
Reading: *Twin lives*	**Preparation for task:** discuss / read about famous people **Task:** design a set of stamps of famous people (extended speaking and writing)	**Task link:** describing people (*He's the sort of person who ..., She's always ...,* etc.) **Real life:** filling in an application form
Reading: *Quiz – how organised are you?* **Listening:** working in something different (people talking about their jobs)	**Preparation for task:** listen to a conversation describing a job vacancy **Task:** select the best candidate for a job (extended speaking)	**Real life 1:** writing a covering letter **Real life 2:** making a formal telephone call *Pronunciation:* connected speech Do you remember?
Listening: television (people talking about types of television programmes) **Reading:** newspaper articles	**Preparation for task:** listen to radio extracts **Task:** prepare a review or entertainment guide (extended speaking and writing)	**Task link:** 'extreme' adjectives (*brilliant, tragic, furious,* etc.) Do you remember?

Part A **Language**

Part B **Task**

Reading / Listening	Task	After the task
Reading: *Going out around the world*	**Preparation for task:** listen to a description of social customs in Thailand **Task:** draw up a list of tips for visitors to your country (extended speaking and writing)	**Task link:** making generalisations (*Quite a lot of people ... / It is quite common for ... / People tend to ...*, etc.) **Real life:** making a social arrangement Do you remember?
Reading: *How to be a successful inventor*	**Preparation for task:** listen to people describing a personal or ideal possession **Task:** describe a personal or ideal possession (extended speaking and writing)	**Task link:** describing objects (*it's round, made of leather, makes a noise*, etc.) **Real life:** writing 'thank you' letters
Reading: *The Lucky Generation* (life in the year 2050)	**Preparation for task:** listen to appeals for lottery money **Task:** decide how to spend lottery money (extended speaking)	**Task link:** ways of saying numbers **Real life:** dealing with money Do you remember?
Reading and listening: *The Knightsbridge Safe Deposit Robbery*	**Preparation for task:** find objects in pictures telling a story (speaking) **Task:** invent a story using pictures (extended speaking and listening)	**Task link:** adverbs for telling stories (*eventually, surprisingly, strangely*, etc.) Do you remember?
Listening: school rules	**Preparation for task:** read article about controversial laws around the world **Task:** discuss the advantages and disadvantages of different laws (extended speaking)	**Task link:** linking words (*also, although, besides*, etc.) **Real life:** agreeing and disagreeing Do you remember?
	Preparation for task: read letters to a problem page **Task:** find solutions to problems (extended speaking)	**Task link:** verbs to describe behaviour and reactions (*deny, threaten, admit, persuade*, etc.) **Creative writing:** a letter / a story / a soap opera script

Language summary (pages 140–151)   **Irregular verbs** (page 152)   **Tapescripts** (pages 153–167)

module 1

About you

Questions and answers
Present Simple and Continuous
Vocabulary: people around you
Speaking and reading: *A quiet revolution?*
Wordspot: *have* (and *have got*)

Language focus 1

Questions and answers

Mini-task

Work with a partner. Find five things you have in common. Ask about:
– your home / family.
– your job / studies.
– your likes / dislikes.
Then tell the rest of the class about what you discovered.

> Neither of us / Both of us like jazz music.

🖵 [1.1] You will hear ten questions that people might ask you when you first meet. Listen and write answers for yourself. Write notes, not full sentences.

a ....
b ....
c ....
d ....
e ....
f ....
g ....
h ....
i ....
j ....

Analysis

1 **Auxiliary verbs in questions**
a To form questions in English we normally need an auxiliary verb. Use one of the auxiliary verbs below to reconstruct the questions on the cassette. Then listen again and check your answers.

> are is do does have has was were did

b Ask and answer the questions with a partner.

2 **Auxiliary verbs in answers**
The long answers below are not very natural. How can we shorten them using auxiliaries?
a Do you live near here?
Yes, I live near here.
b Do the rest of your family speak English?
My brother speaks English, but my parents don't speak English.

Now read Language summary A on page 140.

Pronunciation

1 **1** 🔲 [1.2] Listen to the following questions and answers and underline the stressed (strong) words.

a Do you <u>live</u> near <u>here</u>?
Yes, <u>actually</u>, I <u>do</u>.
b Did you do anything special last night?
No, I didn't.
c Do you come from Spain?
No, I don't – I come from Argentina.
d Do all your family live here?
My parents and grandparents do, but my sister doesn't any more.

What kind of words are stressed?

2 What happens to the pronunciation of *Do you ...?* and *Did you ...?* at the beginning of the questions? Listen again and repeat, paying attention to the stressed and weak words.

Practice

1 Make questions from the following words. Use the pronoun *you* in each case.

For example:
Where exactly / live?
Where exactly do you live?

a How / get here from your house?
b have / any special reason for learning English?
c How long / be / in this class?
d Whose class / in / last year (term, month)?
e do / anything special last night?
f What sort of music / like?
g all your family / live in the same town as you?

2 Choose one question from above or think of another question of your own to ask each student in the class. Walk around the class and ask each student a different question. Then tell the rest of the class what you discovered.

3 Discuss in pairs what questions you would ask in the following situations.

For example:
You don't know what 'eyebrow' means.
What does 'eyebrow' mean?

a You want to know the English word for
b You don't know how to pronounce a word.
c You don't know how to spell 'eyebrow'.
d You don't know which page the teacher is looking at.
e You want to know what tonight's homework is.
f You didn't hear what the teacher said properly.
g You would like your teacher to write 'paperclip' on the board.

🔲 [1.3] Now listen to the questions and check your answers.

4 Think of some other questions you often need to ask in class. Make a poster for the wall to remind you how to ask these questions.

Part B **Task**

Describe a childhood memory
Task link: short questions

Personal vocabulary

Useful language

Beginning the story
"This all happened about ... years ago ..."

"One day, when I was ..."

Telling the story
"Suddenly ..."

"After a while ..."

"So, anyway ..."

"Then ..."

Ending the story
"So, eventually ..."

"In the end ..."

Listening with interest
"How funny / amazing / sad!"

"Really!"

"Oh no!"

"So, what happened?"

Preparation for task

1 📼 [2.6] You are going to hear two people, Tim and Anna, talking about an important childhood memory. The following 'key' words / phrases are important in one of the two stories. Listen and mark them **T** (Tim's story) or **A** (Anna's story).

•	a big sister	❏	• a chocolate bar	❏
•	Czechoslovakia	❏	• stealing	❏
•	a field	❏	• 1968	❏
•	a rose	❏	• a five-year-old son	❏
•	going shopping	❏	• a half-brother	❏
•	1988	❏	• the police	❏
•	burying	❏	• two little girls	❏

2 Listen again and summarise what happened in pairs, using the 'key' words / phrases above.

Task

1 **a)** Think of an incident that happened to you as a child, or when you were much younger. It could be:
– a time when you did something wrong.
– a time when you tried to do something that went wrong.
– a story about a pet or animal you had as a child.
– a point in your childhood when your life seemed to change.
– a time when you met someone important.

b) Spend 10–15 minutes planning how you will tell your story. Make a note of your 'key' words, and ask your teacher about any words or phrases you need and write them in the *Personal vocabulary* box. Do not write out the story yet.

2 Work in groups. Look at the sentences / phrases in the *Useful language* box opposite. Tell your story to the other students. They should listen and ask questions if they want to. When everyone has told their stories, choose an interesting story from the group to tell to the rest of the class.

Optional writing

Either: write your story out for other students in the class to read.

or: write out your story, then record it onto a cassette for your teacher to listen to and correct.

Task link

Short questions

1 [2.7] Look at what the people in the picture opposite are saying. Can you guess what the second speaker's response is? Listen and complete the gaps.

2 How do the following short questions relate grammatically to the first statements?

- There aren't any scissors here!
  Aren't there?
- The photocopier's broken again.
  Is it?

Now read Language summary D on page 142.

3 [2.8] Respond to the following statements with a short question. Listen and check.

a   Robert isn't here today.
b   How strange – Mrs Glover normally comes in on a Tuesday.
c   Don't do that yourself – the new computer can do it all for you!
d   We all went to see the new office at lunch-time.
e   Chris doesn't like her new boss at all, apparently.
f   Where's my bag? It was here a minute ago!
g   You know what? Liz didn't come back to work after lunch today!
h   Oh no! It's three o'clock already!

Pronunciation

The second speaker uses intonation to show that they are interested:

Isn't he?

Does she?

Listen again and copy the intonation on the cassette.

Do you remember?

①

Complete the gaps with the best form (Past Simple or Continuous) of the verbs in brackets. If there is more than one possibility, explain the difference in meaning.

a) It .... (*snow*) when I .... (*come*) to work this morning.

b) Apparently, Tom and his wife .... (*meet*) while they .... (*be*) on holiday.

c) A fox .... (*come*) into our kitchen while I .... (*cook*) dinner last night!

d) Lucy thinks she .... (*drop*) her purse while she .... (*shop*).

e) Your boss .... (*try*) to call you while you .... (*be*) at your mother's.

f) When Jack .... (*arrive*), Max .... (*go home*).

②

a) What are the Past Simple forms of the following verbs?

- think ....
- sleep ....
- fall ....
- get ....
- grow ....
- wear ....
- bring ....
- read ....
- steal ....
- hide ....

b) Work in pairs. Look at the list of irregular verbs on page 152. Test your partner on the Past Simple form of ten more irregular verbs.

③

How many syllables do the –ed forms below have? Where is the main stress? Put the words into the correct columns, as in the example.

- happened
- closed
- used
- wanted
- remembered
- tried
- started
- decided
- imagined
- invented

A	B	C
●	●●	●●●
	happened	

④

Complete the gaps with a suitable word or phrase.

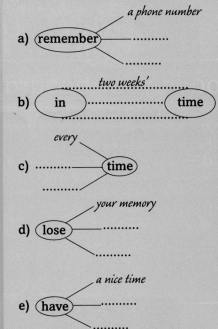

a) remember —— *a phone number* / ....

b) in —— *two weeks'* .... —— time

c) .... / .... —— time *every*

d) lose —— *your memory* / ....

e) have —— *a nice time* / ....

⑤

Look at the following sentences written by foreign learners of English. Which one is wrong?

a) When I was a child, I used to live in the country.

b) Spanish people are used to stay out late at night.

c) Sometimes he used to call me ten times a day – I didn't know what to say!

⑥

Choose the best alternative to complete the following sentences.

a) Trains and buses in this country never leave *in time* / *on time*.

b) Can you *remind me* / *recognise me* to phone Mum later?

c) A: I saw Emma yesterday.
B: *Did you?* / *Have you?*

d) When he died, they *hid him* / *buried him* next to his wife.

e) My brother has *trained* / *learnt* his dog to follow his commands.

⑦

Look back through Module 2 and write two more revision questions of your own to ask other students.

25

Amazing cities!

The oldest ... the biggest ... the most mysterious!

✳ The world's oldest city is Jericho, in the Middle East, which dates back to about 8000 BC. It has been destroyed many times in its history (one such story is described in the Bible), but it has always been rebuilt.

✳ Ancient Rome was the first city in the world to have a population of 1 million. At its height, the entire Roman Empire had a population of 100 million!

[10]

✳ The world's most mysterious cities are to be found in the Indus Valley in modern-day Pakistan. Known as the 'Secret Cities', they are around 4,500 years old, but no one knows who built them or where they disappeared to. Whoever they were, they were so advanced that they invented their own form of writing (at around the same time as the Ancient Egyptians), and built a complete system of drains and plumbing almost two and a half thousand years before they were 'first invented' by the Romans!

Not so modern!

✳ We think of democracy as a modern invention, but in fact the world's most perfect democracy probably existed in Ancient Athens in 500 BC – if you were not a woman or a slave, that is! In the so-called 'Golden Age', all decisions [20] were made by citizens collectively. Even military leaders were elected, and crimes were tried by juries of between 101 and 1001 citizens!

✳ We often imagine that the enormous cities of Asia are a twentieth century phenomenon, but throughout history, they have always been bigger than cities in Europe. Even in 1450, the biggest city in the world was Peking (population [30] 600,000), and most of the other 'top ten' cities were also in

Reading

1 Look at the picture of Ancient Rome above and find **six** things which do not belong there.

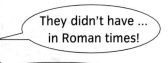

They didn't have ... in Roman times!

... weren't invented until ...!

2 You are going to read an extract from a book of fascinating facts. First check the meaning of the following words and phrases in your mini-dictionary.

> to ban   a jury   welfare
> plumbing and drains   a slave
> smelly   traffic congestion
> a vehicle

3 **Race:** work in pairs. Find the following information in the text as quickly as you can. The first pair to find all the information are the winners.

A two groups of people who didn't have democratic rights in Ancient Greece [ ]

B the first city in the world to have a population of more than 1 million [ ]

C the number of hospitals in medieval Florence [ ]

D the name of the oldest city in the world [ ]

E two incredible inventions made by the civilisation that inhabited the 'Secret Cities' [ ]

F the name of the biggest city in the world in 1450 [ ]

G two 'modern' urban problems that also existed in Ancient Rome [ ]

China. London at the time had a population of just 75,000.

* Tower blocks are not a modern invention either. Buildings over six storeys high existed in many cities in the Middle Ages, and in ancient Rome some blocks were so high that sightseers used to come from the countryside especially to look at them!

* Our typical image of a medieval city `40` is of somewhere smelly and unhealthy! But this is not entirely true – in fact, public services such as bathhouses, drains and hospitals were relatively developed. Medieval Florence, for example, with a population of 90,000, had thirty hospitals with over a thousand beds. Its system of drains was much better than those of many nineteenth century cities! `50`

* Ancient Rome had many of the same urban problems as cities today. Crime was an acute problem – few people dared even to go out after dark for fear of robbers and cut-throats. And even then many of the poor lived on 'welfare' – the Emperor's government regularly distributed bread to more than 200,000 poor people. Traffic congestion is not a new `60` problem either – in the centre of Ancient Rome it was so bad that Julius Caesar had to ban all wheeled vehicles during daylight hours!

4 Read the text again and mark the information (✓) if you already knew this and (!) if you are surprised to discover this. Compare answers with other students. Which information did you find most surprising?

5 Discuss the following questions.

- Have you ever visited any of the historical cities mentioned in the text?
- Are there any famous historical sights that you would especially like to see?
- If you could spend a weekend in any city in the world, which would you choose? Why?

Vocabulary

Describing towns and cities

1 You are going to answer the questions below about a town or city you know well. First check the meaning of the words in **bold** in your mini-dictionary or with your teacher.

2 Work with a partner.
Either: compare answers. Do you share the same opinions?
or: close your book and describe the place to your partner. Answer any questions your partner has.

A place I know well

1. Is it a village, town or city? How big is it, roughly? Describe its location, using some of the phrases below to help you.
- *it's in the west / south-west / centre, etc. of the country*
- *it's on the river / the coast ...*
- *it's about 50 km, etc. away from ...*
- *it's near the **border** with ...*

2. Which of the following features does the place have?
- *a **beach***
- ***docks** or a **harbour***
- *nice walks and **views***
- *beautiful **scenery** nearby*
- ***shopping malls** or street **markets***
- *an **underground** or **trams***
- *an industrial area*
- *a **carnival**, **festival** or other important events*

Does your town have any other important features not on this list?

3. You have to describe the place to a stranger in five words. Which adjectives would you choose?
crowded   exciting   **cosmopolitan**
historical   noisy   **old-fashioned**
peaceful   **polluted**   **touristy**   ugly
Think of two more adjectives of your own to describe it.

4. Which is your favourite area or individual place? Which place do you like least? What are the best and worst things about living there?

Part B Task

Plan a tour of your country or region

Task link: recommending and advising

Personal vocabulary

Useful language

Recommending places

"You must see ..."
"You should definitely visit ..."
"... is worth seeing."
"... is worth a visit."

Describing places

"It's famous for ..."
"It's one of the most famous / beautiful ... in ..."

Times and distances

"It's about ... kilometres from ..."
"It takes about ... hours."
"It's on the way to ..."

Preparation for task

1 What do you know about Ireland? Where exactly is it? What's the capital city? Do you know anything about its language, history, culture and scenery? Why do tourists go there? Read the 'Ireland factfile' below and check.

2 🔲 [3.5] Bob and Isobel are going to spend a week touring the south-west of Ireland by car. They have asked an Irish friend, Helen, to suggest where they should go. Listen to their conversation and follow the route that Helen suggests on the map below. Then answer the following questions.

a Where are Bob and Isobel going to start and finish their trip?

b What order does Helen suggest that they visit the places shown? Number them as you listen.

c How many nights does she recommend that they stay in each place?

IRELAND

FACTFILE

• Ireland is separated into two parts. The north is still part of the UK, while the Republic of Ireland, in the south, has been an independent state since 1921.

• The Republic has three and a half million inhabitants and two official languages, English and Gaelic.

• The capital of the Republic is Dublin, with a population of half a million; the second city is Cork, situated in the south-west. The most important river is the River Shannon.

• Ireland is famous for its beautiful scenery, especially its coastline and green rolling hills. It is often known as the 'Emerald Isle'.

• Ireland is also famous for its traditional music, its many great writers (Oscar Wilde, W.B. Yeats, James Joyce, to name just a few), and finally for its traditional drink, Guinness, a thick black beer.

If you have time, Westport is also worth a visit. It's close to Croagh Patrick, one of the most famous mountains in Ireland.

▲ Westport
Croagh Patrick Mountain

You should definitely see Limerick, which is one of the most beautiful cities in Ireland. It's situated on the River Shannon, and is famous for its cathedral and castle.

River Shannon   Limerick

Killarney is right in the middle of one of the most beautiful areas of Ireland. It's famous for its lakes and mountains.

Kerry

Dingle Bay   Killorglin   Killarney
Kenmare   Blarney   Cork

You must see the Ring of Kerry – it's generally considered to be the most beautiful scenery in the whole of Ireland. You can drive round the coastal road,

visiting a number of beautiful places – Killorglin, Dingle Bay and Kenmare. The drive is about 100 miles and it takes about a day.

Northern Ireland

Republic of Ireland

Dublin ●

Waterford is another famous tourist attraction. It's got a world-famous crystal factory, and the scenery on the journey back to Cork is superb.

● Waterford

Cork is Ireland's second largest city – it's worth seeing, especially the cathedral. There's a famous castle here at Blarney, where you should stop on your way to Killarney. When you visit, it's traditional to kiss the Blarney stone. ①

Task

1 You are going to plan a seven-day tour of your own country similar to Helen's. Work on your own or in pairs.

a Decide who the tour is for:
  • one of the groups of people in the pictures below.
  • the other students in your class.

b Decide if your tour will cover your whole country or just part of it. Decide which places your tourists would most enjoy visiting and for how long.

c Draw a map, and make some notes and illustrations to help explain your tour.

2 Spend a few minutes thinking about the language you need to describe your tour. Look at the phrases in the *Useful language* box. Ask your teacher about any other words and phrases you need and write them in the *Personal vocabulary* box.

3 *Either*: work in groups. Talk through your tour to the other students, using your map to explain and recommend where they should go. Be ready to answer their questions.
or: work in pairs. Imagine you are talking to one of the foreign visitors above, making recommendations as Helen did on the cassette. Be ready to answer their questions.

Optional writing

Copy out your map and tour with an itinerary (*Day one ..., Day two ...,* etc.) Read the other students' tours. Which would you most like to do yourself?

module 4

Life stories

Part A Language

Present Perfect Simple
(and Past Simple)
for, *since* and *ago* (and Present
Perfect Continuous)
Vocabulary: life experiences
Reading: *Twin lives*
Wordspot: *get*

In your thirties

Later in life

In your twenties

In your teens

As a child

Vocabulary

Life experiences

1 The words and phrases below all describe important life experiences. Think about when these things *usually* happen in a person's life, and put them in the correct place on the diagram opposite. If necessary, check the meaning of the words in the box in your mini-dictionary or with your teacher.

> leave home   start work   retire
> move house   settle down
> pass your driving test   get married
> get divorced   leave school
> go to university   get a degree
> bring up your children   fall in love
> get engaged   have an affair
> learn how to read

2 Look at the phrases again and find four things which you:

- have done already, or are doing at the moment.
- would like to do one day.
- would <u>not</u> like to do.
- could do at any time in your life.

Compare answers with a partner.

Reading

1 Do you know any twins? How do you think being a twin affects people's lives and personalities? What do you think the advantages and disadvantages might be?

2 Read the text quickly and look at the pictures. Match one of the following captions with a picture. (There is one caption too many.)

a The coincidences in their lives are truly remarkable. [4]

b They had their own special language. ☐

c They would only speak to each other. ☐

d They got married on the same day. ☐

e They met each other for the first time dressed in exactly the same clothes. ☐

1 June and Jennifer Gibbons

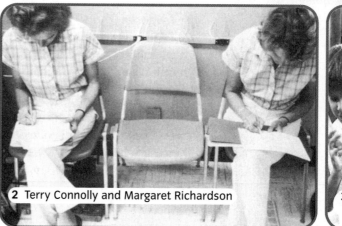

2 Terry Connolly and Margaret Richardson

3 Grace and Virginia Kennedy

Twin Lives

It is well-known that twins are closer to each other than most brothers and sisters – after all, they probably spend more time with each other. Parents of twins often notice that they develop special ways of communicating: they invent their own words and one can often finish the other's sentence. In exceptional circumstances, this closeness becomes more extreme: they invent a whole language of their own, as in the case of Grace and Virginia Kennedy from Georgia in the USA, who communicated so successfully in their own special language that they did not speak any English at all until after they started school. In Britain there was the famous case of the 'silent twins', June and Jennifer Gibbons, who were perfectly capable of normal speech, but for years refused to talk to anyone but each other.

However, these special relationships are the result of lives spent almost entirely in each other's company. What happens when twins do not grow up together, when they are separated at birth for some reason? Are they just like any other strangers, or are there still special bonds and similarities between them? Professor Tom Bouchard, of the University of Minnesota, set out to find the answer to this question. He traced sixteen pairs of twins, who were adopted by different families when they were babies, and often brought up in very different circumstances. Each twin was then interviewed about every small detail of their life.

The results of this research make surprising reading. Many of the twins were found to have the same hobbies or phobias, many have suffered the same illnesses, and some have even had the same type of accident at the same point in their lives. When they arrived in Minneapolis, many were dressed in very similar clothes. One pair of middle-aged women arrived for their first meeting in identical dresses, another pair were wearing identical jewellery. A large number of the twins have had children at almost the same times; sometimes they have even given them the same names. Terry Connolly and Margaret Richardson, British twins who didn't meet until they were in their mid-thirties, found that they had been married on the same day of the same year at almost the same time of the day. Both women have also had four children, all of more or less the same age.

But the most incredible similarities are to be found in the case of Jim Springer and Jim Lewis from Ohio in the USA. The story of the 'Jim Twins' made headline news across USA, and they even appeared on national television. Born to an immigrant woman in 1939, and adopted by different families at birth, both babies were named Jim by their new parents. This was just the first in an almost unbelievable series of coincidences. (see box)

But what can be the explanation for these remarkable similarities? Is it all pure coincidence, or is the explanation in some way genetic? Research into the lives of twins is forcing some experts to admit that our personalities may be at least partly due to 'nature'. On the other hand, analysts are also anxious to emphasise that incredible coincidences do happen all the time, not just in the lives of twins.

4 Jim Twins

4 Jim Twins

The remarkable 'Jim Twins'

- Both grew up with an adopted brother called Larry.
- As children both had dogs called Toy.
- At school both boys liked maths and disliked spelling.
- Since leaving school, both men have worked in fast-food restaurants, as petrol station attendants and as deputy sheriffs.
- Both men have been married twice, first to a woman called Linda and then to a woman called Betty.
- They both named their first son James Alan.
- Both suffer from the same kind of tension headaches.
- Both have had two heart attacks.
- Their homes and gardens are remarkably similar.
- They drink the same brand of beer and chain-smoke the same brand of cigarettes.

3 Read the text again and discuss the following questions in pairs.

a What did Professor Tom Bouchard want to find out? How did he do this?

b Give some examples of the kinds of similarities Professor Bouchard found between the Minnesota twins.

c Why do you think the 'Jim Twins' became famous in the USA?

d How do scientists explain the similarities between the sets of twins separated at birth?

4 Discuss the following questions in groups.

- Which of the coincidences described in the text do you find most surprising?
- Do you agree that personality is partly genetic? Can you see any similarities between the personalities of the people in your family? Are there any important differences?

Language focus 1

Present Perfect Simple (and Past Simple)

Mini-task

Work in groups of three. Each student should try to find three things that he / she has done, but the other two students have not. When you have finished, report back to the class.

I've ..., but neither of the others have ...

I haven't ..., but ...

1 Work in pairs. Close your books and think back to the information on the 'Jim Twins' on page 37. Can you remember at least **seven** of the coincidences they discovered when they met?

2 Choose the best verb form for each of the following sentences.

a They *have been / were* born in 1939.

b As children, both men *have owned / owned* a pet dog called Toy.

c Both the two brothers *have been / were* married to a woman called Linda for several years before divorcing her and re-marrying.

d They *have both lived / both lived* in the same town all their lives.

e Both of them *have suffered / suffered* from tension headaches since they were young.

f Both *have had / had* two heart attacks.

Analysis

1 We use the Present Perfect when a past action is related to the present rather than a time in the past. Choose the correct alternative to complete the sentences below about the use of the Present Perfect Simple and Past Simple.

a If we say exactly when the action happened (or if this is clear from the context), we must use the *Present Perfect / Past Simple*.

b If an action began in the past and continues in the present, we use the *Present Perfect / Past Simple / Present Simple*.

c If the action happens in a period of time which isn't finished, we use the *Present Perfect / Past Simple*.

2 Find examples of each rule from the sentences in Exercise 2.

Now read Language summary A / B on page 143.

Practice

1 The sentences below are all about famous people. Check with your teacher that you know who they are, and then match the beginning of a sentence in column A with the correct ending in column B. (You may need to use the same ending twice.)

A	B
a Steven Spielberg made / Steven Spielberg has made	a new film. / *Jaws* in 1975.
b Jack Nicholson played / Jack Nicholson has played	the Joker in *Batman*. / a mental patient in *One Flew over the Cuckoo's Nest*.
c Julia Roberts starred / Julia Roberts has starred	in *Pretty Woman*. / in more than twenty films.
d Bruce Willis and Demi Moore / Tom Cruise and Nicole Kidman	have been married for several years. / were married for several years.
e Marilyn Monroe / Elizabeth Taylor	has been married several times. / was married several times.
f Jane Fonda / Brigitte Bardot	hasn't made any films for many years. / didn't make any films for many years.

2 Complete the following sentences using the Present Perfect or Past Simple.

a Arnold Schwarzenegger / just / make / a new film.

b James Dean / die / in a car crash when he / be / only twenty-four.

c As well as being an actor, Robert Redford / direct / several films.

d Clark Gable's last film / be / with Marilyn Monroe – it / be / also / her last film.

e Michael Jackson / become / a star when he / be / still / a young child.

f Tom Hanks / win / several Oscars.

3 a) 📼 [4.1] What are the people in the pictures opposite talking about? Listen and match a dialogue with a picture.

b) Complete the gaps in the following sentences from the dialogues with a common phrase in the Present Perfect. Use a verb in the box.

change finish (x 2) go (x 2) lose (x 2) meet see

1 We .... Can we go now?

2 Sorry, I .... yet. Just a minute.

3 You .... your hair – it's really nice!

4 You .... weight, haven't you?

5 She was here – perhaps she .... just .... out for a minute.

6 She .... home. She left about ten minutes ago.

7 .... you .... my glasses anywhere?

8 I .... my glasses.

9 George, ... you .... Silvina?

Pronunciation

1 📼 [4.2] Listen to the main part of dialogue 4 again. You will hear *have* or *'ve* five times.

   a When is the pronunciation of *have* strong?

   b When is the contracted form (*'ve*) used?

2 📼 [4.3] Practise the following phrases, starting with the strong words.

      •   /həvjə/   •   /həvjə/   •

   a seen > Have you seen > Have you seen my glasses?

      •   /aɪv/   •   /aɪv/   •

   b lost > I've lost > I've lost my glasses.

      /hæv/   /hæv/   /hæv/

   c have > I have > I don't know if I have.

a

b

c

d

e

Language focus 2

for, *since* and *ago*
(and Present Perfect
Continuous)

1 a) 📼 [4.4] You are going
to hear a woman, Montse
Pinero, talking about her life.
Listen and say why the following
are important in her life.

- a travel agency
- Pablo
- Tarragona
- Barcelona

b) Complete the missing
information on Montse's
'lifeline' opposite.

2 Use the lifeline and the
information on the cassette
to complete the following
sentences. Complete the gaps
when necessary with the best
form of the verb in brackets.

a   Montse Pinero was born about
.... years ago.

b   She .... (*live*) in
Barcelona since 1988.

c   She .... (*meet*) her
boyfriend when she was at
school.

d   She .... (*know*) her
boyfriend since they were
teenagers.

e   She studied tourism for
.... at university.

f   She's worked in a travel agency
for about ....

g   She .... (*be*) engaged
for nearly six months.

h   She's been going skiing since
she .... (*be*) a child.

i   She's been learning English for
about ....

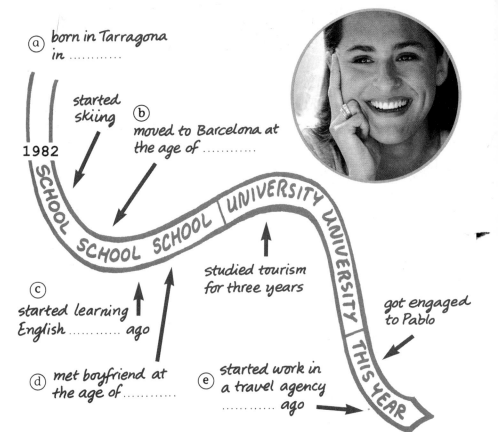

(a) born in Tarragona in ....

started skiing

1982

(b) moved to Barcelona at the age of ....

SCHOOL SCHOOL SCHOOL

UNIVERSITY UNIVERSITY

THIS YEAR

(c) started learning English .... ago

studied tourism for three years

got engaged to Pablo

(d) met boyfriend at the age of ....

(e) started work in a travel agency .... ago

Analysis

Verb forms

1 Look at the sentences in Exercise 2 again. Which sentences are in:
a   the Past Simple?
b   the Present Perfect Simple?
c   the Present Perfect Continuous?

2 a Look at sentences h) and i). Are *going skiing* and *learning English* single or long / repeated actions? Are they complete or not?
b Look at sentences b), d), f) and g). Is it possible to change these sentences into the Present Perfect Continuous? If so, does this change the meaning?

Time words: *for*, *since* and *ago*

1 Which 'time words' are used in the Past Simple sentences?

2 All the Present Perfect Simple and Continuous sentences use *for* and *since*. What is the difference in the use of these two words? Which do you use with the following?
- *twenty years*
- *I was a child*
- *1965*
- *six o'clock*
- *five minutes*
- *ages and ages*

3 Read the tapescript on page 157 and underline any other sentences with *for*, *since* and *ago*.

Now read Language summary C / D on pages 143–144.

Practice

1 a) 📼 [4.5] You are going to hear some questions. Your teacher will pause the cassette after each one. Listen and write answers in your notebook using *for*, *since* or *ago*. Write notes, not full sentences.

For example:
Question 1:
for about six months

b) Look at the answers you have written. How many of the questions can you remember? Choose five of the questions to ask other students in the class.

> ## Pronunciation
>
> Notice the weak pronunciation of *been* in the Present Perfect Continuous:
>
> /bɪn/
>
> • How long have you **been** coming to this class?

2 a) Draw a lifeline like Montse's for yourself. Mark the important dates and events in your life (moving house / schools / relationships / jobs, etc.)

b) You are going to talk through your lifeline. Spend a few moments planning what you are going to say, paying attention to your use of the verb forms and time words *for*, *since* and *ago*.

c) Work in pairs. Explain your lifeline to your partner, answering any questions that your partner has. Write a few sentences about yourself, using the information on your lifeline.

Wordspot

get

1 The diagram below shows some of the most common uses of the verb *get*. Read the phrases with *get* and tick (✓) those that you already know and write (?) next to the ones you are not sure about.

2 📼 [4.6] Look at the following short dialogues and try to think of a word or phrase to complete the gap. Then listen and check your answers.

a A: Oh dear, it's raining – we'll get wet if we walk to the cinema!

B: Shall we get a .... then? Don't worry, I'll pay!

b A: Go inside – you'll get .... !

B: I'm okay, I've got a thick sweater on.

c A: How's Dan's back?

B: I think it's getting .... unfortunately.

d A: Did you have a good journey home?

B: Not too bad – we got .... at about 8.30.

e A: Can't we get .... some of these old records?

B: Oh – I like them all!

f A: Do you get .... your mother-in-law?

B: Yeah, she's really nice actually.

g A: Did you get .... from Liz?

B: Yes, I've just called her back.

3 Work with a partner and write four short dialogues using phrases with *get* like the ones above. Read them out to the class.

4 Copy the diagram above to make a poster for your classroom wall showing the uses of *get*. Add new expressions when you meet them.

Part B **Task**

Design a set of stamps of famous people

Task link: describing people
Real life: filling in an application form

Personal vocabulary

Preparation for task

1 Work in groups. The people in the pictures below are all internationally famous. Where do they come from and what are they famous for? Look at pages 133–134 for more information on these people if necessary.

2 Check the meaning of the words and phrases in **bold** in your mini-dictionary or with your teacher. Then choose a famous person from the pictures who:

a has very **strong principles**.
b is **exceptionally talented**.
c is very **courageous**.
d has made a lot of people happy.
e has **achieved** a lot in his / her life.
f has **suffered** for what he / she **believes in**.
g has done a lot to help other people.
h is someone you really **admire**.

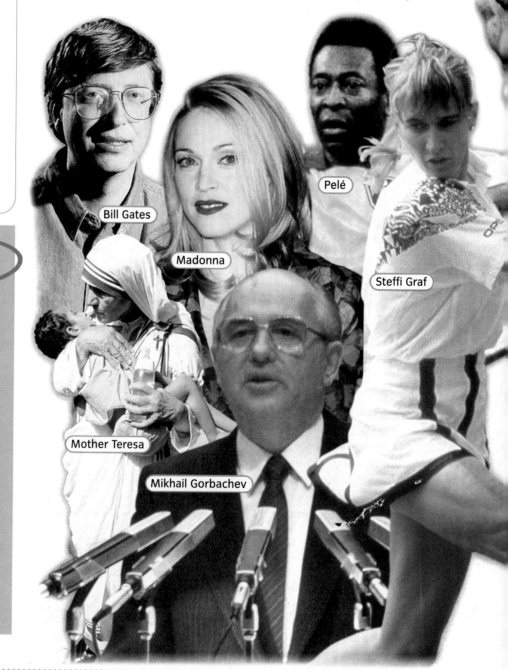

Bill Gates

Madonna

Pelé

Steffi Graf

Mother Teresa

Mikhail Gorbachev

Useful language

Making suggestions
"What about ... (Pelé)?"
"Perhaps we should choose ..."

Using reasons
"I think we should choose ... because ..."
"I think ... would be better because ..."
"... is someone who has (achieved a lot / done a lot to help others, etc.) ..."

Agreeing and disagreeing
"Yes, I agree."
"Sorry, but I don't agree."
"Perhaps you're right, but ..."

Task

1 Your government has decided to issue a set of stamps of famous people. You are on the committee which decides who to put on the stamps and why. Work in groups of three or four. First decide on a title for your set of stamps.

Either: choose one of the following titles.
- Great (Spanish, French, etc.) men and women of the twentieth century
- Great political leaders / sportsmen and women / writers / scientists / philosophers / musicians / artists / actors

or: choose a title of your own.

2 Work on your own. Decide:

- which four people you want to put on the set of stamps.
- which stamp each person will go on (the person you admire most should go on the 100c stamp and so on).

Think about how you will justify your choice to the other students in your group. Ask your teacher about any words or phrases you need and write them in the *Personal vocabulary* box.

3 Look at the sentences / phrases in the *Useful language* box. Work in groups again. Present and explain your suggestions to the rest of the group. Listen to the other students and decide together on the best four people.

4 **a)** You are going to present and explain your choice to the rest of the class. Spend a few minutes thinking about what you will say. What do they think of your decision?

b) Listen to the other groups' decisions and say what you think of the choices they have made.

Optional writing

Write a brief description of a person you really admire (one of the people you have been discussing or someone you know personally). Include:

- brief biographical details
- the person's achievements
- your impressions of what kind of person he / she seems to be
- why you particularly admire him / her.

100c   80c   60c   40c

Aung San Sui Kyi

Nelson Mandela

Gabriel Garcia Marquez

Stephen Hawking

Task link

Describing people

1 The following phrases are all used to describe people. Check the meaning of the words in **bold** in your mini-dictionary or with your teacher. Then mark the phrases as follows:

(+) if they are positive.
(–) if they are negative.
(?) if they can be both positive and negative.

a   **positive** and **enthusiastic** ☐

b   a **good talker** ☐

c   the sort of person who **goes on and on** about their problems ☐

d   someone who's always **cheerful** ☐

e   the sort of person who **gets on your nerves** ☐

f   the sort of person who always **sees the good side of things** ☐

g   someone who really **annoys** you ☐

h   someone who **has** a lot of **confidence** in himself ☐

2 **a)** Look at the people in the pictures below. What kind of personality do you think they have?

b) 🔊 [4.7] Listen to three speakers describe the people in the pictures. Write 1, 2 or 3 next to the person being described. What is the relationship between the speakers and the people in the pictures?

3 The three speakers use all of the phrases in Exercise 1. Which phrases are used in each description? What else do the speakers say about that person? Is their general attitude positive or negative?

4 **a)** Think of a person that you and the other students know. It could be:

* a teacher or student at your school.
* a politician or other famous person.

Write sentences about them starting with the following words:

– He / She's very ...
– He / She's the sort of person who ...
– He / She's someone who ...
– He / She's a good ...
– He / She's always ...
– He / She makes me ...

b) Read out your sentences without saying who the person is. Can the other students guess who you are describing?

Real life

Filling in an application form

1 Ahmet wants to study journalism at a British college. He has completed the application form for the course below. Some of the headings and questions from the form have been cut out. Can you put them back in the correct place?

Signature of applicant

Mr / Ms / Mrs / Miss

For which course are you applying?

List work experience in order of date

Your education and training background

If yes, what was your date of entry to the UK?

West London College
Application form 1998/99

1. a

1st choice *1 year Diploma in Journalism*
2nd choice *none*

b

Day ....✓.... Part-time / Day .... Evening ....

2. Information about you

c *Mr* **d** *Male*

Family name *Kemal*
Personal name *Ahmet*
Date of birth *24-8-76*
Age on 31/8/98 *22*
Address: *17 Birchwood Close, West Norwood, London*

e *SE27 1TZ*

Telephone number *0181 650 7788*

3. Have you ever been resident outside the UK? *Yes*

f *3-4-92*

Is English your first language? *No*
What other languages do you speak? *Turkish (first language), French (beginner)*

---

4. g

(give your last school and any further education)

Dates	School/college
1992 – 1994	Kingsley school, London SE24
1994 – 1997	University of West London

h

Year	Qualifications	Subject	Grade
June 1994	A-level	English, Economics	B and C
June 1997	BA Hons Degree	Media Studies	2:1

5. i

Dates	Types of work	Employer
1993 – 1994	Part-time waiter	Westlands Hotel
1994 – 1996	Part-time waiter	Enzo's fish restaurant
August 1997	Telephone sales	Computing magazine

6. j

I have wanted to be a journalist for several years. I have had considerable experience of working on school and university newspapers and radio, including a year as editor of my college magazine. I would like to pursue a career in newspaper journalism, and believe that this course would give me the necessary skills and practical experience.

k *Ahmet Kemal* Date *3-4-98*

Why do you wish to take this course and what future education / employment are you considering?

List any qualifications in order of date, including exams to be taken before September

How do you wish to study?

Male / Female

Postcode

2 Check your answers with the blank application form on page 134. Then complete the blank form for yourself, choosing from the list of courses at the bottom of the form.

module 5

Making plans

Part A Language

Future plans and intentions
Future clauses with *if*, *when*, etc.
Speaking and reading:
Quiz – how organised are you?
Wordspot: *work*
Vocabulary: training and work
Listening: working in something different

Speaking and reading

1 Discuss the following questions in groups.

- Are you an organised person or not? Do you like to plan carefully in advance or do you prefer to be more spontaneous?
- Do you have any friends or relatives who are very different from you in this respect? Does this ever cause problems?
- Do you think age or sex affect how organised people are?

2 Check the meaning of the phrases in **bold** below in your mini-dictionary or with your teacher. Then read through the quiz *How organised are you?* quickly and match a phrase below with a question in the quiz. (Do <u>not</u> answer the questions yet!)

- **attending a meeting** ☐
- **packing** for a holiday ☐
- filling in an important form ☐
- **arranging** a night out with a friend ☐
- winning money ☐
- **booking a holiday** ☐
- giving someone a message ☐

How organised are you?

Situation: How do you behave? A or B

1 You have an important form to fill in and you know it'll take at least two hours to do it properly. It's Tuesday today and you have to hand it in by nine o'clock on Friday morning at the latest.

A You're planning to do it tonight. That'll give you time to read it through tomorrow night and hand it in early on Thursday.

B You're going out tonight, but you intend to do it tomorrow night. If you're honest though, you know you probably won't even get down to it until about ten o'clock on Thursday evening.

2 You bump into a friend you haven't seen for ages in the street – she suggests a night out together next week.

A You get out your diary to see what you're doing next week, and make an arrangement there and then.

B You agree enthusiastically and promise to ring her tomorrow ... and then forget all about it!

3 To your amazement, you win £500 in a competition that you entered.

A You put the money in the bank towards the new car / holiday / computer that you're saving up for.

B You pay off a few debts, buy a couple of CDs and some new clothes, take a friend out for a meal to celebrate ... and the money's gone!

4 It's the end of June. You have two weeks holiday from work at the beginning of August.

A You have already booked your holiday and are starting to plan what clothes you need. You've borrowed several tourist guides to the area, and are planning various excursions and trips.

B You're thinking of going to Greece, but you haven't really looked into it yet. You're going to start phoning travel agents next week.

3 Now do the quiz in pairs. What do you think your partner's answers show about him / her?

4 Add up your partner's score and read the conclusions on page 135. Are they the same as your own conclusions?

5 You've been given an important message for a friend.

A You phone him straight away, in case you forget about it next time you meet.

B You're sure to see him in the next few days – you'll remember to tell him then.

6 You're due to be at a meeting in another town at three o'clock. You know it'll take you at least thirty minutes to get there.

A You allow an hour for the journey – that way you definitely won't be late. You'd like to have enough time to have a coffee and make a few notes before the meeting starts.

B You allow yourself twenty-five minutes and hope you don't have any problems on the way. If you're late, you can blame the traffic or the public transport system!

7 You're about to go on holiday. It's eight o'clock the evening before. Your friend is picking you up to take you to the airport at eight-thirty tomorrow morning.

A You've finished your ironing and packing. Now you're going to have a nice bath and an early night, so that you're fresh for the journey tomorrow.

B You throw a few clothes into the washing machine and go and have a last drink with a few friends. You're going to pack after that.

Language focus 1

Future plans and intentions

Analysis

1 There are many different future forms in English. Look at the following phrases / sentences taken from the quiz and underline the verb forms used.

 a *... you know it'll take at least two hours to do it properly.*

 b *You get out your diary to see what you're doing next week, ...*

 c *You're going to start phoning travel agents next week.*

2 Complete the following rules with *will + verb*, **Present Continuous** or *going to + verb*.

 • .... is used when there is no special plan – it is something you predict, or see as inevitable.

 • .... is used to describe something you have arranged to do in the future.

 • .... is used to describe a present intention about the future.

Look back at the quiz and find one more example of each of these uses.

3 Sometimes other verbs and phrases are used to express plans and intentions.
 • *You're **planning** to do it tonight.*
 • *You're **about** to go on holiday.*

Find four more phrases like these in the quiz. Can you add any other verbs / phrases to this list?

Now read Language summary A on page 144.

Practice

1 **a)** 🔲 [5.1] Listen and write answers to the instructions. Write notes, not full sentences.

For example:
Question 1: *Friday night – meet friends*

b) Look at your notes and write complete sentences using an appropriate future form. Then tell a partner about what you have written.

For example:
I'm meeting some friends on Friday night.

49

2 🖭 [5.2] Listen to people talking about the same topics and complete the gaps.

a I .... to the gym after work tomorrow night, but I ....
.... I'.......... .... to the pub like I always do!

b I'.......... .... TV and read the newspapers – and my mum' .... me, almost certainly.

c I'.......... .... out all my college notes this weekend.

d I'.......... ....
.... any domestic tasks this weekend. I'.......... ....
.... in bed, read a book and generally be lazy.

e We'.......... .... to Scotland for our holidays this year, but we haven't really decided.

f I'.......... .... a holiday this year, but I can't afford it, unfortunately.

Pronunciation

🖭 [5.3] Notice the pronunciation of the following phrases. Listen and practise saying them.

- *want to* /wɒntə/
  I *want to* go to the gym ...
- *won't* /wəʊnt/
  I probably *won't* go.
- *I'll* /aɪl/
  I'll probably go to the pub ...
- *I'm going to* /tə/
  I'm going to sort out ...
- *thinking of* /əv/
  We're *thinking of* going to Scotland ...
- *I'd like to* /tə/
  I'd like to have a holiday ...

---

3 **a)** The picture below shows a group of friends who have just graduated from university. Read the notes and choose the correct alternative.

'Dan's parents, who are both lawyers, really want (1) *him to become / that he becomes* a lawyer too, but he isn't so sure. He's about (2) *going / to go* on a long holiday to think things over. Who knows what'll (3) *happen / happening* when he gets back.'

'This is Eliza. She's hoping (4) *to work / working* in fashion. Ideally, she'd like (5) *being / to be* a fashion editor for a glossy magazine. A bit strange considering she studied Ancient History!'

'Amanda's just finished a Business Studies course and intends (6) *to work / work* in Personnel Management eventually, but first she's decided (7) *to go / going* travelling for a while.'

'Heather did Drama Studies, and is hoping (8) *become / to become* an actress. She's working at the moment as a waitress, but she's also doing lots of auditions, and she's determined (9) *being / to be* a star one day.'

'This is me, Richard. I have no real plans at the moment. I'm thinking (10) *of going / to go* abroad for a while, but basically I just seem to enjoy being with all my friends! I'm really going (11) *missing / to miss* them.

b) Work in groups of three. Interview each other about your plans and ambitions. Make notes under the following headings.

- career / education   • travel   • home / family life
- money   • other plans / ambitions

c) Write a paragraph about one of the students you interviewed using the verb forms you studied in the *Analysis* on page 49.

Wordspot

work

1 Which of the following sentences with *work* are already correct? Add a preposition from the box to correct the others. (You do not need to use all of the prepositions.)

after	as	before	for	from	like
of	off	out	out of		

a   The thieves stole several valuable works art.

of

b   Have you ever done any office work before?

c   When Jack leaves school, he's going to work his father's company.

d   Can you lend me your pen for a minute? Mine doesn't work.

e   My mother worked a nurse in Africa for several years.

f   My boss is work because he's hurt his back again.

g   Tom's been work for ages – he can't find a job anywhere.

h   We usually have dinner quite early. We're always starving when we get home work.

i   I'll just work how much it cost.

j   Your idea worked perfectly, thank you very much!

2 The diagram below shows some of the most common uses of *work*. Put the phrases with *work* from Exercise 1 in the correct section of the diagram. Practise saying the phrases.

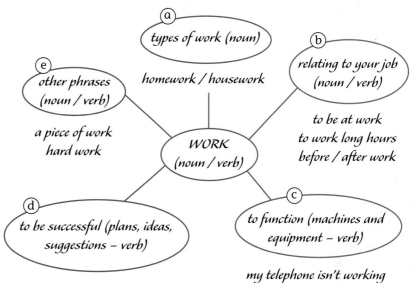

a types of work (noun)
homework / housework

e other phrases (noun / verb)
a piece of work
hard work

b relating to your job (noun / verb)
to be at work
to work long hours
before / after work

WORK (noun / verb)

d to be successful (plans, ideas, suggestions – verb)
his plan didn't work out

c to function (machines and equipment – verb)
my telephone isn't working

3 Match a sentence from column A with a sentence / phrase from column B. Then spend a few minutes trying to remember the sentences / phrases.

A

a   Her suggestion didn't work out at all.
b   It's her mother's funeral today.
c   The whole class complained.
d   This is an excellent piece of work.
e   Unemployment is very high.
f   We'll have to call a plumber.
g   He never does any housework.
h   Don't ask me.

B

1   The shower isn't working again.
2   Work it out for yourself.
3   It was a ridiculous idea.
4   There are over 3 million people out of work.
5   His wife does everything.
6   The teacher gave them too much homework.
7   Well done!
8   She's having the day off work.

4 Work in pairs. Student A should close his / her book while Student B reads out a sentence from column A. Student A should try to say the second sentence from column B. Then change over. How many sentences could you remember?

5 Copy the diagram above to make a poster for your classroom wall showing the uses of *work*. Add new expressions when you meet them.

Vocabulary

Training and work

1 All of the following sentences could be used to describe jobs. If necessary, check the meaning of the words and phrases in **bold** in your mini-dictionary. Then mark each sentence as follows:

(+) if you think it describes a positive aspect to a job.

(–) if you think it describes a negative aspect to a job.

(?) if it could be either positive or negative.

- It's **well-paid**. ☐
- It's **badly-paid**. ☐
- It's **challenging**. ☐
- It's **stressful**. ☐
- It's hard work physically. ☐
- You **work long hours**. ☐
- You have to **work shifts**. ☐
- You need to be **talented**. ☐
- You need special **training** and **qualifications**. ☐
- You need good **people skills**. ☐
- There's a lot of **job satisfaction**. ☐
- There's a lot of **variety**. ☐
- There's a lot of **responsibility**. ☐
- There are a lot of **opportunities**. ☐

2 Work in pairs or groups. Which of the above do you associate with the following jobs?

- a journalist
- a police officer
- a concert pianist
- a supermarket cashier
- an accountant
- a train driver
- a social worker
- a professional footballer

3 Think of one more job that you associate with each of the sentences in Exercise 1.

Listening

Working in something different

1 Look at the pictures opposite and discuss the following questions.

- Do you know anyone who does any of these jobs?
- Are you surprised to see any of these people doing these jobs?
- Which of these jobs would you be suited to / not suited to? Why?

2 🖭 [5.4] You are going to hear four people in the pictures talking about their jobs as part of a television programme called 'Working in something different'. Listen and decide which four people are speaking.

3 Listen again and answer the following questions.

a How did each person start doing his / her job?

b What are the advantages / disadvantages of each job?

c Do the speakers make any other interesting points about their jobs?

4 Discuss the following questions in groups.

- If you could choose any job in the world, what would you choose? Why?
- Can you think of any jobs that you would particularly hate to do? Why?
- Which of the following statements do you agree with?
  - Men and women are both equally capable of doing any job.
  - There are a number of jobs that women are naturally better suited to than men.
  - There are a number of jobs that men are naturally better suited to than women.

Kevin – house husband

Pat – bank manager

Debbie – engineer

Dave – nursery school teacher

Language focus 2

Future clauses with *if*, *when*, etc.

Mini-task

Choose three friends, classmates or relatives whose work plans and ambitions you know about. Think of at least one possible consequence in each case if their plans work out. Tell a partner about it.

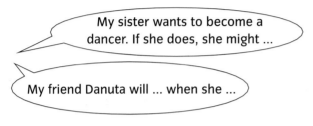

My sister wants to become a dancer. If she does, she might ...

My friend Danuta will ... when she ...

Look at the pictures opposite and below again. Which of the people in the pictures do you think said the following statements?

a   'If my area manager retires next year, I'll probably apply for his job.'
b   'When this school year finishes, I might try and find a job abroad.'
c   'As soon as our youngest child starts school, in about three years' time, I'll go back to my old job.'
d   'I'll be fully qualified in about two years' time – unless I fail my exams, of course!'
e   'I can't train as a surgeon until I've got more experience.'

Anita – doctor

Analysis

1   Look at sentences a)–e) opposite. Each of them has two parts (or 'clauses'). Underline the verb in each clause.

2   Do the sentences refer to the present or future? What do you notice about the verb form in the clause which comes after *if*, *unless*, *until*, *when* and *as soon as*? Is this the same in your language?

3   What kind of verb do you find in the other 'main' clause of each sentence?

Now read Language summary B on page 144.

Practice

1   Here are some more sentences about the same people. Complete the gaps with the best form of the verb in brackets. (There may be more than one possibility in some cases.)

a   Dave .... (*get*) bored if he .... (*not / have*) a change soon.
b   If Pat .... (*become*) area manager, she .... (*be*) under a lot more stress.
c   When Kevin .... (*go*) back to his old job, he .... (*probably / feel*) much closer to his children than before.
d   Debbie .... (*not / earn*) much money until she .... (*finish*) her apprenticeship.
e   If Dave .... (*leave*) the nursery where he works, the children .... (*really / miss*) him.
f   Once Anita .... (*become*) a surgeon, she .... (*not / work*) such long hours.

2   Complete the following sentences so that they are true for you.

a   I'm going to buy ... as soon as ...
b   I'll continue to study English until ...
c   I won't come to class next time if / unless ...
d   I'll be home by ... o'clock today if / unless ...
e   I'd like to ... this evening after I ...
f   I'm going to ... next weekend if / unless ...

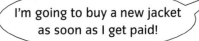

I'm going to buy a new jacket as soon as I get paid!

Part B **Task**

Select the best candidate for a job

Real life 1: writing a covering letter
Real life 2: making a formal telephone call

Personal vocabulary

Useful language

Good points

"He has got plenty of experience of ..."

"The good thing about ... is that ..."

"What I like about ... is that ..."

Bad points

"She hasn't got much experience of ..."

"I'm worried that ..."

"I think ... is too old / too young / isn't experienced enough."

Other

"I get the impression she's ..."

"He seems very energetic / inexperienced ..."

"If ... happens, she will / might ..."

Horizons Unlimited

Fed up with your daily routine?
Looking for something different?
Always wanted to travel?

Horizons Unlimited is an international employment agency, recruiting for positions all over the world. Vacancies include:
- management and office staff
- hotel and restaurant staff
- nannies, private teachers and nurses
- many more!

All applicants must be appropriately qualified. Write for an application form to:
Horizons Unlimited, PO Box 444, Richmond, Surrey, SJ5 4TS
Interviews will be arranged with suitable applicants.

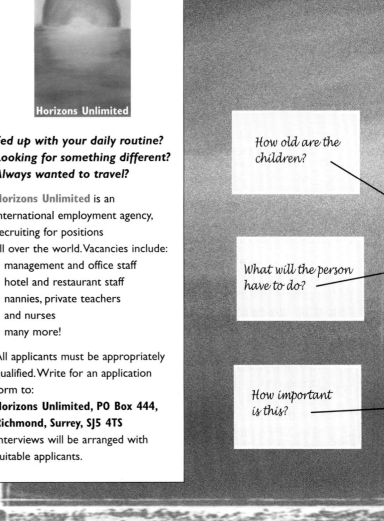

How old are the children?

What will the person have to do?

How important is this?

Preparation for task

1 Read the advertisement on the left above. What is *Horizons Unlimited*? What kind of jobs do they offer?

2 The card above on the right shows information on one of the vacancies the agency has. Read the information and answer the following questions.

a What is the job?
b What are the duties?
c Which skills are essential to the job?
d Which skills are also very useful?

3 📼 [5.5] Marion O'Neill works at *Horizons Unlimited.* She is calling Jean-Luc Bertrand, the owner of the hotel where the vacancy is. She wants to check some of the details of the job. Listen to their conversation and note down the answers to the questions she has noted down above. Does Jean-Luc Bertrand make any other important points?

Position:
General assistant hotel
manager/part-time childminder

Location:
25-bedroom family hotel in
remote ski resort
(French Alps)

Horizons Unlimited

Duties:
During busy 'winter' season:
1) To organise hotel reception/
   office during mornings and evenings
   – hotel experience, computer skills
   and good French essential; experience
   / knowledge of skiing, <u>driving
   licence</u>, other languages (especially
   German and English) also very useful.
2) To organise part-time staff (chef,
   barman, chambermaids) when owner is
   absent on business.
3) To help in kitchen, bar, etc. as
   necessary during busy periods.

When hotel is closed (spring and autumn):
1) <u>To look after owner's two children
   while he is absent on business</u>.
2) To look after premises and organise
   cleaners, etc.

Salary and benefits:
Good salary, free food and accommodation,
6-8 weeks' paid holiday, free ski pass,
use of car.

Contract:
Minimum 1 year, <u>2 years preferred</u>.

Other details:
The owner is a man in his forties, whose
wife died 18 months ago. He is looking for
someone able to take over the work that
she did in the hotel. The person needs to
be friendly, flexible, kind and able to
fit into family life.

Why?

Peter Krajeck, page 135

Brigitte Schumann, page 136

Brenda Macdonald, page 137

John Bailey, page 138

Anne-Sophie Martin, page 139

Task

1 **a)** Marion has short-listed the five candidates in the pictures above for the job. Work in groups of five. Each of you should choose one candidate and read the notes about him / her on the page indicated.

b) Mark the notes as follows:
(+) if you think it is a positive point.
(–) if you think it is a negative point.

2 You are going to present the positive and negative points about your candidate to the group. Spend a few minutes thinking about the language you will use to do this. Look at the phrases in the *Useful language* box opposite. Ask your teacher about any words or phrases that you need and write them in the *Personal vocabulary* box.

3 Work in your groups. Listen to the positive and negative points about each candidate. Decide who is your first and second choice for the job and why.

First choice [   ]
Second choice [   ]

4 You are going to present your decisions to the rest of the class. Spend a few minutes thinking about what you will say. Did everyone agree about the best candidate for the job?

Real life 1

Writing a covering letter

1 Louisa Barry wants to apply for a job through *Horizons Unlimited*, so she is sending her CV and a covering letter. Put the addresses and date in the correct position on the page opposite.

30th April 1998

Horizons Unlimited
PO Box 444
Richmond
Surrey
SJ5 4TS

15 Thayers Farm Road
Abingdon
Northampton
NT12 4PF

ⓐ --------------

ⓑ --------------

ⓒ --------------

2 Put Louisa's letter in the correct order. (There may be more than one possibility.) How many paragraphs do you think the letter should have?

a *I would therefore be particularly interested in any secretarial positions that you have available, especially in France or Switzerland.* ☐

b *I will be available to start work from the middle of June.* ☐

c *I look forward to hearing from you soon.* ☐

d *Yours faithfully,* ☐

e *I enclose my CV, as requested.* ☐

f *I am a qualified and experienced secretary, and am bilingual in Spanish and English. I also speak French fluently.* ☐

g *I am writing in reply to your advertisement for temporary summer positions, which appeared in The Western Mail on 27th April.* ☐

h *Dear Sir or Madam,* ☑

i *However, I am willing to consider any kind of work.* ☐

j *Louisa Barry* ☐

3 Is the layout of a formal letter the same or different in your language? Underline five phrases in Louisa's letter that might be useful in any formal letter that you write in English.

4 Write a similar letter to *Horizons Unlimited* in response to their advertisement on page 54. Mention briefly where you would like to work, and what kind of work you would be interested in. (You can invent qualifications and experience!)

Real life 2

Making a formal telephone call

1 📼 [5.6] Louisa Barry is phoning *Horizons Unlimited* to find out about her job application. Listen and answer the following questions.

a   Why is she phoning?
b   What is the secretary going to do?

2 Complete the missing phrases in the dialogue. Then listen again and check your answers.

TELEPHONIST: Hello, Horizons Unlimited.

LOUISA: Hello, (1) .... Marion O'Neill, please.

TELEPHONIST: (2) ....

SECRETARY: Hello, how can I help?

LOUISA: Er ... (3) .... Marion O'Neill, please?

SECRETARY: I'll just see if she's available. (4)............
....?

LOUISA: Louisa Barry.

SECRETARY: One moment, please ... hello ... I'm afraid she's in a meeting at the moment. (5) ....
....?

LOUISA: Well, (6) .... she interviewed me for a job about two weeks ago, and I haven't heard anything yet. She said she'd let me know last Friday whether or not I'd got it.

SECRETARY: Okay ... (7) .... Will you be at home all afternoon?

LOUISA: I'll be here until about four o'clock, but anyway, (8) ....

SECRETARY: Fine. (9) .... ?

LOUISA: Yes, it's 0165 776 3234.

SECRETARY: Okay then, (10) ....

LOUISA: Thank you, bye.

SECRETARY: Bye.

Pronunciation

1 📼 [5.7] Listen to these telephone phrases again. Some sounds are weak and some words are linked together.

a I'd like to speak to Marion O'Neill, please.
   /tə/   /tə/

b Just a moment, I'll put you through.
   /jʊ/

c Can I ask who's calling?

d Can I take a message, or would you like her to call you back?
   /ə/ /tə/

2 📼 [5.8] Listen for the weak or linked words in some more phrases. Practise saying them yourself.

3 📼 [5.9] Work in pairs. Act out the conversation below. Then listen to the real conversation.

Student A: you are phoning *Bank Direct* about a money transfer you're expecting from the USA. You want to speak to Sharon Elliot, your personal banker, to find out what is happening.

Student B: you are the telephonist at *Bank Direct*. Sharon Elliot is on the other line at the moment.

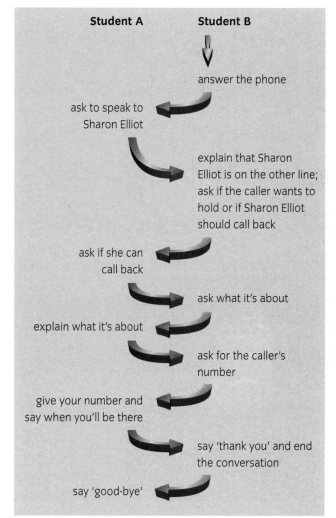

Student A   **Student B**

answer the phone

ask to speak to
Sharon Elliot

explain that Sharon
Elliot is on the other line;
ask if the caller wants to
hold or if Sharon Elliot
should call back

ask if she can
call back

ask what it's about

explain what it's about

ask for the caller's
number

give your number and
say when you'll be there

say 'thank you' and end
the conversation

say 'good-bye'

Do you remember?

①

Answer the following questions using a full sentence.

a) What are you doing:
  – tonight?
  – tomorrow night?
  – at the weekend?

b) What are you going to do with your spare time when this course finishes?

c) Where do you think you will be this time tomorrow?

②

Explain the difference in meaning between the following things.

a) • working **shifts**
  • working **long hours**

b) • the **skills** you need for a job
  • the **qualifications** you need for a job

c) • doing something **challenging**
  • doing something **stressful**

d) • a job with plenty of **variety**
  • a job with plenty of **opportunities**

③

Which *one* of the following sentences is wrong? Can you correct it?

• When this lesson finishes, I'm going home.
• As soon as I will see her, I ask her.
• I can meet you in town if I leave work early.

④

Below are some phrases used for making a formal telephone call. Put the words in the correct order.

a) calling / for / Thanks

b) I'll / moment / Just / a / put / through / you

c) her / and / to / you / call / message / ask / I'll / pass / the / on / back

d) please / number / take / your / Can / just / I?

e) speak / Susan Daniels / to / I'd / like / please / to

f) answerphone / leave / the / you / message / a / Can / on?

g) on / line / other / she's / the / afraid / I'm /

h) available / see / I'll / if / just / she's

⑤

Match a word / phrase in column A with a word / phrase in column B to make phrases from Module 5.

A	B
• pack	• an application form
• save up for	• your holiday in advance
• apply for	• in the bank
• book	• your suitcase
• fill in	• how much something costs
• put your money	• a new job
• work out	• a new car

⑥

Which preposition (*on, to,* etc.) has been blacked out in the following sentences?

a) John's thinking ▨▨▨ buying a fax machine.

b) I'm going swimming ▨▨▨ work this evening.

c) She's hoping ▨▨▨ get away from work early tonight.

d) I am writing ▨▨▨ reply ▨▨▨ your advertisement.

e) Poor Matthew is ▨▨▨ work with flu at the moment.

f) I look forward ▨▨▨ hearing ▨▨▨ you soon.

g) I can't work ▨▨▨ how much this will cost.

h) Can we discuss it when I get home ▨▨▨ work?

⑦

Look back through Module 5 and write two more revision questions of your own to ask other students.

module 6
News and media

Part A Language

> -ing / -ed adjectives
> Passive forms
> Vocabulary and listening:
> television
> Reading: newspaper articles
> Wordspot: by

Vocabulary and listening

Television

1 Discuss the following questions in groups.

- How much television do you watch?
- What are your favourite programmes?
- Are there any programmes that you particularly dislike?

2 Below is a list of things we can watch on television. If necessary, check the meaning of the words and phrases in **bold** in your mini-dictionary. Then mark them as follows:

✗✗ if you think there are too many of these on television in your country.

✓✓ if you think there are about the right amount of these.

✓ if you think there should be more of these.

✗ if you don't have these in your country at all.

a **advertisements** that use attractive people to sell products like cars or perfume ☐

b government **advertising campaigns** against things like drink-driving

c programmes with live **sports coverage** ☐

d children's programmes which include violence ☐

e long complicated **murder mysteries** or **thrillers** ☐

f **interviews** with politicians ☐

g **chat shows** ☐

h **game shows** ☐

i **soap operas** ☐

3 🔊 [6.1] Listen to four people talking about television. Which of the things listed in Exercise 2 are they talking about?

4 Listen to the speakers again. Which of the adjectives in the box below did each one use to describe their feelings? Which form did they use?

> annoying / annoyed interesting / interested
> boring / bored worrying / worried
> shocking / shocked upset / upsetting
> confused / confusing

Language focus 1

-ing / -ed adjectives

... inflation is at 20 per cent ... unemployment is up by 10 per cent ...

Practice

1 If necessary, check the meaning and pronunciation of the adjectives in the box in your mini-dictionary. Can you think of three more adjectives like this?

embarrassed / embarrassing   surprised / surprising   excited / exciting
disappointed / disappointing   pleased / pleasing   terrified / terrifying

2 Choose the correct alternative in the following sentences.

a Did you see that documentary about political corruption last night? It was a really *interested / interesting* programme – I was quite *shocked / shocking*!

b The President said in the news that he was very *pleased / pleasing* with the country's economic progress, but I found some of what he said very *worried / worrying*.

c There was a really *excited / exciting* basketball match on television last night. I was a bit *disappointed / disappointing* that my team lost, though!

d I know that people are always *interested / interesting* in famous people's private lives, but I do think some of the personal questions they ask on chat shows can be a bit *embarrassed / embarrassing* for the guests.

3 Discuss in groups how you would feel in the following situations.

For example:
You switch the television on to watch your favourite soap opera, and discover there's a football match on instead.

> I'd be really pleased – I love football!

> I'd be really annoyed. I find football really boring!

a You find out that there's a chat show on television with your favourite actor or rock star.

b You suddenly see a friend or colleague on television.

c You finish watching a thriller on your own late at night, and then have to go to bed in a dark house.

d You watch a news item about famine in a third-world country.

e One of your friends phones you for a chat in the middle of the news.

Reading

1 Make a list of five common topics for news stories (disasters, elections, etc.) Then discuss the following questions in groups.

- What types of news stories do you find:
  - most interesting?
  - most worrying?
  - most annoying?

- How often do you:
  - watch the news on television?
  - listen to the radio news?
  - read a newspaper?

2 a) Look at the newspaper headlines below. Which article do you think will be about:

- how a Polish fireman and glazier tried to make work for themselves?
- a natural disaster in India and Bangladesh?
- a lucky escape for a young child?
- a man who was very unhappy with his love-life?
- someone who had a serious problem with their nose?
- the death of a very old man?

① **Preacher, 136, meets his maker**

② **Thunder saves girl from crash**

③ *Job creation*

④ **'One sneeze and you'll die!'**

⑤ **LOVE-LORN MAN BEGS TIGER TO EAT HIM**

⑥ **Monsoon flooding kills 200**

b) Work with a partner. Can you predict more details of the stories?

3 Read the articles and check your predictions.

4 Without looking back at the articles, mark the following statements **T** (true) or **F** (false).

a   Millions of people have been affected by the floods in India and Bangladesh. ☐

b   The 6-year-old girl from Oxford was not in her own bed when the car crashed into her bedroom. ☐

c   The Shanghai tiger did not hurt the man who climbed into his cage. ☐

d   The man who died had over a hundred grandchildren. ☐

e   The Polish fireman admitted starting the fires. ☐

f   A Colorado factory worker died in an explosion. ☐

Read the articles again and check your answers.

5 Discuss in groups which article you found:

•   the most interesting or funny.
•   the most shocking.
•   the most difficult to believe.

Monsoon flooding kills 200

Flooding and landslides have killed up to 200 people and made about 2 million homeless in north-east India and north Bangladesh, and monsoon rains are continuing to lash the region, officials said yesterday. In the eastern sector of West Bengal state, at least 70 people have been killed by floods and landslides and 350,000 made homeless.

Thunder saves girl from crash

A girl's fear of thunder saved her life today when a stolen car crashed into her bedroom. Leila Mauger, 6, slipped into bed with her mother during a storm, and as she slept a stolen car crashed into their house in Headington, Oxford, stopping inches from her bed. Her mother Sylvie, 33, said: 'If Leila had been in there, who knows what could have happened.' Two teenagers were injured in the crash, but they are expected to survive.

Preacher, 136, meets his maker

Dubai: a retired mosque preacher, Ali Matar Bin Ghurain, has died, aged 136, Arab Emirates newspapers said. He is survived by 103 grandchildren and great-grandchildren. One of his sons is 98. Villagers said he liked to take long walks.

Job creation

Warsaw: a volunteer Polish fireman has pleaded guilty to setting light to ten buildings to give himself more work. In a similar case last week, a glazier was accused of smashing shop windows in the hope that he would get the job of repairing them.

'One sneeze and you'll die!'

A factory worker was warned he would die if he sneezed, when an explosive device got stuck in his nose after a machine blew up at a factory in Denver, Colorado. Nicolas Villaruel, 29, was taken to a hospital by bomb squad officers and was operated on underwater because air activates the device.

Love-lorn man begs tiger to eat him

A Shanghai man, unlucky in love, climbed into a tiger's cage at the city zoo, knelt in front of the animal and begged it to eat him. The tiger obliged by knocking him down and taking a bite at his neck. Screams from visitors attracted help and a vet shot the tiger full of sedatives, while the injured man was carried to safety.

Articles taken from *The Evening Standard*

Language focus 2

Passive forms

Mini-task

What have been the most important news stories in your country during the last few months? Make a list of three things you would tell a foreign visitor to your country. Then compare your lists in groups.

Either: *look at the other students' lists. Did you choose the same stories or not?*

or: *compare news stories. Are the same kind of issues in the news in your different countries or not?*

The following phrases / sentences come from the newspaper articles on page 61. Look at the verbs in each sentence and <u>underline</u> the active verb forms and (circle) the passive verb forms.

a   ... a vet shot the tiger full of sedatives, ...

b   ... the injured man was carried to safety.

c   Flooding and landslides have killed up to 200 people ...

d   ... at least 70 people have been killed by floods and landslides ...

e   ... a stolen car crashed into (a child's) bedroom.

f   Two teenagers were injured in the crash, ...

g   ..., but they are expected to survive.

Analysis

1   Look at sentences a) and b) above. In sentence a) the subject is 'a vet'; in sentence b) it is 'the injured man'. Is the subject the person who *does* the verb (the 'doer') in both sentences?

2   Below are two reasons why the passive is often used. Find another example of each use in the sentences above.
   a We use the passive when what happened to the person or thing is more important than 'the doer'.

   Examples are sentence d) and sentence ....

   b We use the passive when the 'doer' of the verb is not known or not important.

   Examples are sentence b) and sentence ....

3   How are passive verbs formed in each tense? In the sentences above, find:
   a one example of the Present Simple passive.
   b two examples of the Past Simple passive.
   c one example of the Present Perfect passive.

4   Look back at the other articles on page 61 and underline all the examples of the passive that you can find.

Now read Language summary B on page 145.

1   The Statue of Liberty in New York was designed and built by:
   a the English architect, Sir Christopher Wren.
   b the American architect, Frank Lloyd Wright.
   c the French architect, Alexandre Gustave Eiffel.

2   The sport of ice hockey was invented more than a hundred years ago in:
   a Canada.   b England.
   c Russia.

3   About half of the world's gold is produced in:
   a Canada.   b Russia.
   c South Africa.

4   'Crime and Punishment' was written by:
   a Dickens.   b Tolstoy.
   c Dostoyevsky.

Practice

1 a) 🔊 [6.2] Do the general knowledge quiz above in pairs. Then listen and check. (You will hear quite a lot of information, so listen carefully for the information that you need.)

Pronunciation

1 🔊 [6.3] Listen and notice the stress and weak forms in this passive sentence:
   • *The Statue of Liberty was /wəz/ built in France.*

2 🔊 [6.4] Listen to the other answers to the quiz. Practise saying the weak forms.

b) In teams write your own general knowledge quiz. Use the words / phrases in the box below to help you.

was composed / painted in ... by ...
was discovered / designed in ... by ...
was built / started / completed in ... by ...
was elected / killed in ... by ...

c) Do your quizzes in teams, taking turns to read out questions.

5 How many languages are spoken in India in total?
   a 2   b 14   c over 1,000

6 Who was John Lennon assassinated by?
   a Lee Harvey Oswald
   b Mark Chapman
   c Ringo Starr

7 How many bicycles are sold in the world every year?
   a 1 million   b 10 million
   c 100 million

8 How often has the final of the Football World Cup been played in Asia?
   a never   b once   c twice

Wordspot

by

1 *By* is missing from most of the following sentences. Where should it go? Which sentences need *on* instead of *by*?

a I always go to work train. *(by)*

b You can book your ticket phone if you prefer.

c It's not far – we can go foot.

d All the cooking was finished seven o'clock.

e Food prices have gone up fifteen per cent this year.

f He made a bit of money selling his old books.

g That's Gabriela sitting the door.

h You did it purpose, I saw you!

i Acid rain is partly caused car exhaust fumes.

j My favourite piece of music is 'Clair de Lune' Debussy.

k Since his wife died, he's lived himself in that big old house.

l I think you've taken my coat accident.

2 Draw a diagram for *by* like the ones in the other *Wordspots*. Include the following categories:

a *by* + *-ing* form
b passive + *by*
c ways of communicating / paying
d = near
e = before
f with composers, writers, etc.
g ways of travelling
h other phrases

3 Work in pairs. Student A should read out the questions on page 135. Student B should read out the questions on page 138. Answer your partner's questions using a phrase with *by*.

2 If necessary, check the meanings of the words in the box in your mini-dictionary. Then complete the following true stories with the correct active or passive form of the verb in brackets. (Pay attention to the tense of the verb.)

> an assault   a burglar   a courtroom   a judge   a parking ticket
> a shoplifter   a traffic warden   to sentence

a Seventy-five prisoners in northern Mexico (1) .... (*spend*) over six months digging a tunnel in an attempt to escape from Saltillo prison. Unfortunately for them, however, their tunnel (2) .... (*come*) up in the nearby courtroom, where they (3) .... (*sentence*). All seventy-five prisoners (4) .... (*return*) to prison immediately by the surprised judge.

b Mrs Redwood, from Port Headland in Australia, (5) .... (*attack*) by a burglar while she (6) .... (*talk*) on the phone to her brother in Leeds, England. Her brother (7) .... (*hear*) strange noises, and (8) .... (*phone*) his local police station in Leeds. The Port Headland police (9) .... (*contact*) immediately, and an officer (10) .... (*send*) to Mrs Redwood's house. The woman (11) .... (*rescue*) just eighteen minutes after the attack (12) .... (*happen*)!

c A towel (13) .... (*steal*) from a 'Holiday Inn' hotel in the USA, every twelve seconds – a total of 2.7 million towels a year!

Part B **Task**

Prepare a review or entertainment guide

Task link: 'extreme' adjectives

Personal vocabulary

Preparation for task

1 The words in the box are all things you might hear on the radio. Complete the gaps in the sentences below with one of the words.

review	phone-in	entertainment guide	advert

a An .... tries to persuade people to buy goods or services.

b In a .... a critic gives his / her opinion of a new film, book, play, etc.

c In a .... people call the radio station to express their opinions or ask questions.

d An .... tells you where and when you can see films, concerts, etc.

2 🔲 [6.5] You are going to hear four extracts from radio programmes. Listen and write what each extract is, using a word from the box in Exercise 1.

a .... b .... c .... d ....

3 Listen again and answer the following questions.

a What three types of music are mentioned in the entertainment guide?
b What other form of entertainment does she talk about?
c What kind of film is being advertised?
d What is the phone-in about?
e Is the reviewer talking about a book, a play or a film? Is she generally positive or negative about it?

Task

1 You are going to prepare an item for a radio programme. You can choose:

Either: a review of a television programme, film, video, play, concert or CD that you have seen or heard recently.

or: an entertainment guide to cinemas, theatres, concerts, etc. in your local area, or a guide to programmes on television over the next few days.

Make your choice and then read the appropriate instructions.

Entertainment guide

• Work in pairs. Try to choose programmes, films, plays, etc. that you think will interest the other students. If possible, choose things that you know something about. Include both factual information and reasons why you recommend it.

• Spend about fifteen minutes preparing your entertainment guide. Do *not* write it out word for word, but make notes about what you are going to say. Look at the phrases in the *Useful language* box. Ask your teacher about any words or phrases you need and write them in the *Personal vocabulary* box.

Useful language

"If you like ... you should try / go to / see ..."

"It's on at ..."

"It starts / finishes at ..."

"It's about ..."

"It stars ... "

"It's written / directed by ..."

"It looks good / interesting / exciting / unusual / fun ..."

"There are ... performances every day. Tickets are on sale at ..."

"You can get more information from ..."

Useful language

"It's about ..."

"It stars ..."

"It's set in ..."

"It was written / directed / produced by ..."

"The story / acting / photography is ... excellent / not very good ..."

"The thing I liked best about it was ..."

"Another thing I really liked was ..."

"The thing I didn't like was ..."

"I'd recommend it to people who like ..."

Review

• Work on your own. Try to choose a programme, film, etc. that you think will interest the other students. (Ideally it will be something recent.) Include both factual information (where you saw it / what it's about / who's in it, etc.) and your opinion of it.

• Spend about fifteen minutes preparing your review. Do *not* write it out word for word, but make notes about what you are going to say. Look at the phrases in the *Useful language* box. Ask your teacher about any words or phrases you need and write them in the *Personal vocabulary* box.

2 *Either*: present your review or entertainment guide to the class. The other students should listen and note down:

- which films, programmes, etc. they would like to see.
- any questions they would like to ask.

or: make a radio programme of your own called *News and Reviews*. Record your entertainment guides and reviews onto a cassette. Decide:

- what order to put the items in.
- who is going to be the radio announcer and what he / she will say.

Optional writing

Write a review of the film, play, etc. you have already described, or another one you are interested in.

Task link

'Extreme' adjectives

1 Look at the extracts below from reviews for the film *Ocean Dogs*. What is the film about? Were the reviews good, bad or mixed?

Brad Pick is terrific as the evil modern-day pirate ...

JORDAN JONES' SCRIPT IS UNNATURAL AND ON OCCASIONS RIDICULOUS ...

... hilarious screenplay from Jordan Jones ...

Brad Pick's dullest performance in years ... appalling!

2 Look at the extracts again and find a word which means:

a   very bad   c very good
b   very funny   d very silly

3 **a)** Match an 'extreme' adjective in column A with an 'ordinary' adjective in column B.

A	B
brilliant	frightened
tragic	interested
furious	very bad
fascinated	sad
astonished	cold
boiling	angry
terrified	surprised
freezing	hot
terrible	very good

b) 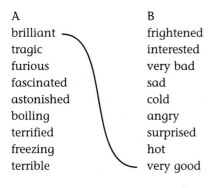 [6.6] Mark the stress on the words in column A. Listen and check.

For example: brilliant

Ocean Dogs STARRING BRAD PICK

4 'Extreme' adjectives are often used in newspapers to make stories sound more dramatic. The headlines below sound rather boring at the moment. Re-write them using an 'extreme' adjective to make them sound more dramatic.

(a) **VERY GOOD RESULT FOR UNITED**

(b) *Very cold temperatures in the North*

(c) **Princess very surprised by kiss on lips**

(d) **Government statistics 'very silly' says expert**

(e) READING AND WRITING STANDARDS IN SCHOOLS 'VERY BAD', SAYS INSPECTOR

(f) **The man who's very interested in slugs**

(g) **Prime Minister very angry about 'interference from Brussels'**

(h) **The very sad story of the boy who had everything**

5 The adverbs *very*, *absolutely* and *really* are used when we want to make adjectives sound stronger. Which **two** are possible before the following adjectives?

(a) .... *interested* ....

(b) .... *furious* ....

(c) .... *surprised* ....

(d) .... *fascinated* ....

Do you remember?

1

Add five more things to this list of things you can see on television.

advertisements, films, ...
....
....
....
....

2

Complete the gaps in the following sentences with an appropriate *-ing / -ed* adjective.

a) Last night you went to a restaurant and your friend was very rude to the waiter – it was so ....

b) You feel .... because you have just found out that you have failed an important exam.

c) A good friend of yours said that he was coming round to your house at eight o'clock. It's already ten o'clock, and he still hasn't arrived – it's very ....

d) You're .... because you have just discovered that your sister is going to have a baby.

e) You're feeling a bit .... because you've just broken up with your boyfriend / girlfriend.

3

a) What is the past participle of the following verbs?

- build
- cause
- discover
- elect
- find
- give
- hold
- hurt
- invent
- produce
- sell
- take

b) Work in pairs. Look at the list of irregular verbs on page 152. Test your partner on the past participles of ten more verbs.

4

Are the verbs in the following article passive or active? Complete the gaps with the correct form of the verb in brackets. Remember to use the correct tense.

Over a million pounds worth of jewellery(1) .... (*steal*) from a private home in Chelsea, London. It (2) .... (*believe*) that the robbery (3)......... (*happen*) late last night while the owners (4) .... (*attend*) a party in another part of London. Three men (5) .... (*see*) outside the house at about midnight last night, but so far no one (6) .... (*arrest*). Police (7) .... (*ask*) anyone who was in the area at the time to contact them at Chelsea police station. A £10,000 reward (8) .... (*offer*).

5

Which phrase does not belong to the following groups? Why?

a) to be surprised / to be frightened / to be terrified / to be worried

b) to be rescued / to be attacked/ to be saved / to be helped

c) to be produced by / to be arrested by / to be directed by / to be written by

d) to be discovered by / to be destroyed by / to be invented by / to be designed by

6

Can you think of an 'extreme' adjective for each of these 'ordinary' adjectives?

- good *brilliant*
- bad ....
- surprised ....
- cold ....
- angry ....

7

Look back through Module 6 and write two more revision questions of your own to ask other students.

module 7

Social matters

Part A **Language**

Polite requests
will (instant decisions and responses)
Speaking and reading: *Going out around the world*
Vocabulary: social occasions
Wordspot: *go*

Speaking and reading

1 Young people all over the world were given the questionnaire opposite about going out. Read the questionnaire quickly. What general topics did it ask about?

2 Look at the words and phrases in **bold** in the box below and mark them:

✓✓ if you already know them.
✓ if you can guess the meaning from the context.
✗ if you need to check the meaning with your teacher or in your mini-dictionary.

popular *(question 1)*
to **treat** people **equally** *(question 2)*
to be **acceptable** *(question 4)*
to **go out on a date** *(question 4)*
to **share** the bill *(question 4)*
a **custom** *(question 5)*
an **attitude** *(question 5)*

Going out around the world

1 Where people go
List the five most popular activities people do when they go out in the evening. Are there differences between age groups?

2 Late or early?
a At what time do the following things usually happen in your country?
   • meeting your friends for an evening out [＿＿＿]
   • bars and pubs closing [＿＿＿]
   • night-clubs closing [＿＿＿]
b What time would parents usually expect their 16-year-old sons or daughters to come home at night?
   • before 9pm ☐   • between 11 and 12pm ☐
   • between 9 and 10pm ☐   • after midnight ☐

   Do parents treat sons and daughters equally in this respect?
c Which of the following statements do you agree with?
   • People expect you to arrive on time ☐
   • It's rude to be more than about twenty minutes late – people will get annoyed if you make a habit of it ☐
   • Most people expect you to arrive at least half an hour late for arrangements ☐

3 Tastes
Do you agree (✓) or disagree (✗) with the following statements?
a American / International films are more popular than films made in my country ☐
b In nightclubs and bars, American / international music is more popular than music from my country ☐
c American / International food like hamburgers and pizzas are more popular than traditional food from my country ☐

4 What's acceptable and what's not acceptable?
Do you agree (✓) or disagree (✗) with the following statements?
a Most young men and women smoke and drink alcohol ☐
b It is not very common for groups of women to go out on their own ☐
c When a couple go out on a date, they normally share the bill ☐

5 Different generations and regions
a Look back at the questions above. Were these customs and attitudes the same or different when your parents were young? And your grandparents?
b Are these social habits the same all over your country or do they vary according to region?

A night out in Tokyo is much the same as a night out in Milan these days, according to a survey about socialising, conducted amongst 16 to 34-year-olds around the world. Whether you live in Korea or Canada, Italy or Ireland, a typical night out is spent eating burgers, seeing American films or listening to English-language music in clubs and bars. Individual differences do survive – the ballet is still particularly popular amongst Russians, while more Japanese favour an evening of Karaoke – but American culture is everywhere.

Differences in the social behaviour of the two sexes are also disappearing. The majority of respondents world-wide felt that it was 'perfectly normal' for groups of young women to go out alone, that it was 'equally acceptable' for young women to smoke and drink, and that a couple should split the bill when they go out together. For most young people these were the biggest differences between their own generation and their parents'.

Interestingly, however, the vast majority of the young people interviewed said that parents are still stricter with daughters than sons about where they go and who they go with. Overall, only 10 per cent thought that parents treat their sons and daughters equally, and almost no one thought parents were stricter with their sons! In most countries, it was also agreed that such rules tend to be stricter outside the big cities.

Important national differences did appear, however, when it came to time-keeping. In the Far East and in Eastern Europe a night out starts – and finishes – much earlier: there seven o'clock was the average time given for meeting up with friends. For many Southern Europeans and South Americans, on the other hand, an evening out doesn't even start until ten or eleven o'clock, by which time many of their Korean and Japanese counterparts are safely home in bed!

Parents' rules reflect this. Most Japanese parents expect their teenagers home by ten o'clock or even earlier, whereas in Europe it is more likely to be eleven or twelve o'clock. The most surprising findings here came from Argentina, however, where it is apparently quite normal for 15 and 16-year-olds to stay out all night. But then perhaps this is because their parents have less to worry about – 80 per cent of Argentine youngsters claimed that they rarely or never drink alcohol!

3 Discuss the questionnaire in groups, comparing and explaining your answers.

4 The article above describes the findings of the questionnaire. Read it and:
– underline any findings similar to those of your class.
– circle any findings different from those in your class.
– write (!) next to anything you found surprising about customs in other countries.

5 Discuss the following questions in groups.
- Is the influence of American culture increasing in your country? Does this worry you?
- Should parents have strict rules about where their teenage sons and daughters go? Do you think that sons and daughters should be treated the same?

Vocabulary

Social occasions

1 In box A is a list of social occasions. In box B is a list of things people do on different social occasions. In your country, which of the things listed in box B would normally be associated with the social occasions in box A? Would it be very unusual to see or do any of the things in box B?

A	B
meeting an old friend / acquaintance in the street being introduced to someone at a party going round to a friend's house going out to a restaurant with a business associate	bow wave bring wine or flowers hold hands kiss leave a tip offer food and drink accept or refuse food and drink say 'hello' shake hands

2 Can you think of any other customs in your country for the social occasions in box A?

Language focus 1

Polite requests

⋯⋯⋯⋯⋯⋯⋯⋯⋯⋯⋯⋯⋯⋯⋯⋯⋯⋯⋯⋯⋯

Mini-task

Think of three common requests you make in your daily life. What are the requests people most often make to you? Compare lists with the rest of the class. Which requests came up most often?

⋯⋯⋯⋯⋯⋯⋯⋯⋯⋯⋯⋯⋯⋯⋯⋯⋯⋯⋯⋯⋯

1 Imagine that you have just arrived in an English-speaking country. Everywhere you go, people are asking things and making requests. Look at the pictures below and opposite. Can you guess what the people are asking?

2 **a)** 📼 [7.1] Listen to what the people are asking. Your teacher will stop the cassette after each question. Decide:

• which person is speaking.
• how you could answer.

b) 📼 [7.2] Listen to how the foreign man answers each request and compare.

Analysis

1 a Listen again to the complete dialogues. Write the phrases used for asking and answering politely in the correct category below.

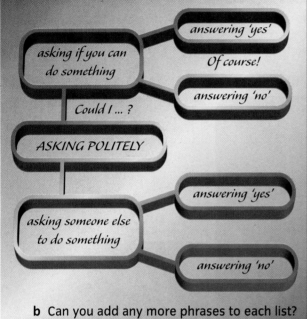

asking if you can do something

answering 'yes'

Of course!

answering 'no'

Could I ... ?

ASKING POLITELY

asking someone else to do something

answering 'yes'

answering 'no'

b Can you add any more phrases to each list?

2 Mark the phrases as follows:
✓ if it is quite casual.
✓✓ if it is more polite.

Now read Language summary A on pages 145–146.

Pronunciation

1 🖾 [7.3] Intonation is very important when you want to ask things politely. Listen to the questions again and notice what happens to the speaker's voice.

• Can you tell me the time, please?

• Is it okay if I sit here?

Listen again and copy the speakers' intonation.

2 Work in pairs. Practise saying the questions and answers from Exercise 2, using the pictures to remind you of what they are saying. (It does not matter if you do not use exactly the same words as on the cassette, but make sure that you ask and answer politely!)

Practice

1 The following short dialogues are not very polite. Re-write them to make them sound better. Then practise the polite dialogues in pairs.

For example:

A: ~~I want~~ to speak to Maria‸.
    Can I   *please?*

B: ‸She's in the bath. ~~Call back later~~.
    I'm sorry   *Can I take a message?*

a A: I want to use your scissors.
  B: Yes.
b A: Pass me my coat.
  B: Here you are.
c A: Lend me £5 until tomorrow.
  B: I haven't got any money with me.
d A: Bring me the bill.
  B: Yes.
e A: Give me a light.
  B: My lighter isn't working.
f A: If you're going into town, give me a lift to the bus stop.
  B: Yes.
g A: Tell me the way to the National Gallery.
  B: I don't know this area very well myself.
h A: Pick my suit up from the dry-cleaner's while you're at the shops.
  B: I don't think I'll be able to carry it – I'll have a lot of other things.

2 a) Think of six things to ask other students in the class politely, using the following verbs.

• lend or borrow
• pass (me)
• turn on / turn off
• open or close
• move
• help (me)

b) Take turns to make your requests to each other. If the other student agrees, he /she must really do it. If your partner refuses, he / she must give a reason. Make sure your requests and answers sound polite.

> Would you mind lending me your dictionary?

> I'm sorry, I need it myself.

> Sure ... here you are.

71

Language focus 2

will (instant decisions and responses)

1 Look at the pictures opposite. Where are the people? What are they talking about?

2 Match the dialogues below with the pictures. Then complete the dialogues in your own words.

a
A: I'm going home now.
B: Oh ... Tony said he needs to speak to you urgently.
A: I'll go and see what he wants quickly.
B: I think he's in a meeting with Kate at the moment, actually.
A: I really need to get home – tell him I'll ...

b
A: This is driving me mad!
B: What are you trying to do?
A: I'm trying to change the flash in this camera, but the instructions are so unclear.
B: Hang on, I'll just finish doing this and then I'll ...

c
A: Oh no, it's ten past eleven! I've missed the last bus!
B: Never mind, I'll take you home, it's no trouble.
A: No, don't do that. It's too far and you've had quite a few glasses of wine. I'll ...

Analysis

In each of the situations above the speakers decide what to do about a small problem.

- When do they decide?
- What verb form do they use?

Now read Language summary B on page 146.

Practice

1 Discuss in pairs what you would say in the following situations.

a Someone tells you that a friend has broken his leg and is at home on his own all day. What would you say?
- I'll phone him next week.   • I'll send him a card.
- I'll go and see him.

b A colleague is complaining that he hasn't got any money to buy lunch. What would you say?
- I'll buy you lunch.   • I'll lend you some money if you want.
- I'll share my sandwiches with you.

c A friend phones up to say he is stuck with his English homework. What would you say?
- I'll come round and help you.   • I'll do it for you if you want.
- I'll meet you later when you've finished it.

d You are round at a friend's house for dinner. Nobody seems to be enjoying themselves. What would you say?
- I'll put some music on.   • I think I'll go now.
- I'll just pop out and buy some more drinks.

2 How would you respond in the following situations?

a You see an elderly neighbour in the street, carrying two very large bags of shopping.
b You're at a cousin's house. It's chaos – the baby's screaming and she's trying to cook lunch.
c A close friend is very nervous because he's going to the dentist's to have several teeth taken out.
d You're visiting your grandmother. Her television isn't working properly, and she's worried about it.

3 Use some of the situations from Exercises 1 and 2 to create dialogues like those on page 72. Act them out with a partner.

Wordspot

go

1 The following diagram shows some very common phrases with *go*. Study the diagram and then answer the questions below.

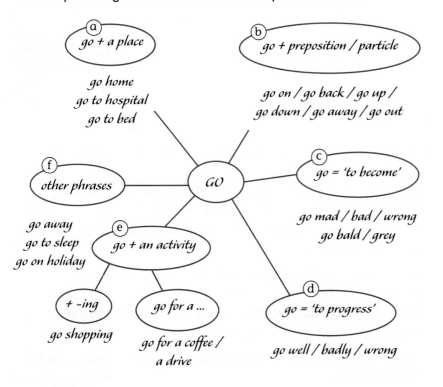

a Find a phrase with *go* that means:
   • to return • to increase • to decrease • to continue
   • to have a holiday
b Who or what can:
   • go wrong? • go bad? • go bald? • go grey? • go mad?
c Imagine a situation where you might say the following phrases.
   • 'Go away!' • 'Go to sleep!' • 'Go on!'

2 Complete the following diagrams with **your own** suggestions.

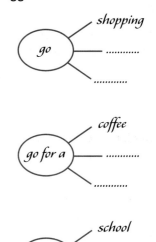
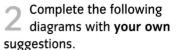
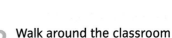

3 Walk around the classroom and find one person who:

a sometimes goes on holiday alone.
b hates going shopping.
c usually goes for a drink / coffee after class.
d usually goes home as soon as the lesson finishes.
e is going out on Saturday night.
f is going away next weekend.
g goes jogging regularly.
h likes going for a walk in the countryside.

4 Copy the diagram opposite to make a poster for your classroom wall showing the uses of *go*. Add new expressions when you meet them.

Part B Task

Draw up a list of tips for visitors to your country

Task link: making generalisations
Real life: making a social arrangement

Personal vocabulary

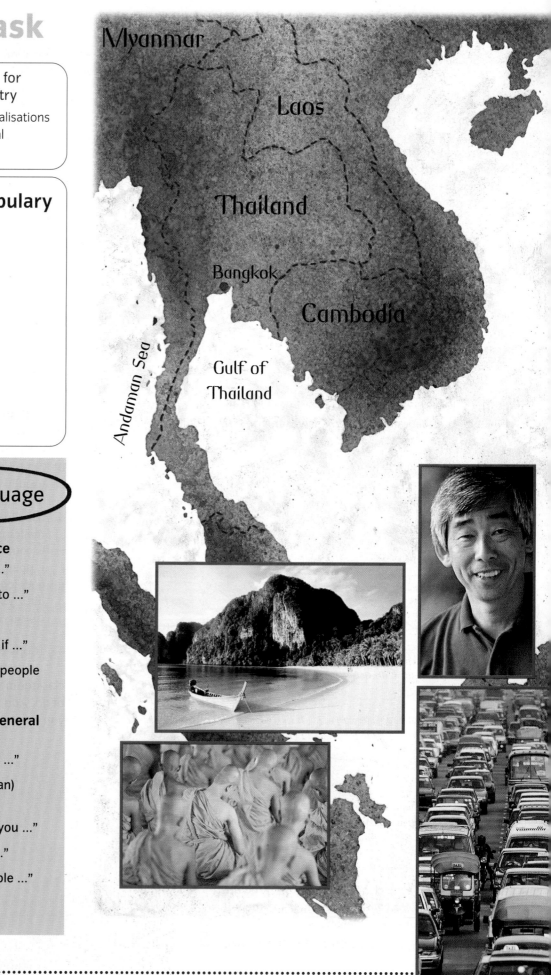

Useful language

Giving advice

"You should never ..."

"Always remember to ..."

"Don't forget to ..."

"Don't be surprised if ..."

"You should expect people to ..."

Describing the general situation

"It is polite / rude to ..."

"Most (French / Italian) people ..."

"Normally / Usually you ..."

"Generally, people ..."

"On the whole, people ..."

Preparation for task

1 Look at the map and pictures of Thailand. What do you know about Thailand? Can you imagine how social customs there differ from those in your country?

2 Below is an extract from a travel guide to Thailand which gives 'tips' to foreign visitors about social behaviour and customs. Read the extract and answer the following questions.

a   Which social situations are mentioned?
b   Some of the tips have two alternatives – can you guess which is the correct one?

3 🖭 [7.4] Nikam Nipotam was born in Thailand, but was brought up in England. You are going to hear him talking about customs to a colleague who is going to Thailand. Listen and underline the correct alternatives in the extract below.

4 Compare your answers with a partner. Were you surprised by anything Nikam Nipotam said?

Tips for foreign visitors to Thailand

Thailand is famous for its hospitality, and the average visitor will have no difficulty in adapting to local customs. The following tips are mostly common sense, but to avoid giving offence, foreign visitors may find them useful.

1.   When addressing a Thai person it is polite to use just *their first name | their surname*.
2.   In more formal situations you should use the word 'Khun'. This is like 'Mr' and is used for addressing *men | both men and women*.
3.   It is not usual to shake hands when you meet a Thai person. Instead you do a 'wai' – you put your hands together as if you are saying a prayer, and bow your head slightly. You should always use this greeting when you meet *older people | your friends*.
4.   Couples should be careful about how they behave. You don't see Thai couples *holding hands | kissing in public*.
5.   The head is very important in Thai culture. It is *very respectful | not respectful* to touch another person's head.
6.   If you're invited to someone's home, you should *always take off your shoes | never take off your shoes*. It's very important to remember this!
7.   When eating a meal with Thai people, you should expect the food to be served in large bowls in the centre of the table. Everyone helps themselves, using *chopsticks | a spoon and fork*.
8.   Finally, you should never insult the Thai royal family. Thais always show respect towards their royalty, and they expect visitors to do the same.

Task

1 Imagine that a visitor from a different culture is coming to your country (a British or American tourist, a Thai person like Nikam Nipotam or one of your fellow students). You are going to draw up a list of eight tips about social behaviour, like the ones in the extract. Make a list of ideas under the following headings:

- addressing people
- meeting and greeting
- gestures
- public behaviour
- an invitation to someone's house
- at a meal
- dress code
- other important 'dos' and 'don'ts'

Ask your teacher about any words or phrases you need and write them in the *Personal vocabulary* box.

2 When you have finished, you can:

Either: listen to the other students' lists to see if they included any useful tips that you didn't think of. Then work with a partner and act out a conversation like Nikam Nipotam's. Imagine your partner is either:
- a foreign guest staying with your family.
- a foreign business associate.

or: give a talk to the rest of the class about social customs in your country. Listen to the tips that other students give you about their countries and note down any customs that are very different from those in your country. Discuss the ones that you find most interesting / surprising and ask questions about anything that you do not understand.

Look at the phrases in the *Useful language* box.

Optional writing

Write up the tips for foreign visitors to your country, as in the extract for people visiting Thailand.

Task link

Making generalisations

A. The majority of Inuit people from Alaska are nomads, moving from one place to another, hunting and fishing to survive. They don't tend to live in houses, preferring tents or houses built from ice, called 'igloos'. Even today, it is quite common for a man to have several wives.

B. In some parts of Kentucky and Virginia, it is quite normal for girls of twelve or thirteen to get married and start a family. Often their husbands are only sixteen or seventeen, so young couples tend to live with their parents until they finish their education. Many schools in these areas have crèches to look after their pupils' babies while they are studying.

C. The Hopi Indians of Arizona generally live in family groups called 'clans'. It is usual for the woman to be the head of the family and the owner of the family home. When a young couple get married, most new husbands go and live with their wife's family and their children become members of her clan, rather than his.

1 The extracts above describe different cultural groups in the USA. The customs described in two of the extracts are still true today, but one is no longer true. Can you guess which it is?

2 In the extracts above the writer is talking *generally* about the customs of different groups of people. Read the extracts again and underline the phrases used to make generalisations. The first extract has been done for you. Then read *Language summary* C on page 146.

3 Circle the best alternative in the following sentences to describe what generally happens in your country. Compare your answers in groups. Did you agree / disagree?

a *Quite a lot of people / Not many people / Nobody* get(s) married in their teens.

b *It is quite common / It is uncommon* for girls in their teens to have babies.

c *It is usual / It is quite normal / It is unusual* for young couples to live with their parents after they get married.

d *The majority of young people / Some young people / Very few young people* stay with their parents until they get married.

e Women *tend to / don't tend to* take their husband's name when they get married.

f *Almost everybody / Many people / A few people / Nobody* still wear(s) traditional dress.

g *Most people / Some people / Very few people* still live(s) in traditional-style houses.

4 In pairs, use the words and phrases in the diagram below to make at least four more sentences about your country.

In my country

it's / it isn't

quite / very

common for / normal for / unusual for / easy for / difficult for, etc.

families / (young) couples / (young / old) people / grandparents, etc.

to live in houses rather than flats
to rent rather than buy a home
to have four or five children
to have a second home in the country
to live with their children and grandchildren
to live in old people's homes

Real life

Making a social arrangement

1 📼 [7.5] Laurence is phoning Roger. Read Laurence's part of the conversation and answer the following questions. Then listen to check.

a What do you think the relationship is between Roger, Laurence and Millie?

b Can you guess what Roger is saying?

ROGER: ....

LAURENCE: Hello, Roger. It's Laurence.

ROGER: ....

LAURENCE: Fine. We've just got back from a few days away with some relatives down on the coast. Anyway how are things with you and Millie?

ROGER: ....

LAURENCE: Yes, I can hear you're busy! Listen, I won't keep you. I was just phoning to ask if you and Millie are doing anything next Saturday night. If not, would you like to come for a meal? Patrick and Colin are coming over, and we thought it would be nice if you were there too.

ROGER: ....

LAURENCE: Yeah, it is a shame ... I know, how about the following Saturday instead? I don't think we've got anything planned that night.

ROGER: ....

LAURENCE: Great! We'll look forward to seeing you. I'll let you get back to the family now. Give me a ring in a week or so to arrange a time.

ROGER: ....

LAURENCE: Yeah, see you!

---

3 **a)** Listen again, paying particular attention to Roger's part of the conversation. Which of the phrases in columns 3 and 4 does he use to accept / refuse Laurence's invitation?

b) Do you hear any other useful phrases for talking on the telephone? Write them in the correct column.

4 **a)** Practise saying the phrases, copying the voices on the cassette. Do you know any other phrases that you could add to these lists?

b) Work with a partner. Choose a situation below and have a conversation like Roger and Laurence's. Invite your partner:

- to go to a concert / football match / club / film / exhibition.
- to come to your house for a meal / drink / party.
- to go out for a drink / meal / coffee.

Suggest a day and a time. Your partner will accept or refuse, giving a reason. Then swap over so your partner invites you.

2 Look at Laurence's part of the conversation again. Write the phrases he uses into columns 1 and 2 of the table below.

1 useful phrases for talking on the phone	2 inviting and arranging	3 accepting an invitation	4 refusing an invitation
Hello, Roger. It's Laurence.		Thank you very much – that would be lovely.	We can't, I'm afraid.
		I think that should be fine.	Sorry, but we're busy.
		That'd be great!	What a shame!
		I'll call you back if there's any problem.	

Reading

1 You are going to read an article about important inventions. Discuss the following questions in groups.

- There is a connection between a picture on the left and a picture on the right. Can you guess what it is?

> Did Caselli invent the telephone?

> No, I think he invented the ...

- When do you think the things on the left were invented?

2 Read the article and see if you guessed correctly.

3 Answer the following questions in pairs.

a Did Caselli's 'fax machine' actually work?

b Who designed the first steam engine?

c Who built the first steam engine?

d Why does the story of the light bulb show that inventors need to be patient?

e Who invented the first telephone?

f What did the inventors of Velcro and of paper have in common?

g What was the purpose of the exhibition at the National Laboratory at Upton in 1958?

h Did Professor Higinbotham understand the potential of his 'computer game'?

4 Discuss the following questions in pairs.

- Which information in the article did you already know?

- Which information did you find most surprising?

How to be a successful inventor

paper factory

Velcro

fax machine

telephone

What do you need for an invention to be a success?

Well, good timing for a start. You can have a great idea which the public simply doesn't want ... yet. Take the Italian priest, Giovanni Caselli, who invented the first fax machine using an enormous pendulum in the 1860s. Despite the excellent quality of the reproductions, his invention quickly died a commercial death. It was not until the 1980s that the fax became an essential piece of
10 equipment in every office ... too late for Signor Caselli.

Money also helps. The Frenchman Denis Papin (1647 – 1712) had the idea for a steam engine almost a hundred years before the better-remembered Scotsman James Watt was even born ... but he never had enough money to build one.

You also need to be patient (it took scientists nearly eighty years to develop a light bulb
20 which actually worked) ... but not too patient. In the 1870s, Elisha Gray, a professional inventor from Chicago, developed plans for a telephone. Gray saw it as no more than 'a beautiful toy', however. When he finally sent details of his invention to the Patent Office on February 14th 1876, it was too late; almost identical designs had arrived just two hours earlier ... and the young man who sent them, Alexander Graham Bell, will always be
30 remembered as the inventor of the telephone.

Of course what you really need is a great idea – but if you haven't got one, a walk in the country and a careful look at nature can help. The Swiss scientist, George de Mestral, had the idea for Velcro when he found his clothes covered in sticky seed pods after a walk in the country. During a similar walk in the French countryside some 250 years earlier, René-Antoine Ferchault de Réaumur had the idea
40 that paper could be made from wood when he found an abandoned wasps' nest.

You also need good commercial sense. Willy Higinbotham was a scientist doing nuclear research in the Brookhaven National Laboratory in Upton, USA. In 1958 the public were invited to the Laboratory to see their work; but both parents and children were less interested in the complicated equipment and diagrams than in a tiny 120cm screen with a
50 white dot which could be hit back and forth over a 'net' using a button and a knob. Soon

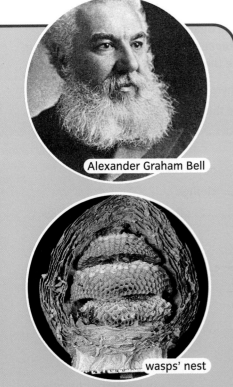
Alexander Graham Bell

wasps' nest

Giovanni Caselli

seed pods

hundreds of people were ignoring the other exhibits to play the first ever computer game – made from a simple laboratory instrument called an 'oscilloscope'. Higinbotham, however, never made a cent from his invention: he thought people were only interested in the game because the other exhibits were so boring!

Vocabulary

Machines

1 🔲 [8.1] Listen to some conversations and decide which of the items in the box the speakers are talking about.

| answerphone   CD player   dishwasher   home computer   fax machine |
| vacuum cleaner   photocopier   video recorder   washing machine |

2 **a)** Match a word / phrase from box A with one from box B.
Listen again to check your answers.

A	B
press	flashes
hold	that button
a red light	the button
	down

A	B
plug	it
unplug	it on
switch	it in

A	B
pick up	the tone
dial	the handset
wait for	the number

A	B
put	the tape out
the tape	a tape in
get	gets stuck

b) Which of the words / phrases above could be used about:

- a cassette recorder? • a telephone? • a camera?

3 Think of a machine you often use and describe to a partner how it works. If you have it with you, show it to your partner as you are explaining.

Pronunciation

1 Notice the stress patterns in compound nouns:

NOUN + NOUN   ADJECTIVE + NOUN
•   •   •
phone message   central heating.

Where do you think the stress will be in the following words?

- mobile phone   • swimming pool   • dishwasher
- dark glasses   • video recorder   • dining room
- electric guitar   • electric cooker   • car radio
- washing machine

2 🔲 [8.2] Listen and check. Practise saying the words.

Language focus 2

Quantifiers (*a few, a lot of,* etc.)

··

Mini-task

Work in pairs. Try to think of as many things as possible which your partner might keep in his / her:
- *bag.*
- *pocket.*
- *desk at work.*
Tell your partner what you think. Were you right? Tell the class about anything unusual you discovered.

··

1 Denise Connor owns a small arts and crafts shop. Look at the picture above and discuss what kind of things it might sell.

2 a) 🔲 [8.3] Listen to Denise talking about her shop. Tick (✓) the things which she sells.

plates	mugs	bowls	ashtrays	brooches	necklaces
earrings	watches	dresses	dressing gowns		cards
handkerchiefs	candles	lamps	mirrors	picture frames	

b) What does Denise say are the good and bad points about the shop's location?

3 Listen to Denise again. When you hear the following sentences, ask your teacher to stop the cassette. Complete the gaps with the words you hear.

a   I've only been here for .... of years.

b   .... the things are imported from abroad.

c   I've got .... ceramics from Greece and Portugal.

d   I sell .... of jewellery.

e   I sell .... clothes.

f   There are .... other little shops and cafés nearby.

g   There are .... students and young people living around here.

h   And I've got .... friends who live or work in this area.

i   There just isn't .... space.

j   I've got far .... things in this tiny little shop.

k   I'd love to have .... space for a little café and a cake shop as well.

Analysis

1 Mark the 'quantifiers' below as follows:
  – **C** if they can only be used with countable nouns.
  – **U** if they can only be used with uncountable nouns.
  – **C / U** if they can be used with both.

• *a lot of / lots of* ☐		• *a little* ☐	
• *too much* ☐		• *not much* ☐	
• *too many* ☐		• *not many* ☐	
• *some* ☐		• *one or two* ☐	
• *a few* ☐		• *no* ☐	
• *(not) enough* ☐		• *loads of* ☐	
• *plenty of* ☐		• *(not) any* ☐	
• *several* ☐		• *a couple of* ☐	

2 Is there any difference in meaning between the following pairs of sentences? If so, can you explain what it is?

a • *The car costs too much money.*
   • *The car costs a lot of money.*

b • *We've got enough time.*
   • *We've got plenty of time.*

c • *We had no problems getting there.*
   • *We didn't have any problems getting there.*

Now read Language summary B on page 147.

Practice

1 In pairs, discuss which quantifiers best complete the following sentences about your classroom or work place.

a   There's .... space for everyone to work.

b   There are .... comfortable chairs.

c   There's .... natural light.

d   There's .... fresh air.

e   There are .... notices on the wall.

f   There are .... plants.

g   There's .... valuable equipment.

h   There are .... stairs.

i   There's .... noise from outside.

j   There are .... people to talk to.

2 In pairs or groups, discuss the features of the city / town / village where you live using appropriate quantifiers. Think about the following things:

- cinemas
- green space
- shops
- theatres
- pollution
- places to eat
- sports facilities
- traffic
- atmosphere

I think there are too many cinemas.

There definitely isn't enough green space.

I don't agree! There are loads of parks!

Wordspot

something

1 The diagram below shows some very common phrases with *something*. Read the following examples of phrases with *something* and add them to the correct section of the diagram. (Some of them have already been done for you.)

a   'And when you've finished that there's **something else** I want you to do as well.'

b   'Can you send someone up to my room to fix the shower? There's **something wrong with it**.'

c   'Did you know that there are **something like** 300 million people in the world who speak English?'

d   'I'm bored! I really must find **something to do**.'

e   'I'm not exactly sure what *voltage* is, but I think it's **something to do with** electricity.'

f   'Mum ... Dad ... Lucy and I have got **something to tell you** ... we've decided to get married!'

g   'I'm not sure exactly how old Clare is, but she must be **thirty-something**, I suppose.'

h   'I really believe the government should **do something** about the problem of unemployment.'

i   'I didn't agree at all with her idea. I really felt I should **say something**.'

j   'There was **something strange** about the way she spoke. I knew there must be a problem.'

l   'Please come in and sit down. Can I offer you **something to drink**?'

ⓐ *for being imprecise*
say something

ⓑ *something + adjective*
something strange

SOMETHING

ⓓ *other phrases*
there's something wrong with it

ⓒ *something + infinitive*
something to do

2 Work in pairs. Student A should read the instructions / questions on page 135, Student B should read the instructions / questions on page 138. Listen to your partner's instructions / questions, and answer them using a phrase / sentence with *something*.

3 Copy the diagram above to make a poster for your classroom wall showing the uses of *something*. Add new expressions when you meet them.

Part B **Task**

Describe a personal or ideal possession

Task link: describing objects
Real life: writing 'thank you' letters

Personal vocabulary

Useful language

Describing things you own

"One of the most precious things I own is ..."

"It's made of ..."

"I bought it in ..."

"It was a birthday present ..."

"It used to belong to ..."

"It reminds me of ..."

Describing things you'd like to own

"What I'd really like is ..."

"I'd love a ..."

"I've always wanted ..."

"Something I'd love to own is a ..."

Emma

Rodney

David

Daphné

Preparation for task

1 Look at the pictures of the objects and people opposite. Which object do you associate with each person? (There is one object too many.)

2 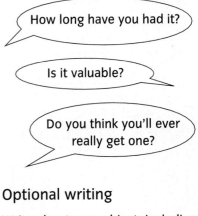 [8.4] *Either:* listen to the four people talking about one of the objects in the pictures. Complete the table below with the information you hear.

	what the object is (do they own one already?)	words / phrases used to describe the object	why the object is important
1 Emma			
2 Rodney			
3 David			
4 Daphné			

or: listen to your teacher talking about an object of importance to him / her, or about something he / she would really like to have. Make notes under the headings in the table above. Ask your teacher questions to find out more about the object.

Task

1 You are going to give a short talk similar to the ones you have heard above. If possible, you will also show the object to the other students or draw a picture of it. Make notes under the following headings. Ask your teacher about any words or phrases you need and write them in the *Personal vocabulary* box. Look at the phrases in the *Useful language* box.

what the object is	description of the object	why it's important to you / why you would like to have it

2 Work in groups. Give your talk and listen to other students' talks. Show your object or draw a picture if possible. Answer any questions other students have, and think of some questions to ask them about their objects.

> How long have you had it?

> Is it valuable?

> Do you think you'll ever really get one?

Optional writing

Write about your object, including the information that was in your talk. (Do not put your name on the piece of paper.) Your teacher will collect the descriptions and read them out. Try to guess who wrote each one.

Task link

Describing objects

1 Choose an object below. Make sure you know the name for it in English. Answer the questions in the table by putting a tick (✓) in the correct box(es).

	Yes, usually or always.	Sometimes, but not usually.	No, never.
Is it round / square / rectangular?			
Is it made of leather?			
Does it make a noise?			
Does it fit easily into your pocket ?			
Does it have a handle ?			
Is it found in the kitchen?			
Is it easily breakable?			
Is it useful for making things?			
Could it be made of wood?			
Does it need batteries or do we plug it in?			

2 Work in pairs. Look at your partner's table and the boxes he / she has ticked. Can you guess which object your partner chose?

3 Work in pairs again. Think of an object which we use every day. Your partner will ask you fifteen questions to find out what the object is. When you have finished, change over.

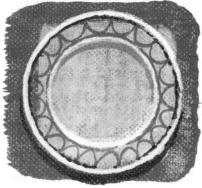

Real life

Writing 'thank you' letters

1 Here are some things we usually do when writing a letter to thank someone for a present.

- Write as soon as possible after receiving the present. ☐
- Mention what the present you received was, why you like it, and how you will use it. ☐
- Include some personal news. ☐
- Ask about the receiver's personal news. ☐
- Sign off in a friendly way. ☐

Read the letter opposite. Tick (✓) the things above which the writer does, and put a cross (✗) next to those he does not do.

2 Look at more extracts from 'thank you' letters and notes opposite. Which one comes from:

a a business letter? ☐

b a card sent to a couple after a dinner party? ☐

c a reply to a party invitation? ☐

d a message written on a card for someone leaving a job? ☐

e a letter from a language student to her former host family? ☐

f a 'thank you' note left on someone's desk? ☐

3 What do you think the writer said before and after these extracts? Choose one and write the complete letter or note. (If it is a letter, remember to put in the address and date, as well as an appropriate beginning and ending.)

October 3rd

Dear Valerie and Walter,

It's been nearly three months since the wedding. So I thought it was time to stop being lazy and finally thank you for your lovely present. It was really kind of you to think of us. We both liked it very much, and Anne has found just the right place for it.

What a pity you couldn't come to the wedding - it really was a great day, and all the guests seemed to enjoy themselves. Still, it is a very long drive from where you are, and I'm sure you were right when you said it might be too tiring for you to come all this way.

I do hope you are both feeling better now, Walter, and that you're both enjoying life. We're both fine - after a lovely honeymoon in Greece (plenty of sun, sea and relaxation!) we're both back at work and settling down in the new flat. Perhaps you'll be able to come and see us one day soon!

Thanks again and take care,
Jeremy and Anne

---

① Thank you for all your hard work in the Accounts Department and your great contribution to ...

② Many thanks for a lovely meal and your hospitality on Friday - we had a great time. We must do it again some time ...

③ Thanks a lot for lending me your leather jacket. It was ...

④ ... thanks for the invitation - we'd love to come! Shall we ...

⑤ ... arrived back safely. I'd like to thank you again for all your kindness during my stay in Edinburgh. I had a really great time and I'll never forget ...

⑥ Thank you for your letter of August 31st concerning your plans to ...

87

Consolidation
modules 5–8

Ⓐ Future forms / future time clauses

Complete the gaps in the following article with the correct form of the verb in brackets, or with a word from the box. (There may be more than one possibility.)

because	before	unless	once	if	when	until

... HOT GOSSIP ... HOT GOSSIP ... HOT GOSSIP

For the hottest, latest gossip on the good, the bad and the famous, read Imelda!!

Actress Glynnis Parsley and tennis star Andy Martinez have finally decided (1) .... (*get*) married – (2) .... Andy's first wife Alana agrees to a divorce!! However, I have heard that Alana (3) .... (*not / give*) Andy a divorce (4) .... he hands over the couple's $20 million mansion in Palm Beach. 'We hope (5) .... (*marry*) later this year,' a smiling Glynnis told me. Or maybe next ...

CSN TV have announced that Britain's Duchess of Cumberland (6) .... (*present*) her own chat show on cable television later this year. The programme (7) .... (*start*) filming (8) .... the Duchess (9) .... (*return*) from her latest skiing holiday in Austria – and (10) .... (*feature*) Hollywood stars as well as many of the Duchess's own friends. 'I really want (11) .... (*do*) the best job as I can as a television presenter,' the Duchess told me last week. 'I'd like people (12) .... (*recognise*) me as a talented media person, and not just one of the best-dressed and most glamorous women in the world.'

Rockstar, actress and mother Myra Meckenridge is about (13) .... (*buy*) a very special holiday home for herself and her baby daughter, Dolores ... the Mediterranean island of Santo Domingo! She is also planning (14) .... (*build*) a copy of the cathedral in Florence at her home in Florida, and is thinking of (15) .... (*convert*) her ranch in Colorado into a private zoo for Dolores and herself. But she will not allow Dolores to have a boyfriend (16) .... she is 21: 'Like any mother, I just want Dolores (17) .... (*have*) a normal life,' Myra told me.

Showbusiness legend Valerie Reinhard, who (18) .... (*hold*) her 70th birthday celebration at the Astoria Hotel, Las Vegas on Friday of next week, says she intends (19) .... (*invite*) all seven of her ex-husbands to the party. 'What if all of them (20) .... (*arrive*) at the same time?' I asked Valerie last week. 'I'm sure that (21) .... they finally all meet each other, they (22) .... (*find*) plenty to talk about!' she replied.

... HOT GOSSIP ... HOT GOSSIP ... HOT GOSSIP

Ⓑ Vocabulary: megamemory

1 Work in pairs. The box below contains twenty-four words and phrases you have studied in Modules 5–8. As quickly as possible find three:

a things you can do over the telephone.
b machines you might have in your home.
c things you might do if you see a friend in the street.
d types of work.
e things you might do in the evening.
f types of television programmes.
g words that can describe a job.
h words that describe negative feelings.

challenging schoolwork
a vacuum cleaner a cartoon
arrange a night out
kiss each other annoyed
well-paid homework
a soap opera depressed
take a message stay in
a documentary terrified
stressful a freezer
book a holiday a dishwasher
shake hands wave
housework go on a date
go round to a friend's

2 You have <u>five</u> minutes to memorise the words / phrases. Close your books. Work with a partner and write down as many of the phrases as you can remember. Which pair remembered the most?

3 Look at the categories of words in Exercise 1 again. Can you add any other words or phrases to each group?

C Listening: famous firsts (passives)

🔊 **[1]** You are going to hear some information about two people and a dog who are famous for being first at something. Listen and complete the first sentence for each one. Then make sentences using the words / phrases given, using the correct passive or active form.

a Harry Belafonte made the first album in history to:

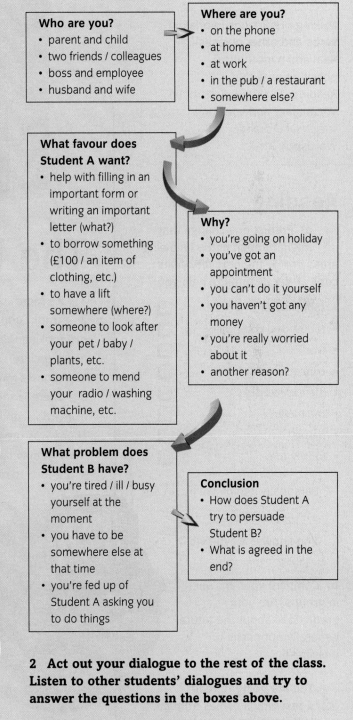

sell a million copies worldwide

• *grow up*

....

• *first album*

....

• *third album 'Calypso'*

....

• *politically active*

....

• *films*

....

b Nadia Comaneci was the first Olympic gymnast to:

....

• *Heroine of the Year*

....

• *escape*

....

• *the United States*

....

c Lakia was the first animal:

....

• *Sputnik 2*

....

• *bring back to Earth*

....

• *die*

....

• *Lakia Foundation*

....

D Role play: asking favours

1 Work in pairs. You are going to write and act out a dialogue in which Student A asks Student B a favour. Choose one thing from each of the boxes below. Spend about fifteen minutes writing and practising your dialogue.

Who are you?
• parent and child
• two friends / colleagues
• boss and employee
• husband and wife

Where are you?
• on the phone
• at home
• at work
• in the pub / a restaurant
• somewhere else?

What favour does Student A want?
• help with filling in an important form or writing an important letter (what?)
• to borrow something (£100 / an item of clothing, etc.)
• to have a lift somewhere (where?)
• someone to look after your pet / baby / plants, etc.
• someone to mend your radio / washing machine, etc.

Why?
• you're going on holiday
• you've got an appointment
• you can't do it yourself
• you haven't got any money
• you're really worried about it
• another reason?

What problem does Student B have?
• you're tired / ill / busy yourself at the moment
• you have to be somewhere else at that time
• you're fed up of Student A asking you to do things

Conclusion
• How does Student A try to persuade Student B?
• What is agreed in the end?

2 Act out your dialogue to the rest of the class. Listen to other students' dialogues and try to answer the questions in the boxes above.

3 🔊 **[2]** You are going to hear some native speakers in two of the situations above. Listen and answer the questions in the boxes. Did they use any words / phrases which might have been useful in your dialogue? Listen again to check.

module 9
Society and the future

Making predictions (modal
verbs and other phrases)
Real and hypothetical
possibilities with *if*
Reading: *The Lucky Generation*
Vocabulary and speaking:
society and change
Wordspot: *make*

Reading

1 **a)** Predict one change that
might happen in the following
areas during the next fifty years.
Look at the pictures to help you.

- space travel   3
- robots and computers ☐
- work   ☐
- education   ☐
- life expectancy   ☐
- the media   ☐
- money   ☐
- family life   ☐

> Personally, I think we'll ...

> Who knows? Maybe we'll ...

b) Compare your answers
in groups. Are your
predictions about the future
generally optimistic or
pessimistic?

2 You are going to read
a text which comes from a
book about life in the year 2050.
Read the text quickly and match
the topics above with a paragraph
in the text, as in the example.

The Lucky Generation

1 It's March, 2050.
2 Frank and Mary Smith wake up in their comfortable house
overlooking the sea and switch on the bedroom computer to give them a
news update. They used to take the Times, but changed to electronic
newspapers many years ago.
3 There is the usual stuff about space: another mission has returned
from Mars and scientists have discovered a new planet. No big deal.
There was great excitement back in 2027, when signals were received
from Titan which indicated that there might be life on a remote moon, but
efforts to make contact came to nothing and no aliens have appeared
on Earth to say 'hello'. The Catholic Church has elected
a black Pope. Interesting, but religion does not play a
significant role in their lives. Financial news: the
Euro has risen sharply in Shanghai, one of the
world's leading business centres. Mary tells the
computer to buy 5,000 Euros, and there is
instant confirmation that the transaction has
been done. Not for the first time she wonders
why Europe ever bothered to have so many
different currencies.
4 As they watch the screen, Frank and Mary take
their usual weight control pills, and order one of the
household robots to make coffee. Frank disappears into
the study to join a live video conference with his colleagues around the

world. He is a computer programmer, working for several companies on a contract basis. This is his third career: he used to be in marketing and then television.

5 Mary has a quick look at the shopping channels — the usual selection of electric cars, household robots and cheap travel offers — before picking up the video phone to talk to a colleague. She also has a job, which she shares with several others. They are doing research into genetic engineering, which has become a major industry. Both she and Frank used to have an office desk in London, but in 2014 they decided to move to the seaside and work from home.

6 Frank and Mary have one child, Louise, who also has her own workstation in the family home. She goes to school only one day a week, mainly to play with other children. Classrooms vanished in 2030 because there was no longer any need for them: interactive communications systems have made it much easier to learn at home. Louise, now thirteen, is currently studying Chinese, which has become as important as English as a world language. Louise has many Chinese friends with whom she communicates by computer.

7 According to medical experts, Louise will live to at least 130. She intends to work for a few decades and then devote her time to music and painting. Louise has given little thought to marriage, which she regards as an old-fashioned concept, and she is not sure whether she will ever want to have a child. She likes the idea of a serious relationship, and thinks there will probably be several during her lifetime, but why should she tie herself down to one person?

from *The Lucky Generation* by **William Davis (1996)**

3 a) Read the text again. How many of the predictions in the text were the same as yours?

b) From the text, find two differences:

a between domestic life in 2050 and the present day.

b between working life in 2050 and the present day.

c between a child's life in 2050 and the present day.

4 Work in pairs and discuss which aspects of the life described in the text:

- seem more attractive than life nowadays.
- seem less attractive than life nowadays.

Do you agree that people in 2050 will be 'the lucky generation'? Why? / Why not?

Language focus 1

Making predictions (modal verbs and other phrases)

Below are some predictions for life in 2050 made by the author of *The Lucky Generation* (some appear in the text on pages 90–91, some in other parts of the book). Read the predictions and mark them as follows:

(✓) if you think they will happen.

(✗) if you think they won't happen.

(?) if you are not sure.

a   You *will* be able to take pills to stop you getting fat. ☐

b   All housework *will* be done by robots. ☐

c   There *will* be no dentists because there will be a vaccine against tooth decay. ☐

d   The government *will* spend less on healthcare because there will be a cure for most diseases. ☐

e   Children *won't* go to school – they *will* be able to study at home using a computer. ☐

f   China *will* be a very important world power and Chinese *will* be a world language. ☐

g   People *will* do all their shopping by computer. ☐

h   There *will* be no more crime as technology *will* make it impossible. ☐

Analysis

All of the predictions above use *will* or *won't*. Below are some more words / phrases we can use to show how sure or not we are about the predictions we make. Put the words / phrases in the correct place on the line.

• *will probably*   • *probably won't*
• *will almost certainly*   • *almost certainly won't*
• *is / are likely to*   • *isn't / aren't likely to*
• *may (not)*   • *might (not)*   • *could*   • *may well*

◄─────────────────────────────►

will definitely   *definitely won't*

Now read Language summary A on page 147.

Practice

1   Look back at the predictions opposite from *The Lucky Generation*. Which of the phrases from the *Analysis* would you choose to replace *will* or *won't*? Discuss your opinions in groups.

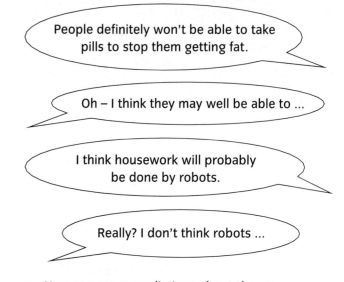

People definitely won't be able to take pills to stop them getting fat.

Oh – I think they may well be able to …

I think housework will probably be done by robots.

Really? I don't think robots …

2   Here are some predictions about the more immediate future. Discuss with a partner the best way to complete the sentences with a phrase from the *Analysis*.

a   Someone *may well* sneeze before the end of this lesson.

b   There .... be a thunderstorm tomorrow.

c   We .... talk in pairs before the end of the lesson.

d   It .... snow this month.

e   My mother .... phone me today.

f   Italy .... win the next World Cup.

g   It .... be dark by the time I get home tonight.

h   I .... win the lottery this week.

i   The teacher .... give us some homework before the end of the lesson.

3   Write your own predictions for the distant or immediate future about:

• yourself.
• a member of your family.
• a close friend.
• one of your classmates.
• your teacher.

For example:

I'll almost certainly get married in the next ten years.

My brother Juan definitely won't pass his exams!

Vocabulary and speaking

Society and change

1 For the topics listed below, which of the two options do you think is happening? Put a tick (✓) next to it. If necessary, check the meaning of the words / phrases in your mini-dictionary or with your teacher.

TOPIC		
HEALTHCARE	is getting worse.	☐
	is getting better.	☐
THE NUMBER OF PEOPLE LEARNING ENGLISH	is decreasing.	☐
	is increasing.	☐
ROADS	are becoming more dangerous.	☐
	are becoming less dangerous.	☐
THE COST OF TRAVEL	is going down.	☐
	is going up.	☐
UNEMPLOYMENT	is falling.	☐
	is rising.	☐
THE QUALITY OF TELEVISION PROGRAMMES	is deteriorating.	☐
	is improving.	☐
THE ECONOMIC SITUATION	is getting worse.	☐
	is getting better.	☐
THE NUMBER OF PEOPLE GOING ABROAD FOR THEIR HOLIDAYS	is rising.	☐
	is falling.	☐
THE EDUCATION SYSTEM	is deteriorating.	☐
	is improving.	☐
THE NUMBER OF PEOPLE WHO TAKE REGULAR EXERCISE	is decreasing.	☐
	is increasing.	☐

2 Why do you think these things are happening? Discuss and explain your opinions.

> Do you think healthcare is getting better?

> Yes, I think it's improving. Technology and doctors' skills are getting better all the time.

3 Close your book and write down as many opposite pairs of words / phrases as you can remember. Mark where the stress falls in each word / phrase.

For example:

to de•crease > to in•crease.

Language focus 2

Real and hypothetical possibilities with *if*

Mini-task

*Look at the questions in **Never say never** below and choose **one** of them. Make a list of all the possible circumstances in which someone might do this. Then work in groups and compare your list with other students. Ask your teacher about any words or phrases you need.*

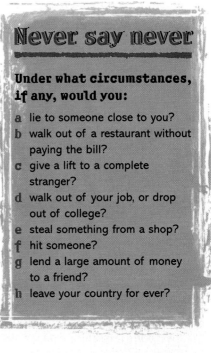

Never say never

Under what circumstances, if any, would you:

a lie to someone close to you?
b walk out of a restaurant without paying the bill?
c give a lift to a complete stranger?
d walk out of your job, or drop out of college?
e steal something from a shop?
f hit someone?
g lend a large amount of money to a friend?
h leave your country for ever?

1 [9.1] You are going to hear some people discussing the questions in *Never say never*. Listen to each part in turn and answer the following questions.

a Which of the topics are the people talking about?
b Under what circumstances would each person do this?

2 Listen again to the three people in Part 1 and complete the gaps in the following extracts.

a "Maybe if it .... a very good friend, who .... a very good reason for borrowing it ... I don't know ... if he or she .... an urgent operation, or something like that."

b "I' .... never lend a friend a large amount of money, because I think it .... almost certainly be the end of the friendship. It's an awful thing to say, but unfortunately I think it's true."

c "I haven't got any money – I never have any money, so it's a completely hypothetical question! But, theoretically, I think I' .... probably lend money to any friend ... if I .... they really .... it, and if I .... sure they .... pay it back!"

Analysis

1 Which sentence below refers to:
a a real possibility in the future?
b an imaginary situation?

• *I'd never lend a friend a lot of money.*
• *I'll never lend her any money again.*

Which verb form is used in each case? Find two more examples with *would* in Exercise 2 above.

2 We often talk about hypothetical situations using *if*. Find three examples of this in Exercise 2 above. Which tense is used after *if*? Does it refer to a past time?

3 Sometimes (but not always) the hypothetical forms in questions 1 and 2 are used together. Which one of the sentences below is incorrect?

• *If he or she really needed it, I'd lend a large amount of money to a friend.*
• *If my friend would need it, I would lend a large amount of money to him or her.*
• *I might lend a large amount of money to a friend if he or she really needed it.*

What is the difference between the two correct sentences?

Now read Language summary B on pages 147–148.

Practice

1 Look back at *Never say never* and write at least one sentence for each situation. Compare answers in groups.

For example:
I would / might lie to a close friend if I didn't want to hurt her feelings.

I'd never lie to a close friend, even if the truth hurt her feelings.

2 Do the following refer to real possibilities in the future or imaginary situations? Make questions from the words given using the pronoun *you* in each case.

a If / can live / anywhere in the world / where / live? What kind of house / choose?
b What / do / if / have some free time this evening?
c If / can / become / famous person for a day / who / be? Why / choose this person?
d If / go shopping next weekend / what / buy?
e Where / go / if / have a holiday next year? Who / go with?
f How / your life / be different / if you / be a member of the opposite sex? What be / best and worst things about it?

3 In groups ask and answer the questions above. Remember – you do not have to answer in complete sentences!

> I'd probably live right in the centre of New York.

> Perhaps I'll phone some friends for a chat.

Pronunciation

1 🔲 [9.2] Listen to some people talking about the topics in Exercise 2, and (circle) the contraction you hear. Which topic are they talking about?
a I probably *won't / wouldn't* do anything special.
b *I'll / I'd* move to a big house somewhere by the sea.
c *I'd / I'll* probably buy some new jeans.
d I expect *I'll / I'd* just go to the beach and relax.
e I think *I'll / I'd* be the Prime Minister ... *it'll / it'd* be really interesting.

2 Practise saying the sentences. Make sure you pronounce the contraction correctly.

Wordspot

make

1
Match a question / statement in box A with a response in box B.

A
a I can't decide what to wear.
b Do you think this car's making a funny noise?
c So, what do you want me to do?
d Have you locked all the doors?
e Did you like that book I lent you?
f What a lovely shirt – what's it made of?
g Sorry, but I don't think that's a very good idea.
h There's a hole in my T-shirt.

B
1 Well, can you make a better suggestion then?
2 Well, don't put your finger in it, you'll make it worse!
3 Well, hurry up and make up your mind!
4 Yes – it was brilliant. It really made me laugh!
5 If I make the dinner, would you mind tidying up a bit?
6 I don't know ... I think it's just cotton.
7 It sounds okay to me.
8 I think so ... I'll just make sure.

2
[9.3] Listen and check your answers. Work with a partner and practise the dialogues (look at the tapescript on page 163 if necessary).

3
The diagram below shows the most important uses of *make*. Underline the phrases with *make* in the dialogues in Exercise 1, and write them in the correct section of the diagram.

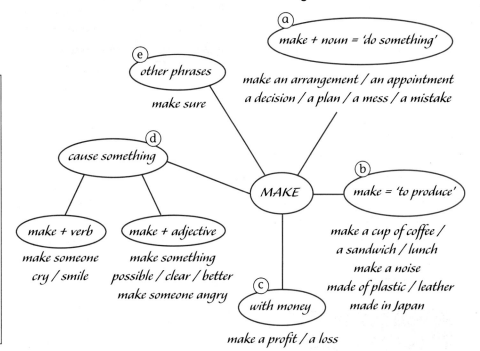

a) *make + noun = 'do something'*
make an arrangement / an appointment a decision / a plan / a mess / a mistake

e) *other phrases*
make sure

d) *cause something*

make + verb
make someone cry / smile

make + adjective
make something possible / clear / better make someone angry

MAKE

b) *make = 'to produce'*
make a cup of coffee / a sandwich / lunch make a noise made of plastic / leather made in Japan

c) *with money*
make a profit / a loss

4
Work in pairs to complete the puzzle below using phrases with *make* from the diagram above. Student A should look at the clues on page 136 and Student B should look at the clues on page 138. Take turns to read out the clues and complete the gaps. What is the hidden message?

5
Copy the diagram in Exercise 3 to make a poster for your classroom wall showing the uses of *make*. Add new expressions when you meet them.

Part B **Task**

Decide how to spend lottery money

Task link: ways of saying numbers
Real life: dealing with money

Personal vocabulary

Preparation for task

1 Do you have a lottery in your country? How does it work? Have you ever entered it? Have you (or someone you know) ever won anything?

2 Read the information opposite about the state lottery in St Ambrosia and answer the following questions.

a Has the lottery been successful or not?
b How much money has it made?
c How will this money be spent?

St. Ambrosia

Six months ago, the independent island republic of St Ambrosia decided to organise a state lottery for the first time. It was agreed that profits from the lottery should go to 'help improve the lives of St Ambrosians'. The lottery has been a great success; SA$10 million have been made in profit. Many applications have been received asking for money to help various projects. Now the Lottery Commission must decide how the money will be spent.

St. Ambrosia

Area: 630 km²
Population: 250,000
Unemployment: 15 per cent
Capital: Port Thomas
(population 55,000)
Climate: warm coastal, 18–30°C
Currency: St Ambrosian dollars (SA$)

Useful language

Giving and explaining opinions

"We should definitely give some money to ..."

"Personally, I don't think we should give any money to ..."

"I think we should spend ... on ..."

"... will make more money for the country because ..."

"It's very important to help / improve / provide ..."

Agreeing / disagreeing

"I agree / don't agree ..."

"Yes, but ..."

"Shall we come back to that later?"

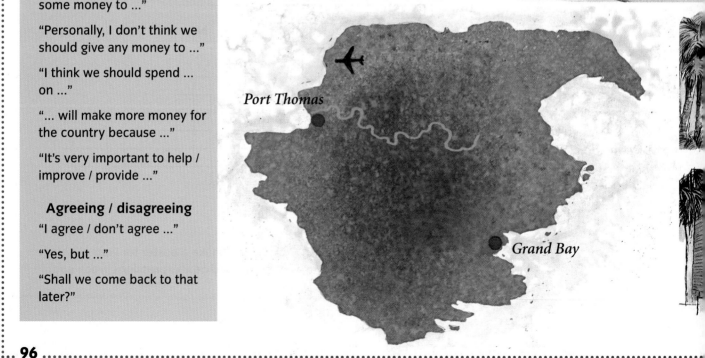

Port Thomas

Grand Bay

3 a) [9.4] You will hear representatives from five groups who would like to receive lottery money. Check the meaning of the words in the box in your mini-dictionary or with your teacher. Then listen and complete the gaps in the first column of the table.

foreign investors	oil deposits
sports facilities	budget
medical equipment	

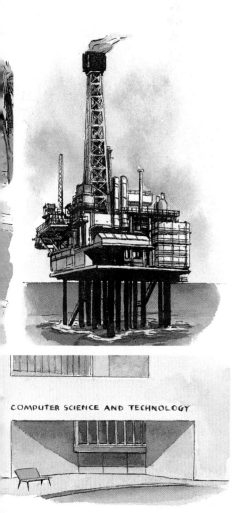

COMPUTER SCIENCE AND TECHNOLOGY

CHILDRENS HOSPITAL

name of organisation	reasons for giving money to this project	your budget (SA$)
1 St Ambrosian Hotel and Tourism Association Need SA$ .... for..................................		
2 St Ambrosian Sports Association Need SA$ .... for..................................		
3 University of St Ambrosia Need SA$ .... for		
4 St Ambrosian Children's Hospital Need SA$ .... for..................................		
5 International Petroleum Incorporated Need SA$ .... for..................................		

b) Listen again and complete the second column of the table.

Task

1 a) Decide how *you* think the SA$10 million should be spent. Note down the amount you think each organisation should receive in the column 'your budget'. You can divide the money between different organisations, or give all of it to one or two of them.

b) You will have to justify how you want to spend the money to other students, so spend a few minutes planning what to say. Ask your teacher for any words or phrases you need and write them in the *Personal vocabulary* box.

2 Work in groups. Discuss how you think the money should be spent and agree on a budget together. Look at the phrases in the *Useful language* box.

3 Present your budget to the class, giving reasons for your decisions. Then listen and note down how much money other groups give to each organisation. Which organisation is the most / least popular? What are the main differences between the budgets?

Task link

Ways of saying numbers

1 [9.5] Look at the following figures. How do you say each one? Listen and practise saying them.

- 71%
- 26,000
- 483,080 m²
- 5.7 billion
- 55,680,000 km
- 300, 000 km / sec
- 199,859
- 99.9999%
- 86,000,000
- –89°C

2 [9.6] What do you think the figures represent? Which do you think is:

a the estimated population of the world in mid-1995?

b the lowest temperature ever recorded (in Vostok, Antarctica)?

c the proportion of the world's surface which is covered in water?

d the closest distance between Earth and the planet Mars?

e the largest crowd ever for a sporting event (the World Cup Final between Brazil and Uruguay in 1950)?

f the speed of light?

g the estimated number of babies born in the world every year?

h the area of the world's largest shopping mall (in Alberta, Canada)?

i the proportion of people who voted for the Communist party in the Albanian elections of 1982?

j the number of murders the average American child has seen on television by the time he / she is eighteen years old?

Listen and check your answers. Write the correct number in the box.

3 **a)** Work in pairs. Student A should look at the information about Russia, the largest country in Europe, on page 136. Student B should look at the information about Monaco, one of the smallest countries in Europe, on page 139.

b) Ask and answer questions to complete the information on your chart about the other country. Do not show each other the numbers, say them! Which statistics do you find the most surprising?

What's the area of Monaco?

It's ...

Real life

Dealing with money

1 Look at the people in the pictures. Where are they and what is the relationship between them?

2 Look at the sentences in the first column of the table below. Which picture does each one relate to? Who says it? Who do they say it to?

Sentence	Picture
a 'Is there a reduction for students?'	3
b 'How would you like to pay, sir?'	
c 'How much do you want for these?'	
d 'How much will it cost roughly?'	
e 'You can have them both for £20 – how's that?'	
f 'It's free for children under twelve.'	
g 'How much do I owe you?'	
h 'I'd like to pay by credit card, please.'	
i 'It's okay, you can keep the change.'	
j 'I'll give you £18 for both of them.'	
k 'If you'd just like to sign there, please.'	

(1)

(3)

(4)

3 📼 [9.7] Listen to the dialogues that go with the pictures and check your answers. Practise saying the sentences in the table, copying the speakers on the cassette.

4 Work in pairs. Choose one of the situations below and decide who you are going to be. Spend a few minutes planning what you are going to say. Then act out a short dialogue like the ones on the cassette.

Customer and shop assistant
Together a Decide what kind of shop you are in.
b Decide what the customer has just bought and how much it costs.
Shop assistant Find out how the customer is going to pay.
Customer Decide how you are going to pay. You don't have much cash.

Taxi driver and passenger
Together Decide where you are.
Driver Decide how much it costs to go to the destination.
Passenger a Decide where you want to go. Try to find out how much it will cost before you start your journey.
b Decide if the taxi driver is polite and honest or not, and whether he / she deserves a tip.

Ticket seller and visitor
Together Decide where you are (a museum, art gallery, cinema, etc.)
Ticket seller Decide the price of the tickets, and whether there is a reduction for students and / or children.
Visitor a Decide how many people you are going to buy tickets for, and how many are students / children.
b Find out the price of tickets, and whether there is a reduction for students / children.

Marketstall holder and customer
Together a Decide what kind of market you are at, and what the stall is selling.
b Find out what article the customer is interested in.
Stallholder Decide how much you will accept for the article which the customer is looking at.
Customer Decide on something you like on the stall, and how much you are prepared to pay for it.

Who said it?	Who did they say it to?
customer	*ticket seller*

Do you remember?

①

a) Mark the stress and /ə/ sounds in the following words.

For example:
   • /ə/
  education

- inflation
- unemployment
- technology
- facilities
- per cent
- pollution
- government
- definitely
- certainly
- probably
- perhaps

b) Practise saying the words.

②

Look back at the words and phrases used for making predictions on page 92. Use these phrases to make predictions about the following topics, as in the examples.

a) Football and other sporting results this year.
Milan may well win the European Cup.

b) Fashions for next season.
The colour red will definitely be in fashion.

c) Stories that are in the news at the moment.
The Social Democrats are likely to win the election.

d) Famous people who are in the gossip columns.
Madonna might have more children one day.

③

Which word does not belong to the following groups of words / phrases. Why?

a) to rise / to increase / to get worse

b) to decrease / to fall / to go up

c) to improve / to deteriorate / to get better

④

Tick (✓) the possible endings to the following sentences with *if*.

a) If I met someone really famous,
- *I probably don't know what to say.* ❏
- *I probably won't know what to say.* ❏
- *I probably wouldn't know what to say.* ❏

b) I'll phone you if
- *I will decide to go out tonight.* ❏
- *I decide to go out tonight.* ❏
- *I would decide to go out tonight.* ❏

c) I might steal if
- *I don't have anything to eat.* ❏
- *I didn't have anything to eat.* ❏
- *I wouldn't have anything to eat.* ❏

d) If I won the lottery,
- *I'll retire.* ❏
- *I might retire.* ❏
- *I'd retire.* ❏

⑤

Work in groups. Say a phrase from one of the columns below. The other students must listen and say if it comes from column A, B or C. Do the same with five other phrases in the table.

A	B	C
• *I see.*	• *I'll see.*	• *I'd see.*
• *They agree.*	• *They'll agree.*	• *They'd agree.*
• *I want to go.*	• *I won't go.*	• *I wouldn't go.*
• *I want to do it.*	• *I won't do it.*	• *I wouldn't do it.*

⑥

Say the following numbers.

- 98.5%
- 48.5 m²
- 76.4 million
- 6,000,000,000
- 455,000
- 100,000 km²
- –5°C
- 29°C

⑦

Look back through Module 9 and write two more revision questions of your own to ask other students.

module 10
Another story

Part A Language

Past Perfect and Past Simple
Reported speech and reported questions
Reading and listening:
The Knightsbridge Safe Deposit Robbery
Wordspot: *say* and *tell*

Language focus 1

Past Perfect and Past Simple

Match the cartoons opposite with the captions below. Which cartoon does not have a caption? Write one with a partner.

a   When they got downstairs, Tom and Fiona were surprised to see that the children had already made breakfast.

b   As soon as she tried it on at home, Amanda knew she had bought the wrong dress.

c   After he had finished his lunch Uncle Albert always liked to have one of his special cigars.

d   Before he got a job in a fast-food restaurant, Fred had been an Olympic discus thrower.

Analysis

1   Underline the Past Perfect verbs in the cartoon captions above. How is the Past Perfect formed?

2   Choose the correct alternative to complete the following rule:
We use the Past Perfect:
a *to describe actions that happened a long time ago.*   ☐
b *to describe a past action which is linked to the present.*   ☐
c *when we are talking about the past and want to describe something that happened further in the past.*   ☐

Now read Language summary A on page 148.

Practice

1   Work in pairs. Student A should read the instructions and information on pages 136–137. Student B should look at page 139 and do the same.

2   **a)** You are going to solve a 'logic puzzle' by asking your teacher questions about the situation described below. Read the situation and draw a rough picture of the scene.

> There was a phone box close to the sea. Inside the phone box a man was lying dead on the floor. The receiver was hanging off the phone, and the glass was broken on either side of the phone box. Why?

b) Make a list of questions to ask your teacher to find out what happened. He / She will only be able to answer 'yes' or 'no'.

> Had the man had a heart attack?

c) 📻 [10.1] Listen to the solution. If you know any other 'logic puzzles', tell the class.

Language focus 2
Reported speech and reported questions

Mini-task

Discuss the following questions in groups.
- *Do you spend much time talking on the phone?*
- *Have you ever spoken in English on the phone? Did you have any problems?*

Think of a phone conversation you have had in which there was a problem or misunderstanding. What did you say to each other? What happened in the end?

1 The story told below is true. Read *Part one* and answer the following questions.

a What had happened to Michael and Harry Findlater when they were young?

b What could Michael remember about his brother?

c Why did Michael look in his secretary's diary on this particular day? What did he find there?

Part one

Michael and Harry Findlater were brothers, separated tragically during the Second World War when they were children. Michael had spent almost thirty years looking for Harry, who was sixteen years older than him. He only remembered one thing about his brother – he had an owl tattooed on the back of his hand.

One morning, Michael arrived at work to find that his secretary had phoned in sick. In order to check his appointments for the day, he looked at his secretary's diary. The first item was a seven-figure number with the name 'Bell' written against it and URGENT written in red ink. He dialled the number, and a woman's voice answered.

2 Opposite is *Part two* of the story. Put the sentences in the correct order to find out how Michael and Harry were reunited.

Part two

On the phone ...

☐ The woman said that it was.

☐ The woman said she was sorry, but she had only just started working there, and she didn't know who Mr Bell was.

☐ She told him that she had – a tattoo of an owl.

☑ Michael asked if he could speak to Mr Bell.

☐ She asked him to ring back later when her boss, Mr Findlater, was there.

☐ Becoming excited now, Michael asked her whether she had ever noticed a tattoo on the back of Mr Findlater's hand.

☐ Michael said he would ring back later, and asked her if Mr Findlater's first name was Harry.

The following day ...

☐ Thanks to this amazing coincidence, Michael found his brother at last.

☐ The secretary told him it wasn't a phone number, it was a bank account number for Mr Bell, one of their customers.

☐ When Michael's secretary came back to work, he asked her who had given her his brother's number.

3 [cassette] [10.2] Below is the beginning of the actual conversations that Michael had. Read the story in Exercise 2 and complete the rest of the conversations. Listen and check.

MICHAEL: Can I speak to Mr Bell ?

WOMAN: I'm sorry, but I've only just started working here, and I don't know who Mr Bell is. Can you ...?

MICHAEL: ...

WOMAN: ...

Analysis

1 Look at the verbs in reported speech in Exercise 2 and compare them with the verbs you have written in direct speech in Exercise 3. Then complete the information below showing how they change.

Direct speech		Reported speech
Present Simple	>	
Present Perfect	>	
Past Simple	>	
Future Simple *(will)*	>	

2 Find four examples of reported questions in the story.
   a What verb do we use to introduce reported questions? When do we use *if* or *whether*?
   b What is the difference between the word order of reported questions and direct questions?

3 Look at this short dialogue between Michael Findlater and someone interviewing him about the reunion.

   INTERVIEWER: *Have you and your brother stayed in contact?*
   MICHAEL: *We're not very close, but we see each other from time to time.*

   Now look at this reported version:

   INTERVIEWER: *I asked Michael if he and his brother have stayed in contact. He admitted that they aren't very close, but he said that they still see each other from time to time.*

   a Why are the verb tenses the same in this case?
   b Is it possible to change the tenses?

Now read Language summary B on page 149.

Practice

1 What can you remember about the Findlater brothers? Which one was Harry? Which one was Michael? Decide who you think said the following sentences when they finally met up. Put them into reported speech.

a 'I can't believe I've finally found you.'
   Michael said he couldn't believe he had finally found Harry.
b 'How did you get my phone number?'
c 'Will you show me that tattoo of yours?'
d 'You're certainly taller than when I last saw you!'
e 'I spent nearly thirty years looking for you!'
f 'Did you ever try to look for me?'
g 'It's lucky that your secretary was off sick that day!'
h 'I think I'll give her a pay rise.'

2 a) Spend a few minutes thinking about how you would answer the following questions.

1 Do you often lose things? Do any of your friends or members of your family have this problem?
2 Have you ever lost:
   – your identity card?
   – your driving licence?
   – anything else valuable?
3 Have you ever found anything valuable in the street? What was it?
4 Have you ever looked for something for a long time? What was it? Did you find it in the end?

b) Choose three of the questions and ask them to another student in the class. Make notes about his / her answers like this:

Name	Question	Answer
Roberto	Question 2	Lost identity card five years ago at concert.
Carla	Question 4	Yes – car keys, this morning. Found them under sofa.

c) Tell the rest of the class what you found out using reported speech.

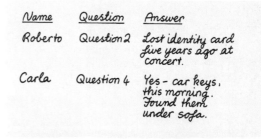

I asked Roberto if he'd ever lost his identity card. He told me he'd lost it five years ago at a concert.

I asked Carla if she's ever looked for anything for a long time. She told me she looked ...

Reading and listening

1 Have any famous robberies ever taken place in your country? What happened? What was stolen? Were the criminals caught?

2 You are going to read about a robbery which happened in London in 1987. Check the meaning of the words in the box in your mini-dictionary or with your teacher.

a safe deposit box   to owe money
a fingerprint   to pretend   to smash
to trace a phone call / a person
insurance money

3 Read the first part of the story only (*Before the robbery*) and answer the following questions.

a What did people use Security Deposits for?

b Who are the two men in the pictures opposite? What problems did each man have?

c What was the relationship between the two men?

4 a) Work in pairs and imagine you are Latif and Viccei. What is your plan?

b) Read part two of the story (*The robbery itself*) and compare your plan to the real crime.

5 a) Work in pairs again and imagine you are Latif and Viccei. Decide what you will do to escape arrest. What do you think the police will do?

b) 🔊 [10.3] Listen to the rest of the story (if you wish to read it as well, look at the tapescript on pages 164–165). Answer the following questions.

• Did everyone do as you predicted?
• What is the importance of pictures 1–5? Describe what happened in your own words.

Viccei   Latif

The Knightsbridge Safe Deposit Robbery

The world's biggest robbery?

Before the robbery

'Security Deposits', situated in Knightsbridge, one of the most fashionable areas of London, was a company which provided lockable safe deposit boxes in a secure building for its rich clients. It attracted the kind of people who preferred not to use banks, where money is easier to trace. Its owners, Z.A. and Parvez Latif had bought the business for nearly a million pounds in 1986, but things had not gone well – and in their first year they lost around £400,000. Latif owed more than £100,000, and had no way of repaying the money.

Around this time, Latif became friendly with a client of the firm, a wealthy young Italian named Valerio Viccei, who had a passion for good living and expensive cars. Viccei was wanted in his native country for bank robbery and had escaped to London, where he also

①

WHITES HOTEL

②

③

④

10 May	9:20 am	01924 761423
10 May	11:40 am	0171 261 498
10 May	12:10 am	0171 264 789
11 May	3:20 pm	0181 926 548

⑤

2 Put a tick (✓) next to the following sentences if they mean the same as the signs in the picture, and a cross (✗) if they do not.

a • You <u>can</u> use a credit card in the duty-free shop. ✓

• You <u>have to</u> use a credit card in the duty-free shop. ✗

b • You <u>have to</u> have a visa to leave the transit lounge. ☐

• You'<u>ve got to</u> have a visa to leave the transit lounge. ☐

c • You <u>can't</u> smoke in the area at the back. ☐

• You'<u>re allowed</u> to smoke in the area at the back. ☐

d • The public <u>mustn't</u> go through the door that says 'staff only'. ☐

• The public <u>aren't allowed</u> to go through the door that says 'staff only'. ☐

e • You <u>mustn't</u> smoke in the area at the front. ☐

• You <u>don't have to</u> smoke in the area at the front. ☐

f • You <u>must</u> have your boarding card ready when you board. ☐

• You <u>should</u> have your boarding card ready when you board. ☐

g • You <u>mustn't</u> leave luggage unattended. ☐

• You <u>shouldn't</u> leave luggage unattended. ☐

h • Passengers <u>should</u> be careful of the wet paint. ☐

• Passengers <u>ought to</u> be careful of the wet paint. ☐

Analysis

1 Look at the underlined verbs in the sentences above. Complete the following lists showing how the verbs are used.

a *it is necessary* *have to*	**b** *it is okay / permitted* *can*	**c** *it is a good idea / the correct thing*
d *it is not necessary*	**e** *it is not okay / it is prohibited*	**f** *it is not a good idea / not the correct thing*

2 What is the difference (if any) in the use of *must* and *have to* in the following pairs of sentences?
  a • *You must finish all the medicine – it's really important.*
    • *The doctor says I have to finish all the medicine – it's really important.*
  b • *You mustn't walk home alone in the dark – it's dangerous.*
    • *You don't have to walk home – we'll give you a lift.*

Now read Language summary A on page 150.

SMOKING

NON SMOKING

Staff only

careful! wet paint!

Practice

1 a) Complete the gaps in the following sentences with *have to, don't have to, should, shouldn't* and *are / aren't allowed to* so that they are true for your country.

- **in city centres**

  You .... park wherever you like.

  Lorries .... drive through the centre.

  You .... pay to use public transport.

  You .... cross the road anywhere you like.

- **on roads**

  You .... wear a seat belt.

  You .... pay to use motorways.

  You .... drive at 150 km / hour.

  You .... drive if you're seventeen years old.

- **on trains**

  You .... reserve your ticket in advance.

  You .... buy your ticket on the train.

  You .... travel in a first class compartment if you have a second class ticket.

  You .... smoke.

b) Compare answers with other students. Do you disagree with any of these laws?

2 a) Can you guess which place is being described below?

You've got to wear trunks and sometimes a cap ... you're not allowed to run about or jump in ... and ... er ... you should never go in the deep end if you can't swim very well ...

b) Work in pairs. Student A should look at page 137 and Student B should look at page 139. For each place on your list think of at least three rules or pieces of advice. Tell your partner and see if he / she can guess which place you are talking about.

Pronunciation

1 [▭] [11.1] Listen and write down the exact words you hear. Which places are the people talking about?

2 Notice the pronunciation of modal verbs in a sentence.
  - can /kən/
  - can't /kɑːnt/
  - must /məst/
  - mustn't /məsənt/
  - should /ʃəd/
  - shouldn't /ʃʊdənt/
  - have to /haəvtə/
  - don't have to /dɒntaəvtə/
  - you're allowed to /əlaʊdtə/
  - you're not allowed to /əlaʊdtə/

3 Practise saying the sentences, paying attention to the pronunciation of modal verbs.

Language focus 2

Obligation and permission in the past

1 There have been some strange laws in the past. Below are some examples. Match them with a picture on the right.

a In the times of Peter the Great in Russia, noblemen weren't allowed to have beards. If they wanted to keep their beards, they had to pay a special tax to the Tsar's government.

b In eighteenth-century England, people had to pay 'window tax' for each window in their house. However, this law was eventually changed because many poor people chose to live in houses without windows just so that they didn't have to pay!

c In the nineteenth century, female teachers in the USA couldn't get married, or even go out with men. If they got engaged, they had to resign from their job immediately. Male teachers, on the other hand, could get married and have children without any problem!

d If you travelled in any motor vehicle in nineteenth-century Britain, the law said that someone had to walk in front of you waving a red flag, or at night time a red lamp. This meant, in practice, that you couldn't travel at more than about eight kilometres per hour!

e In the Midwest of the USA in the 1880s, you were not allowed to eat ice-cream sodas on a Sunday. Restaurant owners solved this problem by serving ice-cream without soda, which became known as a 'Sunday' or a 'sundae'.

① ② ③ ④ ⑤

2 Work in pairs and answer the following questions.

a What exactly were the laws in each case?
b Can you imagine any possible reasons for these laws?
c Which of the laws do you find:
  – the strangest?
  – the funniest?
  – the most unfair?

Analysis

1 Write the past form of the following verbs where possible. Which two verbs do **not** have past forms? Which form is used?
  • *can*   • *must*
  • *can't*   • *have got to*
  • *have to*   • *is / are allowed to*
  • *don't have to*   • *isn't / aren't allowed to*

2 Read the laws described in Exercise 1 and underline any examples of these verbs.

Now read Language summary A (7) on page 150.

Practice

[11.2] Here are some more unusual laws from around the world. Complete the gaps with a verb from the *Analysis* above. Then listen and check.

a In the 1920s in the USA, 'prohibition' meant that you .... produce or consume alcoholic drinks. Eventually, though, the government .... change this law, because it was causing terrible crime, and people were drinking more alcohol than they had done before!

b During the French Revolution, you .... use the polite form of 'you' ('vous'), because this was the word servants used to speak to their masters. Instead everyone .... use 'tu', the familiar form.

c In Italy in the 1930s under Mussolini, Italians .... use foreign words. That's why Italian is one of the few languages which doesn't use the word 'football'!

d In Switzerland, women .... vote until 1971. In New Zealand, on the other hand, females .... vote from 1893 – making it the first country in the world to give women the vote.

e Until a few years ago, pubs in Britain .... stay open all day. They .... open until eleven in the morning and .... shut again at three in the afternoon. In the evening they .... close at half past ten. The laws were even stricter on Sundays!

Vocabulary and speaking

Rules and behaviour

1 Discuss the following questions in groups.

- Were your parents strict with you when you were younger?
- What rules did they have about:
  - homework?
  - household chores?
  - television and music?
  - clothes, jewellery and hairstyles?
  - bedtime / staying out late?
- What happened if you broke the rules? (Give some examples.)

2 **a)** Check the meaning of the words and phrases in **bold** in your mini-dictionary if necessary.

- Parents **let** their children do whatever they like.
- They **punish** their children.
- They **tell** their children **off**.
- They believe that their children have **rights**.
- They expect their children to **obey** them.
- Their children are often **badly-behaved**.
- Their rules are **fair** and **sensible**.
- They don't have any **punishments**.
- They **smack** their children.
- They **treat** their children **with respect**.
- They shout at their children.
- Their children are generally **well-behaved**.

b) Work in groups. Which of the types of behaviour listed above is typical of:

- strict parents?
- liberal parents?

3 If you become a parent how will you behave with your children? Will you bring them up in the same way that you were brought up?

Listening

School rules

1 Look at the photo and read the paragraph below about Joan and Gareth's education.

Joan grew up in the 1930s, in the north of England. Between the ages of seven and twelve, she was sent to boarding school – a convent school in Belgium. Gareth, Joan's grandson, is fifteen, and attends a large comprehensive school near Cardiff in Wales.

2 You are going to hear Joan and Gareth talking about their schools. Which of the following topics do you think Joan will mention and which ones do you think Gareth will mention?

- going to church ☐
- staying at school after class ☐
- snobbery ☐
- mealtimes ☐
- saying prayers ☐
- school uniform ☐
- good manners ☐
- speaking French ☐
- the chemistry lab ☐
- wearing trainers ☐
- being lonely ☐

3 a) 🔲 [11.3] Listen and mark each of the above **J** if Joan mentions it and **G** if Gareth mentions it. (One of them is not mentioned at all.) Did you guess correctly?

b) Can you remember exactly what the rules were for each thing? Listen again and check.

4 Discuss the following questions in groups.

- What are the main differences between Joan and Gareth's schooldays? Do you think they were / are happy at school?
- Do the rules they describe seem sensible and fair to you?
- How do their schooldays compare with your own?
- Describe your last school and how you feel about it. Were the rules strict or not?

Wordspot

do

1 The diagram below shows the most important uses of *do*. Add the following phrases with *do* to the correct section of the diagram.

> do badly   do a course   do economics at university   do your homework
> do the ironing   do nothing   do overtime   do a test   do the washing
> do some work   do yoga

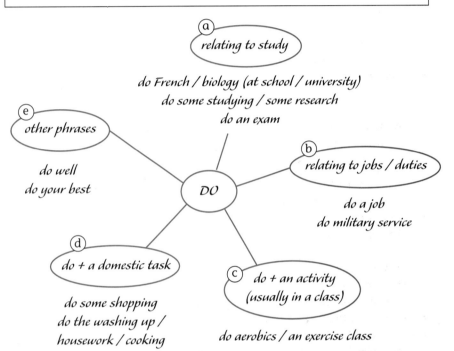

(a) *relating to study*

do French / biology (at school / university)
do some studying / some research
do an exam

(e) *other phrases*

do well
do your best

DO

(b) *relating to jobs / duties*

do a job
do military service

(d) *do + a domestic task*

do some shopping
do the washing up /
housework / cooking

(c) *do + an activity (usually in a class)*

do aerobics / an exercise class

2 a) 🔲 [11.4] Listen to some questions and write your answers *anywhere* in the box below. Do not write complete answers, just one word or a short phrase.

maybe

Yes

about twice a week

b) Work in pairs. Look at your partner's box and ask questions to find out the significance of the words and phrases he / she has written. Then change over, so that your partner asks you questions.

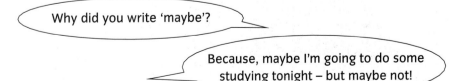

Why did you write 'maybe'?

Because, maybe I'm going to do some studying tonight – but maybe not!

Part B Task

Discuss the advantages and disadvantages of laws

Task link: linking words
Real life: agreeing and disagreeing

Personal vocabulary

Useful language

Introducing opinions

"Personally, I think / don't think it's a good idea because ..."

"It seems to me that ..."

"I agree / don't agree with this law because ..."

Giving opinions

"I think everyone should have the right to ..."

"People should be free to ..."

"I think it's wrong to ..."

"This shouldn't be allowed because ..."

"On one hand ..., but on the other hand ..."

"I don't really have any strong opinions about ..."

FREEDOM OF CHOICE?

Perhaps no issue is discussed more often than the rights and freedoms of the individual – how far should the state decide what is best for us, and how far should we have the right to control our own lives? Even in countries where social and political values are very similar, the laws about some of the world's most controversial issues can be very different.

1 THE RIGHT TO DIE?

In the Netherlands, the law allows doctors to help terminally ill patients to die if the patient states repeatedly that this is their wish. The doctor must follow very strict guidelines, and must be prepared to defend the decision in court. However, unlike in most other countries, he cannot be prosecuted if he has followed the guidelines correctly. Elsewhere in the world 'Voluntary Euthanasia' groups continue to campaign for the right to decide if you no longer wish to live.

2

Recent medical advances mean that, with special treatment, women of almost any age can give birth. In most countries, this is only allowed for women up to about fifty, but in Italy until recently there were no laws to limit this, with the result that several women in their sixties have given birth. Some experts remain convinced that women of this age have the same right to have children as women in their forties, provided they are mentally and physically fit.

3

The second amendment of the constitution of the United States means that every citizen has the right to own and carry a gun if they wish to. In most other western democracies, the law is very different – the ownership of guns is strictly controlled. In Britain following terrible tragedies, all privately owned handguns are now banned.

4

In the Netherlands, people are allowed to carry small amounts of 'soft' drugs such as cannabis for their own personal use. However, only special cafés licensed by local governments are allowed to sell these drugs. The Dutch government believe that this approach has helped to control the abuse of 'hard' drugs, such as heroin. Similar attempts to legalise cannabis in other countries have been opposed by those who believe that this would worsen the drug problem.

5

While some countries rely entirely on a professional army – the USA, Britain and France, for example – in most countries in the world, military service is still compulsory for young men, unless there is some medical reason why they cannot do it. The period varies from country to country: in countries such as Poland, Germany and Italy it is a year to eighteen months. In Switzerland it is only a few weeks a year, but it continues until the man is in his mid-forties. In Israel, on the other hand, both men and women must go into the army: men for three years and women for two.

6

The state of California in the USA has recently introduced a law which means that anyone convicted of three offences – however small – is automatically sentenced to between twenty-five years and life in prison. This has meant life sentences for very minor crimes – stealing a pizza in one case. In Europe, some politicians would like to follow the Californian example in the hope of reducing crime.

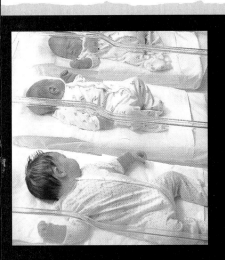

Preparation for task

1 The article opposite describes some controversial laws and issues around the world. The following headings have been taken out of the article. Read the article quickly and match a heading with a paragraph. The first one has been done for you.

a **MUMS AT SEVENTY?**

b **THE RIGHT TO DIE?**

c **A DUTY TO SERVE YOUR COUNTRY?**

d **LEGALISATION OF SOFT DRUGS?**

e **THE RIGHT TO BEAR ARMS**

f **'THREE STRIKES AND YOUR'E OUT'**

2 Mark the following statements **T** (true) or **F** (false). Then correct the false statements.

a Euthanasia is possible in the Netherlands, although it is carefully controlled. ☐

b In Italy, there are no laws stopping women in their sixties from having children. ☐

c In the USA, anyone can have a gun to protect themselves. ☐

d In the Netherlands, anyone can use or sell cannabis. ☐

e In Israel, both men and women have to do the same period of military service. ☐

f In California, even if you only commit a minor crime, you go to prison for many years. ☐

Do you know of any countries in which opposite or very different laws exist?

Task

1 **a)** Work on your own. Look back at the six laws described in the article. Mark them as follows:

✔✔ if you strongly agree with this law.

✔ if you partly agree with this law.

? if you don't know or aren't sure.

✗ if you disagree with this law.

b) Why do you agree or disagree with these laws? Spend a few minutes thinking about how to explain your opinions. Ask your teacher about any words or phrases you need and write them in the *Personal vocabulary* box.

2 In groups explain and discuss your opinions about these laws. Look at the phrases in the *Useful language* box.

3 Now you are going to summarise for the rest of the class the opinions that people expressed in your group. Describe what you agreed about, and explain any differences in opinion.

4 Listen to the other groups' opinions and compare them to your own. Which issues were most controversial in your class?

Optional writing

Write a paragraph or two about one of the laws described in the article, giving your opinion about what should happen.

Task link

Linking words

1 The words in the box are used to join sentences and link ideas. Put them into the correct category below. Then look at *Language summary* B on pages 150–151 to check your answers.

> also   although   besides   for this reason   however
> as a result   therefore   what is more   despite this

similar meaning to *and*	similar meaning to *but*	similar meaning to *so*

2 The following sentences can be continued in two possible ways. Complete the gaps using a suitable word / phrase from the box to link the two ideas. Add or change the punctuation as necessary.

a   Everyone knows that smoking is bad for you.

- *What is more*, *it can be very expensive.*

- .... *thousands of young people take up the habit every year.*

b   Regular exercise can prevent heart disease.

- .... *medical experts recommend that everyone exercises at least three times a week.*

- .... *it can help to control your weight.*

c   Many people nowadays believe that it is wrong to eat animals.

- .... *they believe that eating meat is unhealthy.*

- .... *more and more people are becoming vegetarians.*

d   Doctors agree that too much alcohol is bad for your health.

- .... *small amounts of alcohol may actually be good for you.*

- .... *it can make you depressed.*

e   Doctors have found cures for many serious diseases in the last century.

- .... *the average person is living longer and longer.*

- .... *there is still no cure for the common cold.*

Real life

Agreeing and disagreeing

1 🔊 [11.5] Put the phrases below for agreeing and disagreeing on the line. Listen and mark where the stress falls.

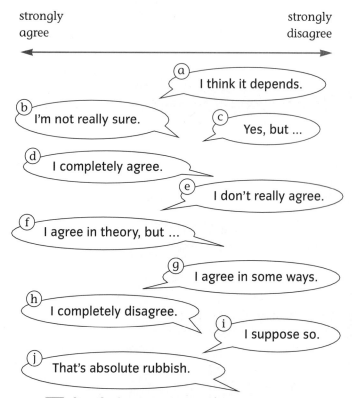

strongly agree ← → strongly disagree

a I think it depends.
b I'm not really sure.
c Yes, but ...
d I completely agree.
e I don't really agree.
f I agree in theory, but ...
g I agree in some ways.
h I completely disagree.
i I suppose so.
j That's absolute rubbish.

2 🔊 [11.6] Listen to six people expressing an opinion about different topics and respond with a phrase from above.

3 🔊 [11.7] Listen to the same opinions again, this time with responses from the listener. Did they agree or disagree with the speakers?

4 Make a list of the phrases used to express opinions (*I think* ... , etc.) Look at the tapescript on page 166 to check your answers. Practise reading the dialogues with a partner.

5 Write *one* strong opinion you have that other students might not agree with. You could write about:

- learning English.
- some aspect of your school.
- things men / women are better at.
- a news story that you have a strong opinion about.

Give the piece of paper to your teacher, who will read out the students' opinions. Listen and respond to each one.

Do you remember?

1

Explain the difference in meaning (if any) between the following pairs of sentences.

a) • You mustn't eat that.
   • You shouldn't eat that.

b) • I must do some studying tonight.
   • I have to do some studying tonight.

c) • You mustn't write anything.
   • You don't have to write anything.

d) • I've got to stay in tonight.
   • I have to stay in tonight.

e) • She ought to be careful.
   • She should be careful.

f) • We must hurry.
   • We had to hurry.

g) • They couldn't sell alcohol.
   • They weren't allowed to sell alcohol.

h) • I didn't have to vote.
   • I wasn't allowed to vote.

2

a) Match word partners in the box. Which word has no partner?

(strict)   well-behaved   housework
a rule   however   to obey
(liberal)   therefore   homework
badly-behaved   to punish
to be alone   to disobey
to be healthy   a law   to be lonely
disadvantage   a punishment
despite this   as a result
to be unhealthy

b) Spend three minutes trying to memorise the words. Close your book and write them down – there are a total of twenty-one! Compare answers with a partner. Who remembered the most words?

3

Which word in the list rhymes with the word in bold?

a) **can't**: want / (aren't) / ant
b) **allowed**: cloud / road / bored
c) **ought**: out / boat / bought
d) **law**: know / four / now
e) **should**: cold / food / stood
f) **although**: so / cough / now

4

There is a word missing in *five* of the following sentences. Find the mistakes and correct them.

a) She's always shouting her children.
b) The teacher told them for being late.
c) In the end, her mother let her go to the party.
d) I'm going to do shopping. Do you want anything?
e) I think it depends the situation.
f) I agree with you.
g) They missed the bus so they had walk home.

5

Think of:

a) two things people usually do in the kitchen.
b) two things you might do this evening.
c) two things people often do when they're at school or university.
d) two things you don't like doing.

All your answers should include phrases with *do*.

6

Join the following sentences using *although, however, therefore, also, for this reason,* or *what is more*.

a) It was the middle of winter. The weather wasn't cold.
b) The train drivers have not had a pay rise this year. They're going on strike.
c) He has been ill recently. He has had a lot of personal problems.
d) There was a bomb in the city centre last night. Most of the shops are open as normal today.
e) There has been a serious accident. There are a lot of traffic jams.

7

Look back through Module 11 and write two more revision questions of your own to ask other students.

module 12
Dilemmas and decisions

Part A Language

could have, should have, would have
Past sentences with *if*
Vocabulary: problems and solutions
Wordspot: *think*

Language focus 1

could have, should have, would have

1 Below is a true story. Look at the pictures and discuss what you think happened without reading the text.

2 Read the story to see if you guessed correctly. If necessary, check the meanings of words / phrases in your mini-dictionary or with your teacher.

3 Discuss the following questions with a partner.

a Pritchard and Larsen were very brave, but did they do anything stupid?

b Larsen decided to risk his life by walking back to the village without any water. Were there any other possibilities for him?

c Imagine yourself in Pritchard's position, waking up at the bottom of the volcano. Describe your actions and feelings.

In the summer of 1985, a young English businessman, Geoffrey Pritchard, and his Danish friend, Peter Larsen, were on holiday in the Sudan. They decided to go on a 3-day trek across the desert to Mount Gimbala, an extinct volcano in a remote part of the country.

Ignoring advice from local people, Pritchard and Larsen travelled without a guide, using only a tourist map of the area, and carrying only a few days supply of water. After three days walking across the desert, in temperatures of 40°C, they reached the volcano and immediately began to climb.

It took Larsen nearly an hour to reach his friend. He found him bleeding and unconscious, but still alive. Larsen had to make the most terrible decision of his life: should he stay with Pritchard and try to attract the attention of a passing aircraft, should he return to the village – three days' walk away – to get help? He decided immediately to return to the village, leaving the little water that remained next to Pritchard's unconscious body.

When Pritchard regained consciousness, he found himself alone. Seeing the water bottle next to him, he guessed that Larsen might return – but would it be too late? Using his last strength, he pulled himself back to the top of the volcano, and collapsed, convinced that he would die.

120

Analysis

1 Tick (✓) the correct answer.

a <u>Larsen and Pritchard should have taken a local guide with them.</u>

Does this mean:

- *it was necessary for them to take a local guide with them.* ❑
- *it was a good idea to take a local guide with them, but they didn't.* ❑
- *they took a local guide with them.* ❑

Write two other things that Larsen and Pritchard *should / shouldn't have done.*

b <u>Larsen could have stayed with his friend.</u>

Does this mean:

- *he stayed with his friend.* ❑
- *he was able to stay with his friend.* ❑
- *it was possible for him to stay with his friend, but he didn't.* ❑

Write two other things that Larsen and Pritchard could have done.

c <u>I would have stayed where I was.</u>

Does this sentence refer to:

- *an imaginary situation in the present?* ❑
- *an imaginary situation in the past?* ❑

Write two other things you *would / wouldn't have done* in Larsen or Pritchard's position.

2 All of the <u>underlined</u> sentences above have a similar construction. Complete the gaps below.

subject + [＿＿＿＿＿] + *have* + [＿＿＿＿＿]

3 Do the <u>underlined</u> sentences above refer to:
a past time? ❑   c future time? ❑
b present time? ❑   d no specific times? ❑

Now read Language summary A on page 151.

As soon as they reached the top, disaster struck: Pritchard slipped on some rocks, and Larsen watched in horror as his friend fell hundreds of metres down ...

Pronunciation

1 🔲 [12.1] Write the sentences you hear.

2 Notice the weak pronunciation of *have* in the middle of the sentence.

- *They should have /əv/ taken more water.*

Listen again and practise saying the sentences, paying attention to the pronunciation of *have.*

Four days passed before Larsen returned – with help. He was amazed to see his friend still alive. Pritchard was immediately flown to hospital, where doctors discovered that he had several broken bones. Everyone agreed that it was a miracle that he had survived, so badly injured and without water.

The experience changed Pritchard's life for ever – he gave up his career in business, and trained as a nurse instead ... so that he too could save lives.

Practice

1 Match the pictures and situations on the right. Complete the sentences which follow.

2 a) Write sentences about at least **four** of the following.

- something you shouldn't have bought
- something you should have done last weekend
- something you should have done sooner
- someone you shouldn't have trusted
- a time when you should have tried harder
- somewhere you shouldn't have gone to
- something you shouldn't have worried about

b) Work in groups. Tell the other students about what you have written and what you could have done instead. Do the other students have any comments or suggestions?

> A few months ago I bought a really expensive jacket, which I've never worn because it doesn't suit me. I definitely shouldn't have bought it. I could've bought lots of clothes for the same money ... or I could've saved it for my holidays ... I'm really annoyed with myself!

> Couldn't you give it to someone else?

> Perhaps you should have taken it back and changed it?

(a) A woman went round to a phone box near her home to phone her sister. Moments later, a young man began banging on the glass, insisting he must use the phone straight away. The woman ignored him for twenty minutes. Eventually, the young man took the phone off her and dialled the Fire Brigade. The woman walked round the corner to see her house on fire.

> The woman should have / shouldn't have ...
> The young man could have ...
> If I'd been in his / her position, I would have.....

(b) A young couple were on a walking holiday in Switzerland. One foggy night, they found themselves in a forest. After walking around lost for three hours in complete darkness, they decided to put up their tent. The next morning, they looked out of the window to see their tent on the edge of a 500 metre drop.

> They should ...
> They could ...
> If I'd been in their position, I ...

(c) A man arrived in London from abroad and hired a car to visit Edinburgh, 400 kilometres away in Scotland. Unfortunately, he took the wrong motorway, finding himself on the M25 – a circular motorway which only goes around London. After twenty-four hours' driving, he began to wonder what was happening when he drove past Heathrow Airport for the sixth time.

> The man ...
> He ...
> If I'd ...

①

②

③

Language focus 2

Past sentences with *if*

Mini-task

• *What do you think are the five most important decisions a person makes in his / her life? Make a list. Then compare your list with other students'.*

• *Think of two important decisions you have made yourself and tell your partner about them. Looking back, do you think you made the right decisions? Why? / Why not?*

1 a) Look at the photos below of Luke and Sandra. What kind of lives do you think they have?

b) 🔲 [12.2] Listen to Luke and Sandra talking about important decisions they have made and answer the following questions.

• What important decision did they each make? Why?

• Do they regret it now?

c) Would you have done the same thing in Luke or Sandra's position? How would you have felt if you were their family?

2 🔲 [12.3] Later Luke and Sandra talk about the differences these decisions have made to their lives. What do you think they will say? Listen to extracts from the interview and check.

3 Complete the gaps in the interview extracts with the correct form of the verb in brackets. Listen again to check.

LUKE:

ⓐ If I .... (*do*) business studies, I .... (*make*) a lot more money by now! On the other hand, I .... (*not / meet*) my girlfriend or any of my best friends.

ⓑ I think I .... (*stay*) abroad if I .... (*not / decide*) to go to drama school.

SANDRA:

ⓒ If I .... (*stay*) in the travel business, I think the whole family .... (*suffer*) from the pressure of my job.

ⓓ If I .... (*be*) at work all day, I .... (*not / be*) there at all the important moments of my children's lives. I .... (*really / miss*) that.

ⓔ We .... (*be*) a lot richer now if I .... (*not / leave*) my old job – that's for sure!

Analysis

1 All the sentences above are *hypothetical*. Look at a), b) and c) – are the situations they describe past or present? What verb forms are used? Complete the following rule.

• **past condition → past result**
  if + ⬚ ,   *would / wouldn't +* ⬚ *+* ⬚

2 Look at each verb in d). Do the verbs refer to a past, present or general situation? What verb forms are used in each case? Complete the following rule.

• **present / general condition →   present / general result**
  if + ⬚ ,   *would / wouldn't +* ⬚

3 Look at each verb in e). Do the verbs refer to a past, present or general situation? Which verb forms are used in each case?

• **past condition →   present / general result**
  if + ⬚ ,   *would / wouldn't +* ⬚

Now read Language summary B / C on page 151.

Practice

1 **a)** Match a fact in box A with a consequence in box B.

A
- Napoleon didn't conquer Russia.
- Karl Mark wrote *Das Kapital*.
- The USA became the most powerful country in the world.
- Kennedy went to Dallas.
- The Berlin Wall came down.
- Nelson Mandela was released from prison.
- Germany lost World War One.

B
- East and West Germany were united.
- He was assassinated.
- Many countries became communist.
- He didn't become Emperor of all Europe.
- English became a world language.
- Apartheid ended peacefully.
- Hitler came to power.

b) Write sentences with *if* about the facts and consequences.

For example:
Perhaps if Napoleon had conquered Russia, he would have become Emperor of all Europe.

2 Complete the following sentences to make them true for you.

a I wouldn't have met ... if ...

b I would've studied ... if ...

c I wouldn't have studied ... if ...

d I would have gone to ... if ...

e I wouldn't have gone to ... if ...

f I would have more money now if ...

g I'd feel more energetic now if ...

> I wouldn't have met my best friend Laura if I hadn't changed schools.

Vocabulary

Problems and solutions

1 The sentences below tell the story of Frank's problem, but they are in the wrong order. In pairs, put them in the same order as the story in the picture. If necessary, check the meaning of the words in **bold** in your mini-dictionary.

- His idea seemed to **work**; he thought he had **sorted the problem out**. ☐
- But the problem gradually became more serious, and eventually Frank decided he would have to **do something about it**. ☐
- He kept **changing his mind** about **the right thing to do**. ☐
- He **talked it over** with some of his friends. ☐
- But in the end he **made up his mind**. ☐
- Frank **had a carefree life** until one day **a problem came up**. ☑
- At first, Frank tried to **ignore the problem** hoping it would just go away. ☐
- He **thought it over** for a long time. ☐
- But he didn't know what to do. ☐

2 a) What do you think Frank's problem was? Was it related to:

– his love life?
– his job or studies?
– money?
– his family?
– his health?
– a secret in his past?

b) In pairs, decide what the problem was and re-tell the story using the words in **bold** from Exercise 1.

> Frank had a carefree life until a slight problem came up. The problem was that ...

Wordspot

think

1 Match a phrase / sentence in column A with an appropriate ending / response in column B. (There may be more than one answer in some cases.)

A		B	
a	What do you **think** ...	1	**I don't think so.**
b	I'm **thinking of** ...	2	**of** the new boss?
c	**Just think!**	3	I'll have to **think it over.**
d	Last night in bed, I suddenly ...	4	Jenny's in Brazil now!
e	Is there a meeting now?	5	help me for a minute?
f	I can't decide now.	6	people should kill animals.
g	Is this Paul's bag?	7	**I think so.**
h	**Do you think you could** ...	8	changing my job.
i	**I don't think** ...	9	**thought of a solution** to our problem.

2 The diagram below shows the most important uses of *think*. Look at the phrases / sentences above and underline the phrases with *think*. Add them to the correct section of the diagram.

(a) *to believe / have an opinion*

I think ...

(b) *to use your mind / consider*

What are you thinking about?

THINK

(d) *common spoken phrases*

Just think!

(c) *to have an idea*

think of a solution

3 Do the following activities in pairs.

a) Take turns to ask and answer the following questions. Respond using either *I think so* or *I don't think so*.

- Is Sydney the capital of Australia?
- Is it going to rain tomorrow?
- Can ducks swim under water?
- Does your teacher speak Chinese?
- Is there going to be a test next week?

b) Give your opinion of the following statements by adding *I think* or *I don't think*. (You may need to change any negative verbs.)

For example:
I don't think the economic situation will improve next year.

- All forms of hunting are wrong.
- All school children should learn a foreign language.
- Cigarette advertisements should not be allowed.
- Men aren't as good at looking after small children as women.
- We don't get enough homework.

125

Part B **Task**

Find solutions to problems

Task link: verbs to describe behaviour and reactions
Creative writing

Personal vocabulary

Useful language

Suggesting possibilities

"He could try ..."

"Alternatively he could ..."

"Another possibility is to ..."

Giving your opinion

"I think / don't think she should ..."

"In her position I would / wouldn't ..."

"If she ..., her mother / husband might ..."

"Personally I would / wouldn't ..."

Your Dilemmas

The column where you send in your questions, and ordinary readers share their experience and advice.
Last week's problem:

I DON'T WANT MY GIRL TO GO AWAY

Question: My daughter, who's just turned seventeen, wants to go travelling around Europe this summer with a group of friends, including her boyfriend, who's several years older than she is. They all seem quite pleasant and responsible, but I'm not happy about the situation. Should I let her go, or insist that she waits until she's older?

(Richard Paxton, Manchester)

Preparation for task

1 Look at the letter above. Where do you think it comes from? Why do people write to columns like this? Would you ever write to a newspaper about a problem? Why? / Why not?

2 Read the problem again and tick (✓) the sentence which best describes it.

a   The man is worried about his daughter leaving home. ❑
b   The man doesn't like his daughter's new boyfriend. ❑
c   The man doesn't want his daughter to go on holiday with her friends. ❑

Your Replies

You are obviously worried that this holiday is the beginning of your daughter's independent, adult life. Perhaps it is – unfortunately, there is nothing you can do to prevent it, unless you want to play the heavy father and risk losing her completely. She is still very young in your eyes, but you have to accept that in her own eyes, she is already an adult. The fact that she is under eighteen will not stop her from doing anything she really wants to do. All you can do is hope that you have given her enough sense of responsibility to cope with whatever happens. I too have had to watch my daughter grow up and leave. We all have to let our girls go eventually.

(Mrs D. Cooper, Edinburgh)

3 Above are three answers sent in by readers. Read them and decide:

a   if the writer thinks the man should let his daughter go or not.
b   what kind of person wrote each letter.
c   which you think is the best answer and why.

I am twenty-one years old. I have been travelling in Europe and Asia since I was sixteen, both with friends and alone. Almost everywhere I have travelled I have met with kindness and friendship. I have had quite a few adventures, but nothing seriously dangerous has ever happened to me. People worry far too much about 'dangers' that they imagine exist abroad. Let your daughter go – she'll probably have lots of fun and come back with experiences that she will always remember. Opportunities like this are too good to miss!

(Mark Hicks, London)

Seventeen is still very young for a girl to go travelling abroad without adult supervision. However pleasant your daughter's boyfriend seems, he is probably not yet mature enough to take care of her. Young people arriving in a foreign country can easily meet the wrong kind of people, who will take advantage of their youth and innocence. We have all heard enough stories recently to make us take more care of our young. Discuss your worries with your daughter and her friends. Ask them to wait at least another year before travelling anywhere exotic together. Suggest a weekend with relatives in another town instead, or an activity holiday closer to home. Either way, it would be better than letting them visit places where they may not yet be able to cope.

(Philip Edmunds, Kent)

4 Below are more problems sent to 'Your Dilemmas'. What is the problem in each case?

(a) I am the assistant manager of a small restaurant owned by a retired couple who have been very kind to me. For the last few months I have suspected that the manager, Alan, who I also get on well with, has been taking small amounts of money from the till. I don't have any hard evidence, but I know that he has had a lot of personal problems. Should I say anything?

(b) Eighteen months ago I became engaged to a woman I had only known for four months. Two weeks before the wedding she broke it off, saying that she was not ready for marriage. Now, after hearing nothing from her for nearly a year, she claims that she's sorted herself out and that she wants to try again. Deep down, I know I still love her, even though she humiliated me in front of my family and friends. Should I give her a second chance?

(c) My husband, in other ways a kind, loving man, is a compulsive gambler. He has promised to give up hundreds of times, but never has. In desperation at all the debts he had run up, a couple of months ago I told him I wanted a divorce. Now I have discovered that I am pregnant. He swears that, with a baby to support, he will never gamble again. Should I believe him?

(d) I am forty-four years old and have looked after my elderly mother for a number of years. Recently, my husband was offered a new job in the United States, a once-in-a-lifetime opportunity; my husband is desperately keen to go, and both our children would love to experience life in a new culture. But I know that my mother would not even consider moving to the USA, and I am so worried about her coping on her own. She has no other children or close relatives and would have to go into an old people's home. What should I do?

Task

1 **a)** Work in groups. Together decide which **one** of the problems from Exercise 4 above interests you most, and make a list of all the **possible** solutions you can think of. Ask your teacher about any words or phrases you need and write them in the *Personal vocabulary* box.

b) Look at your list of possible solutions, and put them in order from best to worst.

2 Form new groups with students who discussed a different problem. Look at the phrases in the *Useful language* box. Describe the solutions to your problem, and tell them what you decided and why. Do the other students agree with your decisions?

Task link

Verbs to describe behaviour and reactions

1 Look at the following descriptions of two television 'soaps'.

Gold follows the adventures of the millionaire Nicholas family – a family which will stop at nothing to extend its power and influence. It is a world filled with corruption, lies and scandal.

Our Street follows the adventures of a group of teenagers in a small town in Australia. It is a world filled with teenage romance, heartbreak, sun, sea and sand.

Below are some extracts from the dialogues of these two soap operas. Read them and mark each one as follows:

G if you think it comes from *Gold*.
O if you think it comes from *Our Street*.

a   'No! I'll never sell my share of the business, no matter how much money you offer me!' ☐

b   'Okay, I'll do business with you … but there's one condition …' ☐

c   'Mom, I don't care what you say – I'm going to wear this dress and that's that.' ☐

d   'If you ever tell the newspapers about this, I'll kill you!' ☐

e   'I think Carl is seeing someone else … another girl in his class … he's so secretive these days.' ☐

f   'I have never offered bribes to politicians. I am a businessman, not a criminal.' ☐

g   'I'll never leave you, Darlene. I'll love you for ever … honest I will.' ☐

h   'That's great news! Let's all have a beach party to celebrate!' ☐

i   'If you sign this, you'll be a rich man … think of all the money … go on, sign … that's it …' ☐

j   'Yes, it's true. I've been in love with Patsy for nearly two weeks now.' ☐

2 Match the verbs below with the speakers' behaviour in Exercise 2.

- deny ☑
- threaten ☐
- admit ☐
- persuade ☐
- refuse ☐

- agree ☐
- suggest ☐
- promise ☐
- suspect ☐
- insist ☐

3 Put the verbs in the correct box below. With which verbs can we also use *that*?

Verbs followed by the infinitive *threaten to do something*	Verbs followed by the -*ing* form *deny doing something*

Verbs followed by an object + infinitive *persuade someone to do something*	Verbs followed by a preposition + the -*ing* form *suspect someone of doing something*

4 Look back at the extracts in Exercise 1 and write a sentence using the appropriate verb.

For example:

refuse > She refused to sell her share of the business.

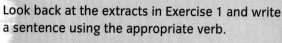

Creative writing

Work in pairs or small groups and choose **one** of the following writing exercises.

Letter

1 Look back at the problems on pages 126–127. Choose one of them and write a letter to the 'Your Dilemmas' page giving your advice. The letter will be more convincing if you include any similar experiences you have had (invent experience if necessary!)

Story

2 Look back at the problems on pages 126–127. Choose one and think about how it might have been solved. Did they work out their problem or not? Write a story describing what happened. (This can be from the point of view of one of the characters if you like.)

Soap opera script

3 Imagine that you are the writers of a television soap opera similar to those described on page 128. Look back at the problems on pages 126–127. Write a scene from a soap opera based on one of them in which the characters discuss their problems, like the one below. Remember to include:

a the characters in the scene and a short description of each one.
b where / when the scene happens ('location').
c stage directions telling the actors what to do and how to say their lines.

When you have finished, act out your scene to the rest of the class.

CHARACTERS

JASON: about 20, a serious, intelligent young man, in love with Charlene.
CHARLENE: about 19, pretty, not very clever.
SCOTT: about 19, handsome and athletic.

LOCATION: the Beach House Café, lunch time. There are a few people at the tables, chatting and drinking coffee.

DIRECTIONS: enter Jason and Charlene. Charlene looks very unhappy about something.

JASON: So what is it, Charlene? Just tell me what's the matter!
CHARLENE: Oh, it's nothing. Nothing you could understand anyway.
(They sit down. Charlene looks angrily at the menu.)
JASON: *(angrily)* That's not fair, Charlene. Why are you behaving like this? Have I done something wrong? What is it?
CHARLENE: You know what the problem is, Jason. I can't believe you don't know. You just don't understand, do you?
(Enter Scott. He looks towards Charlene and smiles.)
CHARLENE: *(in a friendly voice)* Scott, hi! It's good to see you!
SCOTT: *(smiling)* Oh hi, Charlene.
(pause)
Hi, Jason.
(Jason looks suspiciously at Scott, but says nothing.)
Jason there's something you ought to know ... it's about Charlene and me ...

129

Consolidation
modules 9–12

A Verb forms: Past Perfect / reported speech

1 Complete the gaps in the following text with the correct form of the verb in brackets.

Possibly the world's least successful tourist is Mr Nicholas Scotti, an Italian living in San Francisco, who (1) .... (*fly*) back to Italy to visit relatives. During the journey, the plane (2) .... (*make*) a one-hour stop at Kennedy Airport. Thinking he (3) .... (*arrive*), Mr Scotti (4) .... (*get out*), and (5) .... (*spend*) the whole day in New York thinking he was in Rome. The great traveller (6) .... (*notice*) that modernisation (7) .... (*destroy*) many of Rome's ancient buildings and later told friends that he (8) .... (*be*) rather surprised that so many people (9) .... (*speak*) English. In fact, he (10) .... (*speak*) very little English himself, but when he (11) .... (*ask*) a policeman the way, he (12) .... (*manage*) to choose an officer who (13) .... (*be / born*) in Naples, and who (14) .... (*reply*) in fluent Italian. After Mr Scotti (15) .... (*spend*) over twelve hours riding around on a bus, the driver (16) .... (*decide*) to hand over his passenger to another policeman, who (17).................... (*try*) to explain that he (18) .... (*not / be*) in Rome but New York. Mr Scotti (19) .... (*refuse*) to believe him, and said he (20) .... (*be*) very surprised the Rome police (21) .... (*employ*) an officer who (22) .... (*not / speak*) Italian. As he (23) .... (*be / driven*) back to the airport in a police car, racing to catch the San Francisco plane, Scotti told his interpreter that now he (24) .... (*know*) he was in Italy, because that was how they always (25) .... (*drive*)!

2 Underline examples of reported speech in the story. What did the person *actually* say in each case?

B Verb forms: possibilities / obligation and permission

1 Circle the possible alternatives in the following sentences. (There may be more than one possibility.)

a You look really tired – I think you *have to / ought to / should* take a break for a few days.

b The hours of work are quite flexible – the office is open between 8.00 and 6.30 every day, and you *can / have to / must* do thirty-eight hours a week. In the morning, though, you *don't have to /mustn't / shouldn't* start until 10.30 if you don't want to.

c I'm sorry, but it's too late to change my plans now – you *had to / should have / would have* told me earlier.

d The children *aren't allowed to / aren't likely to / aren't supposed* to run inside the school building.

e It seemed that everyone we met in Amsterdam spoke perfect English, so we *didn't have to speak / shouldn't have learnt / couldn't have spoken* any Dutch.

f People *have to / may well / are unlikely* to stop eating meat completely in the next few years.

2 Look back at the sentences in which you have circled more than one possibility. Is there any difference in meaning between them?

C Listening: hypothetical forms

1 ⌷ [1] You are going to hear three monologues. Which person is talking about:

a living in Britain?

b a business venture which failed?

c a tennis tournament?

2 Make notes about what each person says. Discuss your answers in pairs.

3 Each monologue ends with a half-sentence with *if*. Listen again and write down the half-sentence at the end of each monologue. Think of two different ways to complete each one.

D *make / do / say / tell / think*

Match a word / phrase in the box below with *make*, *do*, *say*, *tell* or *think* to make phrases from Modules 9–12.

of a brilliant idea   the truth   something over
about your boyfriend   a noise   a child off you're sorry   someone to go away   your mind up some research   a joke   the washing up   'thank you' someone smile   a test   a prayer   your best   a profit of leaving your job

E Game: just a minute

1 [2] **Listen to three people discussing one of the topics below. Which topic are they talking about?**

a stupid mistake

smoking in public places

a lucky escape

the differences between your town now and when you were a child

the differences between country and city life

things I know now that I didn't know ten years ago

your ideal job

the last long journey you made

2 **Your teacher will give you one of the topics above (or a different topic) and ask you to talk about it for one minute. Spend a few minutes thinking about what you might say about each topic.**

3 **In teams, take turns to talk about the topic your teacher chooses for you. If you complete your one-minute talk, your team will receive ten points. Be careful! The other team(s) can challenge you if you:**

- **hesitate for more than five seconds.**
- **repeat yourself.**
- **go off the subject.**

If your teacher thinks the other team is right, your team will lose ten points!

F Vocabulary puzzle

Read the definitions below and complete the puzzle. The words all come from Modules 9–12. When you have completed the puzzle, you can read the hidden message.

1 If you say you didn't do something, you ..... it.
2 the opposite of *deteriorate*
3 If something happens like this, then it happens slowly.
4 I have thought the problem ..... and come up with a solution!
5 If the law does not allow it, then it's ..... .
6 If you say you won't do something, then you ..... to do it.
7 the opposite of *fall*
8 the opposite of number 3 above
9 If a child does not behave well, his parents might ..... him.
10 If you say you will definitely do something whatever happens, then you ..... to do it.
11 A man with a knife said: 'If you don't give me all your money, I'll kill you.' He ..... me.
12 the opposite of *decrease*
13 If something is prohibited, we can say it's not ..... .
14 If you think a law is right, you could also say that it's ..... .
15 a verb that is similar to *advise* or *recommend*
16 the opposite of *well-behaved*
17 to cry out loudly
18 a kind of long knife that knights wore in their belts before guns were invented
19 the opposite of number 1 above

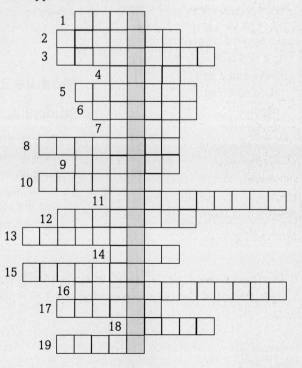

Communication
activities

Module 2: Reading, Exercises 4 and 5, page 18

Student A

Test your memory

1 The following words and phrases all come from Module 1. Try to memorise them by repeating them silently for **one minute**.

- eyebrow
- friends
- neighbour
- divorce
- entertain
- stranger
- have a career
- divorce rate

2 This is your new credit card number: **3853204779**. Try to memorise it by breaking the number into 'chunks' of three or four numbers. Repeat them to yourself a few times. You have **thirty seconds**.

3 The following words and phrases also come from Module 1. Try to memorise them by putting them all into a very short story. You have **a minute and a half**.

- bring up a child
- nephew
- do a course
- work long hours
- mother-in-law
- increase

Module 2: Practice, Exercise 2, page 20

last birthday

1 What day of the week / your last birthday?
2 work / that day?
3 What time / get up?
4 What presents / get?
5 Which present / like best?
6 anyone important / forget your birthday?
7 have / a birthday cake?
8 do / anything special to celebrate?
9 who / with?
10 What time / go to bed?

Total : _____

last plane trip

1 Where / go?
2 Why / travel?
3 How much / ticket / cost exactly?
4 How long / spend / at the airport?
5 What / do / while / wait?
6 What / get to eat on the plane?
7 Who / sit next to during the flight?
8 Have / a conversation with him or her?
9 How long / flight?
10 What time / arrive / destination?

Total : _____

last English lesson

1 When / last English lesson?
2 get there / on time?
3 anybody in the class / arrive late?
4 What / wear that day?
5 What / teacher / wear?

6 listen / cassette?
7 Which new words / learn that lesson?
8 Who / sit next to that lesson?
9 Who else / talk to during the lesson?
10 What homework / teacher / give?

Total : _____

Module 2: Wordspot (*time*), Exercise 3, page 21

Student A

a Do you bring your *Students' Book* with you every time you come to class?
b Give an example of a place where it's hot and sunny all the time.
c Give an example of a place you've been to a few times.
d When was the last time you went shopping?
e Tell me something you're going to do in a week's time.
f Give an example of something you do from time to time.

Module 3: Wordspot (*place*), Exercise 3, page 29

Student A

a car park   a newsagent's   a gym
a sofa   a washbasin   a butcher's

Module 4: Preparation for task, Exercise 1, page 42

Bill Gates

born Seattle, USA, 1955

While at school, he finished among the top ten in the country in a maths aptitude test – despite never taking a book home to study or attending maths classes. He went to Harvard, but left without getting a degree to start up his computer company Microsoft. By the age of forty-one, he was one of the world's richest men – he is believed to be worth about $18 billion. Unlike some millionaires, he is not shy about spending his money: he owns twenty Ferraris, each worth more than £150,000, and a high-tech mansion overlooking Lake Washington.

Mother Teresa

missionary,
born Albania, 1910–1997

The daughter of peasants, she became a nun in 1927 and was sent first to Ireland and then to Calcutta, where she taught in a girls' school for nearly twenty years, before deciding to devote herself to working with the people living in the slums of Calcutta. After a short medical training, she and two other nuns took to the streets, caring for the sick and dying. In 1950 she founded the Missionary Sister of Charity, which now has 775 homes in 120 countries. In 1979 she was awarded the Nobel Peace Prize.

Madonna

singer / actress,
born Michigan, USA, 1959

Originally a dancer, she had her first hit record 'Holiday' in 1983. In 1985 she began her film career and also married actor Sean Penn, but the marriage lasted less than four years. Her 'Blond Ambition Tour' in 1990 – complete with outrageous costumes designed by Jean Paul Gaultier – and her book *Sex* (1993) caused much controversy. Her career took a more respectable direction, however, with the birth of her first child, Lourdes, in 1997, and her performance in the title role of *Evita*.

Mikhail Gorbachev

Soviet leader,
born Stavropol, Russia, 1931

After becoming Secretary General of the Communist Party in 1985, he began his policy of 'Perestroika', which brought greater freedom to the Soviet Union and eventually enabled countries such as Hungary, Poland and Romania to form their own democratic governments. His policies were much admired in the West and he was awarded the Nobel Peace Prize in 1990. However, his popularity declined in his own country and he resigned a year later. By 1996 he was so unpopular that he gained only 0.5 per cent of the vote in Russia's first presidential election.

Pelé

footballer,
born Edson Arantes do Nascimento, Tres Coraçoes, Brazil, 1940

Considered by many to be the greatest footballer of all time, he became a world star at the age of only seventeen, when Brazil first won the World Cup in Sweden. Perhaps his greatest triumph was captaining his country to their third World Cup triumph in Mexico in 1970. He played in four World Cup competitions, and scored over 1,200 goals in his career before finally retiring in 1977. He was appointed Brazilian Special Minister for Sport in 1994.

Steffi Graf

tennis player,
born Neckerau, Germany, 1969

After turning professional at the age of thirteen, she won her first major tournament in 1986 and became the world's number one a year later. In 1988 she became the first woman since 1970 to win 'The Grand Slam' (Wimbledon, the US, Australian and French Open tournaments). She has won over 100 titles in her career and earned up to $20 million. She remained the world's number one throughout 1996 and 1997, despite a recurring back injury and investigations into tax evasion.

Aung San Sui Kyi

Burmese political leader,
born 1945

Educated in India and at Oxford University, she returned to Burma (for many years a military dictatorship) in 1988 to found the National League for Democracy. She was elected President, but the Burmese military did not allow her to form a government, and placed her under house arrest. She won the Nobel Peace Prize in 1990, and was finally freed in 1995. Since then she has continued to criticise the military Government, risking imprisonment and even death.

Stephen Hawking

physicist,
born Oxford, England, 1942

Considered the most brilliant cosmologist of his time, he is an advocate of the 'Big Bang' theory about the origins of the Universe. He is a Cambridge professor and the author of many scientific books, including the best-selling *A Brief History of Time* (1988). His achievements are especially remarkable because for over thirty years he has suffered from a neuromotor disease, which has meant he is confined to a wheelchair and can only speak with the help of a computer.

(continued on page 134)

Communication activities

Nelson Mandela

African National Congress leader and South African President, **born** Transkeu, 1918

Mandela trained to be a lawyer before joining the ANC in 1944. For the next twenty years he played a leading part in their campaign against apartheid, until he was arrested and sentenced to life imprisonment in 1964. He was not freed until 1990. In the years following his release he worked with President de Klerk to end apartheid, and in 1993 the two men were awarded the Nobel Peace Prize. In 1994 he became President of the new South Africa.

Gabriel Garcia Marquez

writer,
born Aracataca, Colombia, 1928

After studying at the University of Bogotà, he worked as a journalist in Colombia and as a foreign correspondent in Italy, France, Spain and the USA. He has written several novels and collections of short stories, including the international best-seller *Cien Años de Soledad* (*One Hundred Years of Solitude*). He was awarded the Nobel Prize for Literature in 1982. He has lived in Mexico City since the late 1970s.

- 1-year Diploma in Computing and Information Technology
- Diploma in European Literature
- 1-year Diploma in Travel and Tourism
- Certificate in Film, Video and Photography
- Certificate in Child Care
- 1-year Diploma in Business Studies

Module 4: Real life, Exercise 2, page 45

West London College
Application form 1998/99

1. a **For which course are you applying?**

   1st choice ....
   2nd choice ....

   b **How do you wish to study?**

   Day .... Part-time / Day .... Evening ....

2. **Information about you**

   c Mr / Ms / Mrs / Miss ....   d Male / Female ....

   Family name ....
   Personal name ....   Date of birth ....
   Age on 31/8/98 ....
   Address:

   e **Postcode** ....
   Telephone number ....

3. **Have you ever been resident outside the UK?** ......

   f **If yes, what was your date of entry to the UK?** ....

   Is English your first language? ......
   What other languages do you speak? ....
   ....

4. g **Your education and training background**

   (give your last school and any further education)

   Dates   School/college

   h **List any qualifications in order of date, including exams to be taken before September**

   Year   Qualifications   Subject   Grade

5. i **List work experience in order of date**

   Dates   Types of work   Employer

6. j **Why do you wish to take this course and what future education / employment are you considering?**

   k **Signature of applicant** ....   Date ....

134

Module 5: Speaking and reading, Exercise 4, page 48

Conclusions to quiz

Mostly As: you are an extremely well-organised person, who has every aspect of their life carefully planned. There are many advantages to this. Make sure, however, that you do not become inflexible, or ignore other people's needs because they do not fit in with your plans.

A combination of As and Bs: you try hard to be organised, yet flexible and sensitive to other people. On the whole you manage to get the balance right, though sometimes perhaps you need to prioritise more carefully, and be more determined about achieving your goals.

Mostly Bs: you are a very spontaneous person, who hates too much organising and planning ahead. This can have a very positive side – you often have great fun. But because you refuse to make plans, you may also miss out on the things other people do. Be careful, too, that your spontaneity doesn't mean more work for someone else.

Module 5: Task, Exercise 1, page 55

Peter Krajeck

Age: 28
Nationality: Slovak
Native language: Slovak
Marital status: single

Skills/ background
• Ex-professional skier
• A lot of experience working with small children as ski instructor in summer camps
• Speaks good French, some German
• Driver
• Good computer skills

Interview notes
• Retired from skiing because of knee injury
• Plans to open own hotel in ski resort - wants to get experience of all aspects of hotel work
• Very friendly, enthusiastic, seems hard-working

Horizons Unlimited

Module 6: Wordspot (by), Exercise 3, page 63

Student A

a   Tell me two ways in which you can become a millionaire. Answer like this:
    You can become a millionaire by ...
b   Can you name one famous piece of music / book / painting? Who are they by?
c   Tell me a phrase which is opposite in meaning to *on purpose* and *with other people*.
d   Which of the following sentences is false?
    • The radio was invented by an Italian.
    • The telephone was invented by an Englishman.
    • The first car was built by a German.
e   Can you tell me three different ways to get from where we are now to your house?

Module 8: Practice, Exercise 2, page 79

Student A

a wasp   a shopping mall   an orphan   a flag
an acquaintance   a sweater   a fireman   a degree

Module 8: Wordspot (something), Exercise 2, page 83

Student A

a   Tell me the name of a country with a population of something like 55 million.
b   Where do you go when there is something wrong with your car?
c   Recommend something to do for a visitor to your town / region.
d   Imagine you want to buy your teacher something special for his / her birthday. What could it be?
e   Tell me the name of something to eat which is typical of your country or region.
f   Say this sentence in another way, using *something*:
    This soup is rather strange.

Module 9: Wordspot (*make*), Exercise 4, page 95

Student A

a   What could you do if you suddenly feel hungry in the middle of the day?

c   If you drop your food all over the floor, you will ...

e   You can use the 'delete' button on a computer or typewriter if you ...

g   A successful business has to ...

i   If you are studying some difficult grammar, your teacher tries to ...

k   If a friend comes round to visit you, you might ...

Module 5: Task, Exercise 1, page 55

```
Brigitte Schumann

Age: 33
Nationality: Austrian
Native language: German
Marital status: divorced

Skills / background
• 8 years as assistant
manager of ski-resort hotel
• Speaks good French and
English
• Good skier
• Driver
• Good computer skills

Interview notes
• Recently divorced and 'wants a
complete change in her life'
• Has 7-year-old daughter and 4-year-old
son she will bring with her if she gets
the job
• Seems very efficient (a bit cold?)
• Obviously has very strong personality
and opinions
```

Horizons Unlimited

Module 9: Task link, Exercise 3, page 98

Student A

	Russia	Monaco
• **Area**	17,075,400 km²	....
• **Population**	147.5 million .	....
• **Life expectancy**	(*male*) 58 years (*female*) 71 years	(*male*) .... (*female*) ....
• **Average January temperature**	(*Moscow*) −15°C (*Siberia*) −46°C	....
• **Religion**	60% no religion 25% Russian Orthodox	....
• **Gross National Product (per person)**	£2,680	....
• **Number of telephones**	26,000,000	....
• **Number of cinemas**	120,000	....

Module 10: Practice, Exercise 1, page 101

Student A

a) Read a half-sentence in the 'Situation' box to Student B. He / She will respond with a half-sentence from his / her 'Explanation' box. Then listen to Student B and respond with a half-sentence from your 'Explanation' box.

Situation	Explanation
• We couldn't get into the rock concert because ...	• ... I'd forgotten to go to the supermarket.
• When I got home, my father was angry because ...	• ... my uncle had reserved a table.
• My grandparents were a little nervous when they got on the plane because ...	• ... she'd studied it at school for many years.
• We got really wet because ...	• ... they'd lived in the same house for forty years.

b) Read these situations to Student B, who will invent an explanation using the Past Perfect. Then listen to Student B's situations and invent your own explanations with the Past Perfect.

- I didn't get up until 12 o'clock because ...
- I knew what would happen at the end of the film because ...
- The telephone company cut off our telephone because ...

Module 11: Practice, Exercise 2, page 112

Student A

a library   on a bus   in church   in a bar

Module 5: Task, Exercise 1, page 55

Brenda Macdonald

Age: 46
Nationality: British
Native language: English
Marital status: widow

Skills/ background
- Several years' experience as hotel receptionist / secretary, but has not worked for 15 years
- French good, but not used for a long time
- Driver
- No experience of computers
- No knowledge of skiing
- Very good cook

Horizons Unlimited

Interview notes
- Husband died 15 years ago so stopped work to bring up three sons, all now grown up
- Wants to do something different and adores France
- Very friendly - good fun!
- Seems capable and flexible

Module 2: Reading, Exercises 4 and 5, page 18

Student B

Test your memory

1 The following words and phrases all come from Module 1. Try to memorise them by forming a picture in your mind that you associate with each word or phrase. You have **one minute**.
- eyebrow
- stranger
- divorce
- entertain
- neighbour
- divorce rate
- friends
- have a career

2 This is your new credit card number: **3853204779**. Try to memorise it by writing it down two or three times on a piece of paper. Then read it through a few times. You have **thirty seconds**.

3 The following words and phrases also come from Module 1. Try to memorise them by repeating them to yourself for **a minute and a half**.
- bring up a child
- work long hours
- nephew
- mother-in-law
- do a course
- increase

Module 2: Wordspot (*time*), Exercise 3, page 21

Student B

a Did you arrive on time for class today or were you late?
b What will you bring with you next time you come to class?
c Tell me something you learned to do a long time ago.
d Where would you recommend for someone who wants to have a great time on holiday?
e Give an example of something you think is a waste of time.
f Give an example of something you have no time to do at the moment.

Module 3: Wordspot (*place*), Exercise 3, page 29

Student B

a bookshelf   a chemist's   a wardrobe   a library a park bench   a greengrocer's

Module 6: Wordspot (*by*), Exercise 3, page 63

Student B

a Imagine that a member of your family goes to live in another country. Tell me two ways you could keep in contact with him / her.

b How good are you at mathematics? Can you answer these questions (without using a calculator)?
   - What is 168 divided by 8?
   - What are the approximate measurements of the room we are in now?

c You're in a shop and have just bought an expensive present for someone. You haven't got enough cash with you. How can you pay for it?

d Are the following sentences true or false?
   - It'll be dark by seven o'clock this evening.
   - You'll be home by midnight tonight.
   - You'll speak very good English by the time we finish this book.

e Look at the room you are in now. Who is sitting by the door? Is there anyone by the window?

Module 5: Task, Exercise 1, page 55

```
John Bailey

Age: 55
Nationality: Canadian
Native language: English
Marital status: single

Skills / background
• 35 years in hotel
business (including 15
years as assistant manager
of Toronto Hilton)
• Excellent French
• Good skier
• Driver
• Computer experience

Interview notes
• Retired from Hilton 2 years ago
because of nervous problems (doctor's
letter says now fine)
• Has never worked with children but
has many nephews and nieces and
'loves children'
• Seems friendly and sympathetic
```

Horizons Unlimited

Module 8 : Practice, Exercise 2, page 79

Student B

| an answerphone   a vet   a concert hall   a stranger housework   a driving test   a neighbour   research |

Module 8: Wordspot (*something*), Exercise 2, page 83

Student B

a Tell me the name of a person you know who is forty-something.

b Tell me a word which is something to do with computers.

c If your teacher makes a spelling mistake on the board, should you ignore it or is it better to say something?

d Do you think the public transport system in your town is good, or do you think that they should do something about it?

e Tell me the name of something to drink which is typical of your country or region.

f Say this sentence in another way using *something*.
   Liz, I've got some important news for you ...

Module 9: Wordspot (*make*), Exercise 4, page 95

Student B

b Shoes are usually more comfortable if they're ...

d A lot of cars and electrical equipment are ...

f When children are playing they usually ...

h Sometimes very sad films ...

j If you want to go to the doctor's or dentist's, you usually need to ...

l If someone in the street shouted something rude at you, it would probably ...

Module 9: Task link, Exercise 3, page 98

Student B

	Monaco	Russia
• **Area**	1.95 km²	....
• **Population**	30,600	....
• **Life expectancy**	(*male*) 73.1 years (*female*) 81.2 years	(*male*) .... (*female*) ....
• **Average January temperature**	10°C	(*Moscow*) .... (*Siberia*) ....
• **Religion**	95% Catholic	....
• **Gross National Product (per person)**	£16,000	....
• **Number of telephones**	53,877	....
• **Number of cinemas**	2	....

Module 5: Task, Exercise 1, page 55

<u>**Anne-Sophie Martin**</u>

Age: 21
Nationality: Swiss
Marital status: single
Native language: French

Skills / background
• 2 years as nanny
• 2 years as receptionist in Geneva hotel
• Good skier
• Very good German, good English
• Computer experience
• Doesn't drive

Horizons Unlimited

Interview notes
• Rather quiet (shy?) but very nice
• Experience of small children
• Excellent references

Module 10: Practice, Exercise 1, page 101

Student B

a) Student A will read a half sentence from his / her 'Situation' box. Listen and respond with a half-sentence from your 'Explanation' box. Then read a half-sentence from your 'Situation' box to Student A, who will respond in the same way.

Situation	Explanation
• She spoke French quite well because ... • There was no food in the house because ... • My grandparents didn't want to move because ... • We didn't have to queue at the restaurant because ...	• ... I'd left my umbrella at home. • ... they'd already sold all the tickets. • ... they'd never flown before. • ... I hadn't phoned him.

b) Student A will read out some more situations. Listen and invent an explanation using the Past Perfect. Then read out the following situations for Student A to respond to.

• I couldn't get into my house last night because ...
• When we got home, the house was very cold because ...
• She knew all the answers in the exam because ...

Module 11: Practice, Exercise 2, page 112

Student B

a hotel   in a taxi   on a motorway   on an aeroplane

Language summary

Module 1

A Auxiliary verbs *be*, *have* and *do*

The auxiliaries *be*, *have* and *do* are used:
– to form questions and negatives.
– on their own (in short answers and questions, question tags, etc.)

1 Auxiliary verbs to form tenses

a   *be* (+ verb + *-ing*) is used to form **continuous** tenses:
Present Continuous: *He's studying to become a doctor.*
Past Continuous: *I was talking to Charles the other day.*

b   *have* (+ past participle) is used to form **perfect** tenses:
Present Perfect: *We have been here for three months.*

c   *do* is used in **simple** tenses (but only in the question and negative form):
Present Simple: *Do you like football?*
Past Simple: *I didn't get your letter.*

> **REMEMBER!**
> 1   **Third person singular forms**
>   do → he / she / it **does**
>   have → he / she / it **has**
> 2   **Contractions**
>   She **is** waiting → She**'s** waiting
>   You **are** joking → You**'re** joking
>   He **has** left → He**'s** left

2 Auxiliary verbs in questions and negatives

a   **Questions** are formed by inverting the subject and auxiliary verb.
Is he studying to become a doctor?
How long have your brother and sister lived here?

b   **Negatives** are formed by adding *not* to the verb. We often shorten this to *n't* (especially when we speak).
She is not working. → She isn't working.
He has not come home. → He hasn't come home.

> **REMEMBER!**
> 1   Modal verbs: we form questions using the modal auxiliaries instead of *do*, *be* or *have*.
>
>   **Can** I come in?
>   I **mustn't** stay long.
>
> 2   We form questions and negatives with **have got** using the auxiliary verb **have**.
>
>   **Have** you **got** any money with you?
>   She **hasn't got** many friends.

3 Auxiliaries used on their own

a   **Short answers:** these can make the speaker sound more polite / interested.
A: **Have you** been to this restaurant before?
B: *Yes, actually, I have.*

We also use them to avoid repeating long sentences.
A: **Do** *your parents both work in Paris?*
B: *My mother does, but my father doesn't.*

b   **Short questions and question tags.**
A: *My brother's gone to live in Australia.*
B: **Has he**?

You were in this class last year, weren't you?

> **REMEMBER!**
> When we use auxiliaries on their own, they must match the tense of the main verb.

B Present Simple and Present Continuous

1 Present Simple

Positive form	Negative form	Question form
I / you / we / they **work**	I / you / we / they **don't** (= do not) **work**	**Do** I / you / we / they **work**?
he / she / it **works**	he / she / it **doesn't** (= does not) **work**	**Does** he / she / it **work**?

We use the Present Simple for:
a   repeated actions or habits.
We go out on Saturday nights.

b   something we see as permanent.
My brother works in a bank.

c   describing a state that doesn't change.
She looks like her mother.

[handwritten margin note: But also "she is in a good mood today! :)"]

2 Present Continuous

Positive form	Negative form	Question form
I'm (= am) working	**I'm not** (= am not) working	**Am I working?**
you / we / they **'re** (= are) working	you / we / they **aren't** / **'re not** (= are not) working	**Are** you / we / they **working?**
he / she / it **'s** (= is) working	he / she / it **isn't** (= is not) working	**Is** he / she / it **working?**

We use the Present Continuous for:
a   things in progress now, at the moment of speaking.
Look! It's raining again!

b   temporary actions that are happening 'around now', or for a limited period, but not necessarily right now.
I'm reading a very good book at the moment.

c   describing a state which is changing.
Families are getting smaller.

3 Present Simple versus Present Continuous

In many cases, either form is possible. The one we choose depends on *how we see* the state or action.

Compare the following pairs of sentences:

*Paola is the student who **sits** at the back of the class.*
(= she always does this)
*Paola is the student who **is sitting** at the back of the class.*
(= she is there now)

*I **stay** at the Metropole Hotel.*
(= I do this every time I visit the town)
*I'm **staying** at the Metropole Hotel.*
(= an action happening around now)

4 'State' versus 'action' verbs

a Some verbs are almost never found in continuous forms: these are verbs which describe states (things which stay the same) rather than actions (things which can change). Some of the most common are:
  – verbs connected with emotions: *like, love, hate, want, need*
  – verbs connected with understanding: *understand, know, prefer, agree, believe*
  – verbs connected with possession and unchanging qualities: *belong, cost, weigh*
  – verbs connected with the senses: *taste, hear, smell, sound*

b Some verbs can describe both states and actions. Notice the difference between:
  *I **think** you're right.* (= a state)
  and
  *What **are** you **thinking about?** (= an action)
  *Our apartment **has** three bedrooms.* (= a state)
  and
  *Claire **is having a shower** at the moment.* (= an action)

Module 2

Ⓐ Past Simple

Positive form	Negative form	Question form
I / you / we / they he / she / it **worked**	I / you / we / they he / she / it **didn't** (= did not) **work**	**Did** he / you / they, etc. **work?**
I / you / we / they he / she / it **left**	I / you / we / they he / she / it **didn't** (= did not) **leave**	**Did** she / it / they, etc. **leave?**
Regular verbs: base form + **-ed** Irregular verbs: *see list of irregular verbs on page 152.*	Regular and irregular verbs: subject + **didn't** (= did not) + base form	Regular and irregular verbs: **did** + subject + base form

1 We use the Past Simple for states and actions which happened in the past. We often say **when** the action happened.
  *I **saw** someone famous in the street **yesterday**.*

2 The action can be short or long, single or repeated.
  *I **dropped** the glass and it **broke** on the floor.*
  *He **took** the same train to work **every day**.*

3 We also use the Past Simple to talk about states in the past.
  *When I **was** young, I **loved** playing with my toys.*

Ⓑ Past Continuous

Positive form	Negative form	Question form
I / he / she / it **was working**	I / he / she / it **wasn't** (= was not) **working**	**Was** I / he / she / it **working?**
you / we / they **were working**	you / we / they **weren't** (= were not) **working**	**Were** you / we / they **working?**

1 We use the Past Continuous for actions in progress at a time in the past.
  *I **was living** in London then.*

  Sometimes this includes a specific time or another (completed) past action.
  *I **was having** breakfast at 7.30 this morning.*
  *I **heard** the news on the radio while I **was driving** home.*

2 The Past Continuous often describes the situation or background to a story (the main events are told in the Past Simple).
  *The sun **was shining** and I **was walking** along happily. Suddenly I **noticed** something on the pavement.*

3 Sometimes the Past Continuous action is interrupted.
  *They **were talking** about him when he **came** into the room.*
  (= they stopped talking)

4 Past Continuous actions are not seen as complete.
  *I **read** a book about Napoleon.* (= I read all of it)
  *I **was reading** a book about Napoleon.*
  (= I probably didn't read all of it)

Similarities with other continuous forms

1 Continuous forms show activities in progress.
  *He**'s reading** the paper.* (= he is in the middle of it)
  *He **was reading** the paper.* (= he was in the middle of it)

2 They emphasise that actions are temporary.
  *She**'s staying** with me at the moment.* (= temporary in the present)
  *I **was sleeping** on my friend's sofa.* (= temporary in the past)

3 They are not used with 'state' verbs.
  *I **hated** vegetables when I was young.*
  not:
  I ~~was hating~~ vegetables when I ~~was being~~ young.

Ⓒ Contrasting past and present

1 used to

Positive form	Negative form	Question form
I / she / we, etc. **used to work**	I / she / we, etc. **didn't** (= did not) **use to work**	**Did** I / she / we, etc. **use to work?**

a *Used to* is for habits and states in the past.
  *I **used to smoke** before I was ill.*
  *She **used to have** really long hair.*

  There is no equivalent form in the present.
  *I **usually go** to my mother's on Sundays.*
  not:
  I ~~use to go~~ to my mother's on Sundays.

b We can always use the Past Simple instead of *used to*.
   I **smoked** before I got married.
   She **had** really long hair.

But we cannot use *used to* for actions that happened only once.

2 *not ... any longer / not ... any more*

These phrases mean that an action or state was true in the past, but is not true now.
   He **used to be** a very good footballer, but he **doesn't play any longer**.
   I **don't drink** coffee **any more** – it gives me a headache.

3 *still*

We use *still* when we want to emphasise that an action or state has not stopped, but continues up to the present.
   I **still** remember how frightened I was.
   I hated spinach when I was a child – I **still** don't like it much!

Still normally goes between the subject and the verb.

D Short questions to show interest

1 These are formed by inverting the auxiliary verb and the subject in the first sentence.
   A: *Shirley's having a baby!*
   B: **Is she?**

2 In Present Simple / Past Simple affirmative sentences (where there is no auxiliary), we use *do*, *does* or *did*.
   A: **My brother works** in a circus.
   B: **Does he?**

   A: **Her parents went** to China last year for their holidays.
   B: **Did they?**

Module 3

A Comparative and superlative adjectives

1 One-syllable adjectives and two-syllable adjectives ending in *-y*

adjective	comparative	superlative
	adjective + **-er**	(the) adjective + **-est**
old	old**er**	the old**est**
big	big**ger**	the big**gest**
large	larg**er**	the larg**est**
friend**ly**	friend**lier**	the friend**liest**

2 Other two-syllable adjectives and longer adjectives

crowded	**more** crowded	**the most** crowded
boring	**more** boring	**the most** boring
interesting	**more** interesting	**the most** interesting
polluted	**more** polluted	**the most** polluted

3 Irregular forms

good	**better**	**the best**
bad	**worse**	**the worst**
far	**further / farther**	**the furthest / farthest**

> **REMEMBER!**
> 1 With short vowels the final consonant doubles.
> thin   thi**nner**   the thi**nnest**
> 2 If the adjective already ends with **-e**, we just add **-r** or **-st**.
> fine   fin**er**   the fin**est**
> 3 *-y* changes to *-i*
> bus**y**   bus**ier**   the bus**iest**
> pretty   prett**ier**   the prett**iest**

B Large and small differences

1 If there is a large difference between two objects, we can use *far*, *much* and *a lot*.

Russia is	far / a lot / much / much, much	**bigger** than Belgium.

2 For small differences, we can use *a little (bit)* or *slightly*.

France	**is a little (bit)** / **slightly**	**bigger** than Spain.

C Common phrases with superlatives

1 *by far the most ... / -est*

Brazil is **by far the largest country** in South America.

2 *one of the most ... / -est*

Baghdad is **one of the oldest cities** in the world.

3 *the second / third most ... / -est*

Birmingham is **the second biggest city** in England.

4 *the least*

I decided to buy **the least expensive** bag in the shop.

> **REMEMBER!**
> The superlative phrases above are followed by in.
>
> Shanghai is the biggest city **in** China, and one of the biggest **in** Asia.

D Other ways of making comparisons

1 *not as ... as*

Silver **isn't as** expensive **as** gold.

If there is only a small difference, we can use *quite*.
Linda **isn't quite as tall as** her sister.

> **REMEMBER!**
> The sentence above does not mean the same as:
>
> Gold **isn't as expensive as** silver.

2 Comparing two things which are the same

Cats are **as intelligent as** dogs.
Now I've mended it, it's **just as good as** before.

3 *less*

Less is the opposite of *more*.
Is life **less expensive** in the country than in the city?

4 Making comparisons with nouns

*Rome has **more historic buildings** than any city I know.*
*There's **less space** in this classroom than in the other room.*
*There are **fewer people** who smoke nowadays.*

We use *fewer* with countable nouns and *less* with uncountable nouns. Nowadays, many people use *less* in both cases, but this is considered to be incorrect by many people.
*There are **fewer students** in my class than in yours.*
not:
There are ~~less people~~ in my class than in yours.

5 Other useful expressions for comparing things

a If two things are nearly the same:
*Their new car is **very similar** to their old one.*
*The train times are **more or less the same** on a Sunday.*

b If there is no difference between two objects:
*George looks **exactly the same as** his twin brother.*

c If there is a small difference between two objects:
*Her hair is **slightly different from** before.*

d If there is a big difference between two objects:
*Computers are **completely different from** how they were twenty years ago.*

Module 4

A Present Perfect Simple

Positive form	Negative form	Question form
I / you / we / they **'ve (= have) worked**	I / you / we / they **haven't (= have not) worked**	**Have** I / you / we they / **worked?**
he / she / it **'s (= has) worked**	he / she / it **hasn't (= has not) worked**	**Has** he / she / it **worked?**
subject + **have / has** **+ past participle**	subject **+ haven't / hasn't** **+ past participle**	**have / has +** subject **+ past participle**

We use the Present Perfect to talk about the **past and the present together**. The past action or situation is related to the present in various different ways.
1 The action continues from the past to the present.
I've known her for many years. (= I still know her now)
We've lived here all our lives. (= we still live here now)

2 The results of the past action are important in the present.
He's lost his key. (= he doesn't have it now)
I've tried to open it. (= but I can't now)

3 The time reference in the sentence includes the present.
He's been ill all this week.

4 We don't give any specific time, but we mean 'in my whole life'. The information is important now for some reason.
I've been to Spain lots of times.
(= in my whole life, so I can give you lots of information about it)
I've never seen Citizen Kane.
(= in my whole life, so I can't discuss it)

B Present Perfect versus Past Simple

1 We use the Past Simple for **completed actions** that are in the past.
*Marilyn Monroe **was married** three times. (= she is dead)*
*As a child, I **spent a** lot of time with my grandparents.*
(= I am an adult now)

Compare these to similar Present Perfect sentences.
*My friend **has been married** three times – and she's only thirty!*
(= her life is not finished)
I've spent a lot of time abroad this year. (= this year is not finished)

2 Whether we use the Present Perfect or Past Simple often depends on **how we see the action**. If we see it as related to the present, we use the Present Perfect. If we see it as finished and in the past, we use the Past Simple.
*Jan **has had** an accident – they've taken her to hospital.*
(= the accident is important now – she's in hospital now)
*Jan **had** an accident – don't worry she's okay now.*
(= the accident is no longer important – she's okay now)

C Time words with the Present Perfect and Past Simple (including *for*, *since* and *ago*)

1 Time words found with the Past Simple

a dates and times: *ten minutes ago, three months ago, four years ago,* etc.
b questions with *When ...?*: *yesterday, last night, last week*, etc.
c words that sequence stories: *then, before, after, after that, afterwards, later, next,* etc.

2 Time words often found with the Present Perfect

– *all day, all week, all my life,* etc.
– *today, this morning, this afternoon, this month,* etc.
– *already* (= before now)
– *yet* (= before now)
– *just, recently* (= a little before now)
– *ever, never*
– *for, How long...?*
– *since* (= from a time in the past until now)
– *once, twice, lots of times,* etc.

With many of these words / phrases we can use the Past Simple if the context is in the past.
*I **saw** her **this morning**.*
(= now it is evening, the morning is finished)
*I went to tell him the news, but he **already knew**.*
(= the context is a story in the past)
*He **was** in prison **for twenty-five years**.*

D Present Perfect Continuous

Positive form	Negative form	Question form
I / you / we / they **'ve been (= have been) working**	I / you / we / they **haven't been (= have not been) working**	**Have** I / you / we / they **been working?**
he / she / it **'s been (= has been) working**	he / she / it **hasn't been (= has not been) working**	**Has** he / she / it **been working?**
subject **+ have / has** **+ been + -ing**	subject **+ haven't / hasn't** **+ been + -ing**	**have / has** **+ subject** **+ been + -ing**

The Present Perfect Continuous is like the Present Perfect Simple in all the ways mentioned above. However we use the continuous form if:

1 we want to emphasise that the action is long or repeated.
*She's **been trying** to pass her driving test for years.*

2 the action is in progress / not complete.
Compare the following sentences:
*I've **been doing** some work. (= perhaps it is not finished)*
*I've **done** my homework. (= it is finished)*

3 the action is temporary.
*He's **been working** in a bar this summer.*
(= but afterwards he's going to university)

Note that we often use *for* and *since* with the Present Perfect Continuous. Like other continuous forms we cannot use it with 'state' verbs.
*I've **known** Ann all my life.*
not:
~~I've been knowing~~ Ann all my life.

Module 5

Ⓐ Future plans and intentions

1 *going to*

am / is / are + going to + verb		
Positive form	Negative form	Question form
I'm / he's, etc. **going to help**	I'm not / he isn't, etc. **going to help.**	Is he / Are you, etc. **going to help?**

We use *going to* to talk about present intentions about the future (near or more distant).
*I'm **going to have a bath** in a few minutes.*
(= I intend now to have a bath in the near future)
*She says she's **going to be** a ballet dancer one day.*
(= she intends now to be a ballet dancer in the future)

In general *going to* is used for future actions related to the present.

2 Present Continuous

a We use the Present Continuous to talk about things we have arranged for the future.
*I'm **meeting** Toni this weekend. (= I've arranged this)*
*What **are** you **doing** tonight? (= what have you arranged?)*

b Sometimes it doesn't matter whether we use the Present Continuous or *going to*.
*I'm **playing** football tonight .*
*I'm **going to play** football tonight.*
*I'm **going shopping** on Saturday.*
*I'm **going (to go)*** shopping on Saturday.*

* Some people think it is bad English to repeat *go* like this.

c It is wrong to use Present Continuous for a general intention.
*They **are going to get married** one day.*
(= this is a general intention, but has not been arranged)
*They **are getting married**. (= the wedding is already arranged)*

3 *will*

Positive form	Negative form	Question form
I / you / he, etc. **'ll (= will) + verb**	I / you / he, etc. **won't (= will not) + verb**	**Will** I / you / he, etc. **+ verb**
I'll see her.	*I won't see her.*	*Will I see her?*

We use *will* for talking about things that we think will happen **without** any particular intention or arrangement. We predict they will happen or think they are inevitable.
*I can give it to her – I'll **see** her at work.*
(= I don't need to arrange this)
*I know I'll **forget** if I don't write it down.*
(= this is inevitable / what I predict)

See page 146 B for more information on *will* and *going* to.

4 Other verbs and phrases

a Verbs
• *decide: She's **decided to leave** her job.*
• *hope: We're **hoping to buy** a flat later this year.*
• *intend: I **intend to phone** her tonight.*
• *would like: He'd (= **would**) **like to start** his own business.*
• *plan: I'm **planning to sell** it soon.*
   *He's **planning on leaving** next year.*
• *think: We're **thinking of having** a party soon.*
• *want: I **want to finish** this by tomorrow.*

b Phrases
• *to be due (to do): for something that is arranged or expected*
   *The plane's **due to take off** in a couple of minutes.*
   *I'm **due** at the dentist's in half an hour.*
• *to be about to do: when something will happen very soon or immediately*
   *She's **about to have** a baby.*

5 Modal verbs

Many present modal forms actually refer to future plans and intentions.
*I **can see** him in half an hour.*
*We **must talk** later.*

Ⓑ Future clauses with *if, when*, etc.

Even when we are talking about the future, after *if, unless, when, before, after, as soon as, until, once, next time*, etc. we use a present verb form. It is wrong to use a future form in these clauses.
***If** she **fails** her exam again, she'll be really upset.**
*I'll continue as planned **unless** you **phone** me.**
*I'm going to stay here **until** I **find** somewhere else to live.*
***When** I **find** it, I'll bring it for you.*
***As soon as** we **get** home, I'm going to have a bath.*
***Once** we **finish** the decorating, we'll have more time.*
*Can you look at this **before** you **leave**?*
*He's going to explain it all to you **next time** he **sees** you.*

Notice in the other clause (part) of the sentence, a future verb is used (*will, going to, can*, etc.)

* Sentences with *if* and *unless* like this are often called the 'first conditional' in grammar books.

Module 6

A -ed / -ing adjectives

1 -ing adjectives

Adjectives ending in -ing describe the thing or person that has an effect on us.

*Today's lesson was very **interesting**.*
(= the lesson interested me)

2 -ed adjectives

Adjectives ending in -ed describe our feeling about something or someone.

*I felt **bored** at the party.* (= I found the party boring)

B The passive

Simple tenses

	Positive form	Negative form	Question form
Present	It's (= is) done.	It isn't (= is not) done	Is it done?
Past	It was done.	It wasn't (= was not) done.	Was it done?
Present Perfect	It's (= has) been done.	It hasn't (= has not) been done.	Has it been done?
Future	It'll (= will) be done.	It won't (= will not) be done.	Will it be done?

Continuous tenses

	Positive form	Negative form	Question form
Present	It's (= is) being done.	It isn't (= is not) being done.	Is it being done?
Past	It was being done.	It wasn't (= was not) being done.	Was it being done?

1 The difference between active and passive

In active sentences the subject is the 'doer' of the verb (the person who makes the action happen).

*The Italian, Marconi, **invented** the telegraph.*
(subject) (verb)

In passive sentences the 'doer' of the verb is **not** the subject.

*The telegraph **was invented** by the Italian Marconi.*
(subject) (verb) ('doer')

2 Reasons for using the passive

a the main topic of the sentence
The main topic normally comes at the beginning of the sentence. Compare the following sentences:

An American *won the Olympic 100 metre race again.*
(main topic = an American)

The Olympic 100 metre race was won *by an American again.*
(main topic = the Olympic 100 metre race)

If the main topic is not the 'doer' of the verb, we need to use the passive.

b the 'doer' of the verb is unknown
*My handbag **has been stolen**.*
(= we don't know who did this)

c the 'doer' of the verb is not important in this context
*The Eiffel Tower **was built** in 1889.*
(= we are interested in **when** it was built, not **who** built it)

d it is obvious who the 'doer' is without saying
*Thousands of young people **were arrested**.*
(= it is obvious that the police arrested them)

e the 'doer' of the verb is 'people in general'
*Spanish **is spoken** in twenty countries around the world.*
(= it is not necessary to say 'by people')

> **REMEMBER!**
>
> 1 *We use the passive more in **formal** contexts (like newspaper reports) and less when we are talking informally.*
>
> 2 *We can still mention the 'doer' in a passive sentence, using by:*
>
> *The accident was caused **by a lorry**.*
> *The telephone was invented **by Alexander Graham Bell**.*

3 Verbs often used in the passive

a verbs relating to accidents / injury, etc.:
was injured / was killed / was damaged / was destroyed, etc.

b verbs relating to crime:
was arrested / was sentenced / was found guilty / was sent to prison, etc.

c verbs relating to inventions, books, films, etc.:
was invented by / was discovered by / was produced by / was directed by / was written by, etc.

Module 7

A Polite requests

1 Asking if you can do things (asking for permission)

Asking	Saying 'yes'	Saying 'no'
Can I ...? *Could I ...?* *Could I possibly ...?*	*Yes, sure.* *Yes, of course.*	*Well, I'm afraid ...* (+ reason)
Is it alright / okay if I ...? *Do you think I could ...?*	*That's fine.* *Certainly.*	*Well, the problem is ...* *Sorry, but ...*
Do you mind if I ...?	*No, not at all.*	

2 Asking other people to do things (making requests)

Asking	Saying 'yes'	Saying 'no'
Can you ...? Could you ...? Could you possibly ...? Do you think you could ...? Will you ...? Would you ...?	Yes, sure. Yes, of course. Yes, that's fine. Certainly.	Well, I'm afraid ... (+ reason) Well, the problem is ...
Would you / Do you mind + -ing?	Of course not!	

- We use *Do you mind if I ...?, Could I possibly ...?, Could you possibly ...?, Do you think you could ...?* when we want to sound particularly polite.
- *Could you ... / Would you ...?* are a little more polite than *Can you ...? / Will you ... ?*
  In all these questions, however, intonation is often more important for showing politeness.

> **REMEMBER!**
> 1 After Would you mind...?, *we use the -ing form of the verb.*
> 2 With Would you mind ...? *and* Do you mind ...?,
>   *if we answer* Of course not! *it means 'yes!'*
>
> A: **Do you mind doing** the washing-up! I'm in a bit of a hurry.
> B: **Of course not**. It's my turn, anyway!

B *will* for instant decisions and responses

1 If we make a decision as we are speaking, we use *will*.
  I suddenly feel a bit tired ... I think I'll stay in tonight.

2 Very often these decisions are offers.
  A: *I'm stuck with my homework.*
  B: *I'll help you in a minute, just hang on!*

This use of *will* is often contrasted with *going to* (used if you've already decided). Compare the following dialogues.
A: *Do you want to play squash tomorrow some time?*
B: *Sorry, I can't – we're going to paint the living room this weekend. I've promised Sue.* (= it is already decided)

A: *Do you want to go and have a quick coffee?*
B: *Why not? I'll just finish this ... I'll do the rest later.*
A: *Okay, I'll wait for you outside then.* (= they decide as they speak)

C Making generalisations

1 Impersonal or 'empty' *it*

We often use *it* + adjective + infinitive to describe a general situation or experience.
It's normal to get married young.
It's difficult to study in this weather.

In this construction, we talk about people using *for*.
*It's common **for couples** to get married late.*
*It's difficult **for children** to study in this weather.*

2 *tend to* + verb

We use *tend to* + verb to describe general situations / tendencies.
*Italian people **tend to make** a lot of gestures.*
*Young people **don't tend to eat** traditional food so much.*
*Children in my day **tended to play** out in the street more.*

3 *most people, a lot of people, not many people, very few people*

Most people live in flats rather than houses.
A lot of people go to the coast at the weekend.
Not many people stay in the city during August.
Very few people speak English there.

> **REMEMBER!**
> *Don't forget that* people *is a plural noun!*
>
> Most people **are** quite interested in world news.

Module 8

A Defining relative clauses

Defining relative clauses give us information about things, people, possessions, places and times using a **relative pronoun**.

1 Things (*that, which* or *nothing*)

*A modem is a piece of equipment **which** sends information along telephone wires.*
*A calculator is a little machine **that** does arithmetic.*

> **REMEMBER!**
> What *is not possible here.*
>
> A calculator is a little machine ~~what~~ does arithmetic.

2 People (*who, that* or *nothing*)

*A technophobe is a person **who** doesn't like machines.*
*A newscaster is a person **that** reads the news.*

The pronoun *that* is less common here than *who*.

> **REMEMBER!**
> *We can leave out* which, who *and* that *if they are the <u>object</u> of the relative clause.*
>
> Career councillors are people **(that)** you go to if you need advice about jobs.
> Gloves are things **(that)** you wear on your hands.
>
> *Notice that in the examples above* which, who *and* that *are the <u>subject</u> of the relative clause, so they <u>cannot</u> be left out.*

3 Possessions (*whose*)

*He's a person **whose** life is dominated by computers.* (= his life)
*An orphan is a child **whose** parents have died.* (= his / her parents)

4 Places (*where, which / that* + preposition)

We can refer to places in the following ways:
*This is the house **where** I grew up.*
*That's the house **which / that** I grew up **in**.*

5 Times (*when*)

*Easter is a time **when** families get together.*
*The evening's a time **when** I can relax.*

B Quantifiers (*a few*, *a lot of*, etc.)

1 Countable, uncountable or both?

With uncountable nouns only	With countable nouns only	With both countable and uncountable nouns
much a bit a little	many a few a couple (of) several (of) one or two loads of	a lot of / lots of some (not) any (not) enough plenty of no

2 Some problems with meaning and use

a *some* and *any*
Some refers to a limited or particular group or quantity of something. It is therefore most often used in positive sentences.
*I like **some** modern art.* (= but not all modern art)

We also use it in some questions.
*Can you pass me **some** plates from that cupboard?*

We do not use *any* in such a limited way. We use it most often in negative sentences and in many questions.
*I don't like **any** modern art.*
*Have you got **any** earrings at all?*

b *a lot of* and *much / many*
A lot of is usually used in positive sentences.
*We have **a lot of** Spanish and Portuguese ceramics.*

Much and *many* are generally used in questions and negatives.
*Do you sell **many** pictures?*
*There isn't **much** space in here to have a café.*

c *a lot of* and *too much / many*
We use *too much / too many* to say that there is more of something than we want or need.
*Shall we go somewhere else? There are **too many people** here.*
(= it's too crowded)
*Do you want some of this pizza? There's **too much** here for me.*
(= I can't eat it all)

d *enough*
We use *enough* to mean 'as much as we need'.
*Have we got **enough cups** for everyone?*

e *plenty of*
We use *plenty of* to mean 'more than enough'. It has a positive meaning.
*You don't need to hurry – we've got **plenty of time**.*
*We've got **plenty of biscuits** at home – we don't need any more.*

Module 9

A Making predictions

1 Using *will* or *won't*

We often use adverbs with *will* and *won't* to show how certain we are.
*Our team **will probably lose** on Saturday.*
*I think he**'ll almost certainly** pass the exam.*
*We **definitely won't** be there on time.*

These adverbs come <u>after</u> *will* but <u>before</u> *won't*.

2 Using *may (not)* / *might (not)* / *could*

These modal verbs all mean that something is possible in the future. We add *well* if we are more sure it will happen.
*Inflation **may** / **might** / **could** go up this year.* (= it is possible)
*Inflation **may** / **might** / **could well** go up this year.* (= it is more sure)

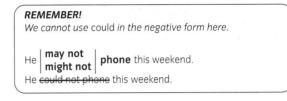

> **REMEMBER!**
> *We cannot use could in the negative form here.*
>
> | He | may not
might not | phone this weekend. |
> | He | ~~could not phone~~ | this weekend. |

3 *likely to*

We use *likely to* when we think something will probably happen. We can also use the negative form.
*People in the next century **are likely to live** longer.*
*The economy **isn't likely to improve** next year.*

B Real and hypothetical possibilities with *if*

1 Hypothetical possibilities

a If we are talking about an imaginary / hypothetical situation, we use *would* / *wouldn't* + verb.
*I **wouldn't like** to be famous.*
*I **would** never **hit** a child.*

b Often when we talk about a hypothetical situation, we need a longer sentence with *if* to explain it.
*If I **were** Prime Minister, I **would cut** taxes.*

Notice that we use the Past Simple (or Continuous) after *if* even though we are talking about the present in general.
*If I **found** a lot of money, I would take it to the police.*
*He wouldn't know what to do all day if he **wasn't working**.*

> **REMEMBER!**
> 1 *It is not correct to use* would *in the if clause.*
>
> *If I **had** enough money, I'd go abroad on holiday.*
> *not:*
> *If I ~~would have~~ enough money, I would go abroad on holiday.*
>
> 2 *We can use* were *instead of* was *after I and he / she / it*
>
> *If **I were** a man, this would never happen.*
>
> *This is especially common in the phrase* If I were you ..., *which we use to give advice.*
>
> *I would be very careful **if I were you**.*
>
> *However, we can also use* was *in this phrase.*
>
> 3 *We can change the order of the if clause and the main clause.*
>
> *I would probably lend money to a friend **if** he or she really needed it.*
> ***If** he or she really needed it, I would definitely lend money to a friend.*

c Instead of *would* we can use *might* or *could*.
*If Sue relaxed a bit more, she **might be** happier.*
*I **could help** you more if I had more time.*

2 Real versus hypothetical possibilities

a To talk about a real possibility in the future, we use *will* not *would*.

I'll be really worried if he doesn't phone me.

> **REMEMBER!**
> *We cannot use a future form in the second clause of the sentence with* will.
>
> I'll be really worried if he ~~won't~~ phone me.

b Sometimes the difference between a real and imaginary possibility is very clear.

I'll be really worried if he doesn't phone me. (= a real possibility)
I'd be terrified if I saw a ghost. (= an imaginary possibility)

Sometimes, however, it depends on **how the speaker sees the situation**. Compare these two sentences:

*If I **have** enough time, I'll help you .*
*If I **had** time, I'd help you.*

In the first sentence, the speaker believes it is a *real possibility* that she will have time (this is sometimes called a 'first conditional').
In the second sentence, the speaker sees it as unlikely or impossible that she will have enough time, so a situation is *hypothetical* or *imaginary* (this is sometimes called a 'second conditional').

> **REMEMBER!**
> *There are many different types of if sentences (conditionals). In most conditionals, we use verbs in the normal way.*
>
> If I wake up early, I usually go for a jog.
> If you're phoning Sue, give her my love.
> If we went to our grandmother's house, she always gave us sweets.
> If he's broken his leg, he can't come on holiday.
>
> *We only study 'first' and 'second' conditionals separately, because they have special verb forms after* if.

Module 10

Ⓐ Past Perfect

had + past participle		
Positive form	Negative form	Question form
I / you / she, etc. **'d (= had) done it**	I / you / she, etc. **hadn't (= had not) done it**	**Had** I / you / she, etc. **done it?**

The Past Perfect links one time in the past to another time further in the past (it is 'the past of the past').

*When we **got** there, everyone **had left**.*

1 Similarities to the Present Perfect

If the Past Perfect is 'the past of the past':

the Present Perfect is 'the past of the present':

He's already been to New York.

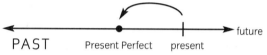

2 Time words with the Past Perfect

With the Past Perfect, we use many of the same time words that we often use with the Present Perfect.

> *He had been in Paris **for two months** / **since August**.*
> *He found that his flight had **just** / **recently** / **already** left.*
> *It was **the first** / **second** / **third time** I'd met her.*

In addition, we use the following words / phrases:

a *by / by the time*
By 5.30 everyone **had left**. (= they left before this time)
By the time I arrived, the film **had finished**.

b *when / after / before / as soon as*
With these words we use the Past Perfect for the first action in each case.
When I got up, Julia **had** already **gone** to work.
We did the washing-up **after** / **as soon as** the guests **had left**.

> **REMEMBER!**
> *If we use* when *with the Past Perfect, it means the first action was finished when the second action happened.*
>
> The play **had** already **started** when we **sat down**.
>
> *With two Past Simple verbs, the two actions happen more or less at the same time.*
>
> When we **sat down**, the play **started**.

3 Cases where the Past Perfect is optional

We do not usually use the Past Perfect when the sequence of events in the past is clear.
*I **had** a shower and **went** to bed.*

If we use *when* with two Past Simple verbs, the first action happened just before the second action.
When we **sat down**, the play **started**.

However, if we use the Past Perfect, it means that the first action was completed when the second action happened.
*When we sat down, the play **had** (already) **started**.*

Ⓑ Reported (indirect) speech and reported questions

1 Change of tenses

When we report someone's words afterwards, the verb forms often move into the past. This is because what they said is now in the past.

Direct speech (the actual words)	Reported (indirect speech)
Several years ago, John said to me:	Several years ago John told me that:
*'I **want** to get away.'* Present Simple	*... he **wanted** to get away.* Past Simple
*'I **had** an awful time last year.'* Past Simple	*... he **had had** an awful time **the year before**.* Past Perfect
*'I**'ve found** a new job in Canada.'* Present Perfect	*... he**'d found** a new job in Canada.* Past Perfect
*'I**'m leaving** tomorrow.'* Present Continuous	*... he **was leaving the next day**.* Past Continuous
*'I**'m going to start** a new life.'* am / is / are going to	*... he **was going to start** a new life.* was / were going to
*'I**'ll write** to you when I get there.'* will / won't	*... he **would write** to me when he got there.* would / wouldn't
*'You **can come** and see me.'* can / can't	*... I **could come / go** and see him.* could / couldn't

Notice the following:
a changes in time references in the reported statement
   last year → *the year before*
   tomorrow → *the next day*

b other modal verbs (*would, could, should, ought, might*) do not change in the reported statement

c changes in pronouns used in direct speech
   (*I* → *he*, etc.)

> **REMEMBER!**
> 1 If what a person said is still true / relevant, it is **not** necessary to change tenses or time references.
>
> *'I**'ve booked** the table for Friday night.'*
> She said she**'s booked** the table for Friday night.
>
> *Many cases of reported speech are like this.*
>
> *2 It is still possible to change tenses in such cases, but it sounds formal.*
>
> PRIME MINISTER: 'The election **will be** on May 1st.'
> NEWSREADER: The Prime Minister told Parliament that the election **would be** on May 1st.

2 Word order in reported questions

Reported questions are not real questions, so the word order is the same as in a normal statement.

Direct	Reported
*'**Can you come** early tomorrow?'*	*She asked if **I can come** early tomorrow.*
*'**Did you see** anything suspicious?'*	*The policeman wanted to know if **I had seen** anything suspicious.*

These verbs can be followed by *that*, but this is not neccessary.

3 Verbs and conjunctions used for reporting

a In statements *say* and *tell* are the most common reporting verbs. Look at how they are used:

He **said** it was true. ✓	He ~~told~~ it was true. ✗
He **said** ~~me~~ it was true. ✗	He **told me** it was true. ✓
He **said to me (that)** it was true. ✓	He **told** ~~to~~ **me (that)** it was true. ✗

b In statements *ask* and *want to know* are common reporting verbs. In *yes / no* questions the verb is joined to the reported words with *if* or *whether*.

She **asked** / **wanted to** know | *if* / *whether* | it was true.

In *wh-* questions, we do not need *if* or *whether*.
A: *'**What** do you think?'*
B: *He **asked me what** I thought.*

> **REMEMBER!**
> *In reported speech we do not usually repeat everything the person said – we just summarise it.*
>
> **Direct speech:** 'I wonder if ... perhaps ... can she call me back? ... If that's okay maybe ... this afternoon?'
> **Reported speech:** He **asked** if you could call back this afternoon.
>
> *There are many verbs for summarising people's words in this way:*
>
> **Direct speech:** 'Okay, so first you put the powder in ... then you shut the door ... and you turn this dial round to 3 ... then you turn it on ...'
> **Reported speech:** She **explained** how to use the washing machine.
>
> *Other useful verbs used for summarising / reporting what people say are:*
>
> – promise (to do something)
> – refuse (to do something)
> – agree (to do something)
> – suggest (doing something)
> – advise (someone to do something)
> – recommend (doing something)
> – deny (doing something)
> – warn someone (not to do something)

Module 11

Ⓐ Obligation and permission

Positive forms	*can / must / should* + verb	
	You	can **must** should	go now.
	have to / have got to / ought to + verb	
	You	*have to* *have got to* *ought to*	go now.
	be + allowed to + verb You **are allowed to** go now.	
Negative forms	You	*can't / cannot* *mustn't* *shouldn't* *don't have to* *haven't got to* *aren't allowed to*	go now.
Question forms	Can Must Should	I go now?
	Do I have to Have I got to Am I allowed to	go now?

> **REMEMBER!**
> 1 *Have to is a normal Present Simple verb – it has the auxiliaries* do / does *in the question form and* don't / doesn't *in the negative form.*
> 2 Ought to *is not often used in the negative and question forms.*

1 *must / have to / have got to*

We use *must*, *have to* and *have got to* to talk about something that is necessary or important.
*We **must be** at the airport by seven.*
*He **has to take** medicine every day for his asthma.*
*I've **got to find** a telephone – it's urgent!*

2 Differences between *must, have to* and *have got to*
The meaning is very similar, but:

a *must* often shows that the obligation comes from the person speaking.
*We **must be** more careful. (= I, the speaker, say)*
*I **must take** more exercise. (= I think this)*

Have to *and especially* have got to *show that the obligation comes from some other person, not the speaker.*
*Men in this country **have to do** military service.*
(= the government says)
*Jake's **got to do** his exam again. (= his teacher says)*

b there are differences of formality. *Must* is often written down, for example on public notices.
*Passengers **must have** a valid ticket.*
(= a written notice at a station)

Have to is mostly used in speech. Have got to *is informal.*

3 *don't have to* and *mustn't*
These are _not_ the same:
- *must / have (got) to* = it is necessary
- *mustn't* = it is prohibited / not allowed
- *don't have to / haven't got to* = it is not necessary
  *You **mustn't eat** any more chocolate. (= it is not allowed)*
  *You **don't have to eat** it if you don't like it. (= it is not necessary)*
  *We **don't have to walk** if you're tired. (= it is not necessary)*
  *We **mustn't walk** on the grass. (= it is not allowed)*

Haven't got to is the same as don't have to.

4 *should / ought to*

a We use *should* to say something is a good idea, or if it is correct / right; we use *shouldn't* for something that is not a good idea or not correct / right:
*You **should try** this ice cream – it's delicious.*
*Teachers **should be** a lot stricter.*
*You **shouldn't work** so hard – you'll be ill.*

Should is weaker than have to *or* must. *It is often used to give advice, suggestions and opinions because it sounds more polite. Again, we often use* ought *for giving advice, suggestions and opinions.*

b *Ought to means the same as* should; *we use it for something that is a good idea or the right thing.*
*You **ought to try** that new restaurant.*
*The government **ought to do** something about pollution.*

5 *can*

We use *can* to talk about something that is permitted; we use *can't* to talk about something that is prohibited.
*You **can park** here after 6.30.*
*In England you **can't drink** in pubs until you're sixteen.*

6 *allowed to*

We use *allowed to* to talk about things we are permitted to (can) do; we use *not allowed to* to talk about things we are not permitted to (can't) do.
*My brother**'s allowed to use** his boss's car.*
*In some countries, women **aren't allowed to vote**.*

7 Past forms

a *I **must go** home.*
 *I **have to go** home.*
 *I've **got to go** home.* } *I **had to go** home.*

b *They **can** vote. > They **could** vote.*
*They **can't** vote. > They **couldn't** vote.*

c *We **were** (**weren't**) **allowed to** wear what we wanted at school.*

Ⓑ Linking words (*although, however,* etc.)
1 Meaning

a Similar meaning to *and*:
*My cousin's a professional footballer. He's **also** an excellent tennis player.*
*I haven't got time to go on holiday this year. **Besides**, I can't afford it.*
*Yoga is excellent exercise. **What is more**, it helps you to relax.*

There are many other such words and phrases, for example *as well as this, in addition, furthermore.*

b Similar meaning to *but*:
Although *she's much younger than me*, *we get on very well together.*
The economy seems to be improving. **Despite this,** *unemployment is not getting any better.*
Her father was extremely angry with her. **However,** *he didn't say anything.*

Other such words and phrases include *though, even though, in spite of (this).*

c Similar meaning to *so*:
More and more people are moving to the city. **As a result,** *housing is terribly expensive.*
At least you haven't lied to me. **For this reason,** *I'm not going to punish you.*
The government increased taxes by over ten per cent, and **therefore** *became very unpopular.*

Other such words and phrases include *that's why, consequently.*

2 Word order

a *Although* is a conjunction – it joins two clauses / smaller sentences. There are two possible positions.
Although *I don't like him, I respect his opinion.*
I respect his opinion **although** *I don't like him.*

Though and *even though* are used in the same way.

b All the other words and phrases listed above are adverbials. There are three possible positions for them in the sentence(s).
• at the beginning of the second sentence
She loved him very much. **However,** *she knew that they could never get married.*
• at the end of the second sentence
She loved him very much. She knew that they could never get married, **however**.

c in the middle of the second sentence
She loved him very much. She knew, **however,** *that they could never get married.*

Notice the use of commas with these adverbials and conjunctions.

Module 12

Ⓐ Past modal verbs (*could have / should have / would have*)

1 *could have* + past participle

This is used for events which were possible in the past, but didn't happen.
He **could've drowned**!
(= it was possible for this to happen, but it didn't)
Compare:
Frances **could walk** *before she was a year old.*
(= she was able to do this)
with:
Frances **could have walked** *to work, but she took a cab instead.*
(= it was possible for her to do this, but she didn't)

2 *should have / shouldn't have* + past participle

This means it was a good idea, but you didn't do it.
I **should have worn** *a tie when I went for the job interview.*
(= it was a good idea for me to do this, but I didn't)

You **shouldn't have been** *so rude.*
(= it was a good idea for you to be polite, but you weren't)

3 *would / wouldn't have* + past participle

We use this for imagining something in the past that didn't happen.
In his position, I **would have waited** *for help.*
(= I wasn't in his position – I am imagining)

Ⓑ Talking hypothetically about the past with *if*

If you are imagining possibilities in the past, we often use *if* to describe the hypothetical situation.
If I **had fallen** *into a volcano, I wouldn't have moved.*

Notice that after *if* we use the Past Perfect not the Past Simple. This form is often called the 'third conditional'.

if + **Past Perfect** + *would have* + **past participle**

> **REMEMBER!**
> *We can also use* might have *or* could have *instead of* would have.
>
> *If I'd worked harder at school, I* **could have gone** *to university.*
> *She* **might have passed** *her exams if she hadn't had so many personal problems.*

Ⓒ Talking hypothetically about the past and present together

Notice the difference in these two forms:
a imaginary situations generally / in the present

if + **Past Simple** + *would* + **verb**

If he **wasn't** *an actor, he'**d be** a teacher.*

b imaginary situations in the past

if + **Past Perfect** + *would have* + **past participle**

*If I'**d gone** to the party, I* **would have seen** *him.*

Sometimes we want to talk about the **past and present together.** In this case we can 'mix' these two forms.
    (past)   (present)
If she **hadn't left** *her job, she* **wouldn't see** *her children.*

    (present)   (past)
If I **didn't trust** *you, I* **wouldn't have lent** *you all that money.*

Irregular verbs

Verb	Past Simple	Past Participle
be	was / were	been
beat	beat	beaten
become	became	become
begin	began	begun
bend	bent	bent
bite	bit	bitten
blow	blew	blown
break	broke	broken
bring	brought	brought
build	built	built
burn	burned / burnt	burned / burnt
burst	burst	burst
buy	bought	bought
can	could	been able
catch	caught	caught
choose	chose	chosen
come	came	come
cost	cost	cost
cut	cut	cut
dig	dug	dug
do	did	done
draw	drew	drawn
dream	dreamed / dreamt	dreamed / dreamt
drink	drank	drunk
drive	drove	driven
eat	ate	eaten
fall	fell	fallen
feed	fed	fed
feel	felt	felt
fight	fought	fought
find	found	found
fly	flew	flown
forget	forgot	forgotten
forgive	forgave	forgiven
freeze	froze	frozen
get	got	got
give	gave	given
go	went	gone / been
grow	grew	grown
hang	hung	hanged / hung
have	had	had
hear	heard	heard
hide	hid	hidden
hit	hit	hit
hold	held	held
hurt	hurt	hurt
keep	kept	kept
kneel	knelt	knelt
know	knew	known
lay	laid	laid
lead	led	led
learn	learned / learnt	learned / learnt
leave	left	left
lend	lent	lent

Verb	Past Simple	Past Participle
let	let	let
lie	lay	lain
light	lit	lit
lose	lost	lost
make	made	made
mean	meant	meant
meet	met	met
must	had to	had to
pay	paid	paid
put	put	put
read / riːd /	read / red /	read / red /
ride	rode	ridden
ring	rang	rung
rise	rose	risen
run	ran	run
say	said	said
see	saw	seen
sell	sold	sold
send	sent	sent
set	set	set
shake	shook	shaken
shine	shone	shone
shoot	shot	shot
show	showed	shown
shut	shut	shut
sing	sang	sung
sink	sank	sunk
sit	sat	sat
sleep	slept	slept
slide	slid	slid
smell	smelled / smelt	smelled / smelt
speak	spoke	spoken
spend	spent	spent
spill	spilled / spilt	spilled / spilt
spoil	spoiled / spoilt	spoiled / spoilt
stand	stood	stood
steal	stole	stolen
stick	stuck	stuck
swim	swam	swum
take	took	taken
teach	taught	taught
tear	tore	torn
tell	told	told
think	thought	thought
throw	threw	thrown
understand	understood	understood
wake	woke	woken
wear	wore	worn
win	won	won
write	wrote	written

Tapescripts

Module 1

Recording 1

a What's your full name?
b Where do you come from?
c What's your date of birth?
d Where were you born?
e What do you do for a living?
f Are you married or single?
g How many brothers and sisters have you got?
h How long have you been at this school?
i How far away from here do you live?
j Do you speak any other languages apart from English?

Recording 3

a What's the English word for one of these?
b How do you pronounce this word?
c How do you spell 'eyebrow'?
d Which page are we on?
e What's for homework tonight?
f Could you say that again, please?
g Could you write 'paperclip' on the board, please?

Recording 4

a Choose a shape and write in the name of your oldest relative.
b Choose a shape and write in the name of a neighbour or a colleague.
c Choose a shape and write in the number of aunts you have.
d Choose a shape and write 'yes' if you have nephews or nieces, and 'no' if you haven't.
e Choose a shape and write in how many years you've known your best friend.
f Choose a shape and write in the number of cousins you have.
g Choose a shape and write 'yes' if you have a mother-in-law, and 'no' if you haven't.
h Choose a shape and write in the name of someone who's an acquaintance, but not really a friend.

Recording 5

E = Erica   F = friend

E: So this is my family having Christmas lunch ...
F: Oh right, is that your mum?
E: Yeah.
F: She looks so much like you ... it's incredible!
E: Everyone says that.
F: Her name's Carol, isn't it?
E: Mmm ...
F: And that's your dad?
E: My step-father.
F: Oh, I see ... do you get on okay with him?
E: Oh yeah, he's great, he's been just like a real father to me and my brothers.
F: Oh, that's nice.
E: Actually we haven't seen much of him recently – he's got a new job with this American company, and they're sending him abroad a lot.
F: Oh ...
E: I don't think he likes being away that much and Mum absolutely hates it, so I think he's hoping that next year, when he knows the job a bit better, he won't have to travel quite so much.

F: It can't be very nice for your Mum ... um, these must be your two brothers ... which one's which?
E: That's Dan the elder one.
F: Mmm ... he's nice. Does he still live at home?
E: He doesn't really know what he's doing at the moment. He's doing a computer course in Manchester – he's living with my aunt and uncle for a while – but I don't know what he wants to do after that.
F: And what's your younger brother's name ... Tom?
E: Tom ... yeah – he's thirteen now.
F: Only thirteen? He looks older than that, doesn't he?
E: I know, he's growing up really fast, isn't he? He's a lot taller than me now.
F: Oh, and this must be your granny – she lives with your family, doesn't she?
E: Yeah ... she's getting a bit old now, poor thing. She hardly ever goes out of the house. It's a bit sad really.
F: It must be quite difficult for your mum, too.
E: Yeah, I suppose it is, but she doesn't seem to mind ...

Recording 6

(missing words only)

a lunch   b look   c accident   d rest   e problems
f great time   g baby girl

Recording 7

P = Philip   S = Sonia   K = Kate

K: Sonia! Hi! How are you? This is Philip, my brother – Sonia's on my course at college.
S: Katie ... hello.
S: Hi, Philip.
P: Pleased to meet you.
K: Sonia's from Milan, Philip – you can try out some of your Italian. Philip's studying Italian at evening classes. Oh, look, I think that's Ian over there ... excuse me, I must just go and say 'hello'.
S: Parli un'po l'italiano?
P: Un po ... I can understand a few words, but I'm finding it quite difficult. I only go to classes once a week – it's not really enough.
S: Oh, I'm sure you will learn to speak very good Italian! It's a very beautiful language.
P: Yeah, I've always liked the sound of it. Unfortunately, I don't have a lot of time to study ... I'm working very long hours at the moment.
S: Oh ...
P: Yes, I'm in the import / export business ... we do a lot of business with Italy – that's why I'm trying to learn a bit of the language.
S: So does that mean you travel a lot?
P: Not yet, unfortunately ... I'm in the London office most of the time, but I'm hoping to travel more in the future ... to Europe and the United States.
S: Yes, I love travelling too. I've travelled round Europe quite a lot ... to France and Greece ... but I'd really like to go to the USA too.
P: So, how are you finding London? You're doing the same course as Katie ... textile design?
S: Yes, it's a really good course. I'm really pleased I'm doing it.
P: And is that ... hard work?
S: Well, we have to spend a lot of time on project work ... which is very practical and useful for the future, but it takes up a lot of time ... and we have some essays and reading to do as well.
P: So do you have any time for a social life?
S: Yeah ... I go out with my friends from college quite a lot. The thing I like most in London is the theatre. I go at least once a week ... I love it. Are you interested in the theatre?
P: Yes ... I go occasionally ... I see a musical once in a while. I prefer

the cinema ... films.

s: What kind of films do you like?

p: Actually, I really haven't seen anything for ages. I don't seem to have time at the moment ... with work and everything. I just come home and put my feet up and watch football on TV. It's terrible really.

s: Oh, do you like football?

p: Yeah.

s: I play football.

p: Really? In Milan?

s: No, here in London. We've got an Italian women's team called Forza Italia. We play every Sunday.

p: Great! Where do you play?

s: Just near Tuffnell Park.

p: That's where I live. I'll have to come and watch you play one Sunday.

k: Philip ... look who's here – it's Carrie. She wants to talk to you. Come and say 'hello'.

p: Excuse me ... Hi, Carrie ...

Module 2

Recording 1

(correct verb forms only)

1 met   2 was spending   3 was doing   4 decided   5 arrived
6 started   7 thought   8 were having   9 began   10 told
11 were talking   12 thought   13 hated   14 liked
15 was wearing   16 didn't suit   17 didn't tell

Recording 2

(missing verbs only)

1 met   2 were travelling   3 started   4 discovered   5 had
6 lived   7 were going   8 were training   9 was working
10 talked   11 fell   12 decided   13 reached   14 were   15 was
16 are

Recording 5

(missing phrases only)

a for a long time   b a great time   c haven't got time
d by the time   e on time   f all the time   g in two days' time

Recording 6

Tim

Right, well, this was really my first experience of crime ... and I can still remember it really well. It happened when I was about eight ... eight years old ... and ... um ... I was out shopping with my mother, and my big sister ... my big sister who was always horrible to me 'cos I was the little one, I suppose ... she still is horrible to me as a matter of fact, but anyway ... we were at our local shop in the village where we lived ... and on the way to the checkout ... it was a sort of little supermarket type of place ... on the way to the checkout, I picked up this chocolate bar ... a Mars Bar to be precise ... and I picked it up, and I thought my mother was going to pay for it, I honestly did, I swear. I thought she knew I'd picked it up, even though I didn't tell her ... so anyway I picked it up, I didn't try to hide it or anything ... we got through the checkout with me still holding this Mars Bar ... which was probably starting to melt by now ... and then as soon as we got outside the shop, my sister came over to me and whispered to me in this really horrible voice: 'You stole that Mars Bar. I saw you.' And I honestly thought mum had paid for it. So we got home ... and ... well, I was just mortified, I couldn't tell my mum or anything, I just thought: 'Oh well, that's it then ... the police are gonna come and get me, and put me in prison and all that ... I'll never see my family again ... complete shame!' ... and when it came to bed-time, my mum kissed

me good night and everything ... and I still had this Mars Bar which I'd hidden. I was just waiting for the police to arrive ... and that night, I thought: 'Well, there's only one thing for it, I'm gonna have to leave home, run away!' So I waited until I thought everyone had gone to bed ... put on some clothes ... and went out into the fields near where I lived ... with this Mars Bar ... and buried it in a field, sort of destroying the evidence, you might say. And I just sort of sat in this field for hours, just not knowing what to do next. I thought, you know, I'll never see my family again ... I'll just be a tramp all my life, you know, wander about from town to town ... and the next thing I remember, of course, there's this police van stops just on the road near where I was ... and these policemen all get out and start walking towards me ... and I thought: 'Oh my God! They've come for the Mars Bar! Run!' So, I start running away, which wasn't all that fast, 'cos I was only eight ... but of course they caught up with me ... and in fact, my parents had called the police 'cos they'd found I wasn't in my bedroom, and they'd all gone out to look for me ... and I just burst into tears. I never managed to find the Mars Bar again, though ... it's ... erm ... it's probably still buried there somewhere.

Anna

I = interviewer   A = Anna

a: One of the most memorable moments in my life was in fact when I was about fourteen, when I met my brother – or rather my half-brother – for the first time.

i: First time?

a: Yeah.

i: How was that?

a: Well ... erm ... in fact my mum ran away from Czechoslovakia in 1968 and she had to leave behind a five-year-old son ...

i: God!

a: ... which I think must have been quite difficult.

i: Poor her! Well how did it happen?

a: Well, you know that in 1968 there was a big movement in Czechoslovakia to get more freedom from the Communists ...

i: Yeah ...

a: ... and eventually the Russian tanks were sent in to bring things back under control. Well, anyway, my parents were staying in London at the time that it happened, and they were terrified that if they went back to Prague, they'd be sent to jail ... so, they decided to stay in London, but my mum's son from her first marriage was left in Czechoslovakia.

i: I see ...

a: So, in fact, we didn't meet until 1988.

i: Yeah?

a: Yeah ... we went back as a family ... oh, it was a pretty strange experience.

i: I'm sure ...

a: I was really nervous ... and ... erm ... well, we actually went to meet him in his flat in Prague where he was living with his wife and two children ... two sweet little girls ... and we went up there and my sister and I were really nervous and ... well ... he and his wife they were very kind to us ... really sweet ... very hospitable ... and he actually gave my sister and I a rose each as a welcoming gesture which was lovely ... erm, but I do remember one thing that struck me most was ... erm ... when he called my mum 'mum'. I suddenly got really protective of her, and thought: 'You can't do that – that's my mum.' That was quite bizarre.

i: Do you still see your ... err ... half-brother?

a: Yes, I do – he phones up quite regularly and we've been in close contact ... he still lives out there ... and we're obviously settled here, but, yeah, we see each other from time to time.

i: But you still remember that first time?

a: I do, very much ... we laugh about it now, but it was certainly important at the time.

Recording 7

a A: I'm afraid the fax from the bank didn't arrive.
   B: Oh, didn't it? That's annoying!
b A: You know that file I lost? I found it at home last night.
   B: Did you? Thank goodness for that!
c A: Apparently the new area manager's going to be here this afternoon.
   B: Oh no! Is he?
d A: I still haven't finished that report.
   B: Haven't you? Oh dear!
e A: Mrs Adams was really annoyed with me for missing the meeting yesterday.
   B: Really? Was she?
f A: It took me two hours to get home yesterday. My train was cancelled again!
   B: Was it? Not again!
g A: Mr Martin wants you to phone him as soon as you can.
   B: Does he? Right.

Recording 8

(answers only)
a Isn't he? b Does she? c Can it? d Did you? e Doesn't she?
f Was it? g Didn't she? h Is it?

Module 3

Recording 1

1 The Nile is the longest river in the world at 6,741 kilometres – slightly longer than the Amazon, which is the second longest at 6,440 kilometres.
2 The Vatican City is the smallest country in the world, with an area of only 0.44 square kilometres, and a population of just 738. The second smallest is Monaco, which has an area of just 1.8 square kilometres.
3 Monaco is actually much more densely populated than Hong Kong – there are approximately 6,000 people per square kilometre in Hong Kong, whereas there are 16,500 in Monaco. At the other extreme, Canada has an average of fewer than three people per square kilometre!
4 Even excluding the part which is in Asia, Russia is still by far the largest country in Europe, with an area of over 4.5 million square kilometres. The second largest is Ukraine, also part of the former Soviet Union, at about 600,000 square kilometres.
5 The biggest city in the world is Tokyo-Yokohama with a population of about 28.5 million. The second biggest is Mexico City, the third biggest São Paulo in Brazil, the fourth biggest Seoul in South Korea, and the fifth biggest, at the moment at least, is New York, though it will soon be overtaken by Bombay, in India.
6 The answer is actually the obvious one – it's a lot further from New York to London than from New York to Los Angeles. New York to London is around 5,500 kilometres, whereas New York to Los Angeles is less then 4,000 kilometres.
7 Officially the largest island in the world is Greenland – with an area of over 2 million square kilometres. Australia is much larger, but is regarded as a continent, rather than an island.
8 The Andes, which reach 6,960 metres, are actually much higher than the Rockies, which reach only 4,399 metres. The highest mountains in the world are of course the Himalayas, reaching 8,848 metres.
9 The country in the world with the most neighbours is the Republic of China, with a total of sixteen neighbours, including Mongolia, Russia, Vietnam, and many others.
10 Canada has by far the longest coastline – it's approximately 151,000 kilometres. The second longest is Indonesia, but it's a long way behind at a mere 33,000 kilometres.

Recording 2

1 Mark the biggest room.
2 Mark the second biggest room.
3 Mark the second smallest room.
4 Mark one of the most comfortable places to sit.
5 Mark the worst place to relax.
6 Mark the best place to study or work quietly.
7 Mark one of the messiest places.
8 Mark the sunniest room.
9 Mark one of your favourite pieces of furniture.
10 Mark one of your least favourite things or places.

Recording 3

I = interviewer   J = Judit

I: So what was it like going back to Budapest after all that time? You hadn't been back since the communist days, had you?
J: It was really interesting ... I really enjoyed it. I'd heard a lot about all the changes, so I went expecting everything to be completely different ... but actually many things didn't seem so different.
I: Really?
J: I mean, a lot of the things that I really love about the city were exactly the same – all the beautiful old buildings, the river, the trams, the old coffee shops – the general atmosphere of the place was still as wonderful as ever. Of course, once I started looking more closely a lot of things were very different, as you'd expect.
I: So what were the differences?
J: Probably the most obvious thing is the shops ... there's much, much more choice in the shops – you can find whatever you want now ... if you can afford to buy it, of course. Before it was much more difficult to find luxuries like, I don't know, Japanese cameras or Swiss chocolate or whatever. There just seem to be a lot more shops ... and of course a lot more places like McDonald's and Burger King, which you didn't see before very much. In fact, generally, there seem to be a lot more restaurants and night-clubs and places to go out.
I: Well, it's become a very popular tourist destination, hasn't it?
J: Yeah, it's amazing ... there are so many tourists and foreigners around the place now. It used to be very unusual to hear people speaking English or French in the street – now they're all over the place ... so that was quite a big difference too.
I: And what about prices – did you notice a big change?
J: You're not joking! Absolutely everything is more expensive – everything! The thing I noticed particularly was transport – public transport used to be incredibly efficient and incredibly cheap. It's still just as efficient as it was, but it's a lot more expensive. And taxis are terribly expensive now – I only took one taxi and it was a real shock!
I: Were there any other changes you noticed, you know, just walking about the streets?
J: Erm ... people looked better dressed, I think, because the shops are better, I suppose ... oh, and the cars ... they were another thing that were really different. There are more cars on the roads now, and, you know, bigger, smarter cars ... that does give the whole place a different atmosphere.
I: Yeah ...
J: One thing that hasn't changed, unfortunately, though, is the pollution ... it's just as bad as it always was.
I: And I suppose with all these new cars it'll get even worse.
J: I don't know ... maybe ...

Recording 4

a They're a lot better than before.
b It's just the same as before.
c They're completely different from before.
d It's not as cheap as it used to be.
e They're more or less the same as before.
f It's very similar to how it was before.

Recording 5

H = Helen   B = Bob   I = Isobel

H: So you're flying to Cork, right?

I: Yeah, right. We arrive there Monday evening and we already have a hotel booked for Monday night. Then we pick up our hire car on Tuesday morning.

H: Well, Cork itself is worth looking around – there's a nice cathedral there, but personally I wouldn't stay there too long if I were you. I'd head straight for the lakes for the second night – it's a beautiful drive through the mountains, and you can stop at Blarney Castle, and you know, kiss the Blarney Stone.

B: Kiss the Blarney Stone!

H: Yes, it's a tradition, didn't you know? If you kiss the Blarney Stone, you get the Irish gift of eloquence. You know, we're very famous for our eloquence and our ability to talk. So, that's what you have to do.

B: Right, we won't forget. We'll definitely kiss the Blarney Stone!

I: And can we stay there – at Blarney Castle?

H: Well, there's not really much there. I'd recommend that you go on to Killarney – it's right in the middle of the Lakes, one of the most beautiful areas of Ireland. You could spend two or three nights there easily, just driving round. There's so much beautiful scenery to see – the lakes and the mountains. You'll love it!

I: Right ... Killarney ... that's here ... and do you recommend anywhere special to visit while we're there?

H: Well, you've got to see the Ring of Kerry – it's the most spectacular coastline in the whole of Ireland, I would say. You just drive along the coast road through places like Killorglin – that's lovely – and Dingle Bay, and Kenmare ... there's lots of beautiful spots where you can stop.

I: So, how long do you think that would take?

H: Oh, you could do it in a day. It's about a hundred miles altogether, I should think.

B: And is there anywhere else to visit while we're in Killarney?

H: There are so many places it's hard to say. You can just drive round and stop wherever you like. You'll find the people terribly friendly in all those little places – and they love Americans, Bob!

B: Sounds great! So where do you think we should head after that, Helen?

H: Well you should see Limerick, for sure – it's something like the fourth biggest city in Ireland, and it's really lovely. It's on the River Shannon, and there's a very nice cathedral. I can't remember the name ... and King John's Castle ... it's really one of the prettiest cities in Ireland.

I: So how long do you think we should stay there?

H: I don't know ... one night's probably enough.

B: And from there?

H: Well, if you've got the time you could drive up to Westport – it's about three or four hours' drive, so it's quite a journey, but it's a wonderful drive, and Westport is right by Croagh Patrick, which is one of the most famous mountains in Ireland. Or if you don't want to go that far north, you could drive across to Waterford here on the south coast.

B: Isn't that the place where they make the glass?

H: That's right, that's right – they make some of the best crystal in the world – Waterford crystal. You can visit the factory there. It's quite interesting!

I: And is it a pretty place?

H: Yes, it's quite nice. You could stay there overnight, and then it's the most wonderful drive back from Waterford to Cork, along the coast road ... and that takes you back to where you started.

B: Great! Thank you very much for your help.

I: Yes, that's fantastic, Helen! Thanks.

H: You're welcome. I hope you have a great trip!

Recording 6

Z = Zelda   F = friends

Z: Can you recommend anywhere to stay – something fairly cheap?

F: Actually, I'd really recommend the place where we stayed – the hotel Nadir. The owners were really friendly, and it was right near the beach and we thought it was very reasonable.

Z: It sounds great!

F: I think I've got the address somewhere. I'll find it for you.

Z: Oh, thanks! I'd really appreciate that.

Z: What about the food? What should I try?

F: Well, you must try the fish, it's wonderful – really fresh and tasty. And they have the most fantastic cakes, so you should definitely try them. What else? All the wine we had was awful, so I wouldn't recommend that. The beer's much better ... oh and be careful with the water – a few people we met had problems, so it's probably best just to drink bottled water.

Z: Oh, right ... I'll remember that. Thanks.

Z: ... and what about travelling around?

F: Well, personally I wouldn't use the taxis. The taxi drivers are terrible with tourists ... you know, charging double the fare, and driving round miles ... and they're terrible drivers – they drive incredibly fast!

Z: Oh, dear! So what do you suggest instead?

F: Well, I would recommend the local buses. We thought they were excellent, they were really cheap and reliable, much better than in this country.

Z: Oh, right. Thanks for telling me.

Z: Have you got any other tips?

F: I can't think of anything ... oh, yes, there is one thing – be really careful with your money when you go into the city centre. It's famous for the pickpockets, so don't carry too much money if you can help it.

Z: Yes, I've heard that before. I'll have to be careful.

Module 4

Recording 1

1   A: Barbara? Catherine? What are you two doing?
    B: We've finished. Can we go now?
    A: Well, just wait a minute. Frank, how about you? How are you getting on?
    C: Sorry, I haven't finished yet ... just a minute ...
    A: Well hurry up, then.

2   A: ... didn't even recognise you for a minute – you look so different. You've changed your hair – it's really nice, I like it.
    B: Oh, thanks ... and you look really well, too. You've lost weight, haven't you?
    A: Well, yes, a bit. I've been on a diet for about three months, and I've joined a gym ...

3   A: John, is Daniela still here?
    B: Well, she was here. Perhaps she's just gone out for a minute.
    C: If you're looking for Daniela, she's gone home. She left about ten minutes ago.
    A: Oh, never mind. I'll talk to her tomorrow.

4   A: What's the matter?
    B: It's my glasses ... have you seen my glasses anywhere?
    A: I don't know if I have ... I can't believe you've lost them again!
    B: Okay, so I've lost my glasses! Will you help me look for them, please?

A: Have you looked under the ... look! They're just there on the table.
B: Well, who put them there?

5 A: Let me see ... err ... George ... have you met Silvina ... Silvina Ramos?
B: Yes, I think we have – we met at the Conference last year, didn't we?
C: That's right, I remember. Nice to see you again.

Recording 4

Okay ... so I was born in Tarragona, a small town not far from Barcelona in 1977. I had a very happy childhood there with my brother and my parents, and then when I was about eleven years old my father got a new job and we moved to Barcelona, where I've lived ever since. I went to secondary school there ... and then I studied tourism for three years at university. After that I spent some time unemployed looking for a job and doing a few temporary jobs ... and then I finally got a job in a travel agency, which is what I've always wanted to do. So I've been working there for about three months now. What else? I've got a boyfriend, Pablo, who I've known since I was at school. I think we met when I was about sixteen ... actually we're engaged now. We got engaged in January, and we're planning to get married next year, hopefully, when we've got a bit more money. And apart from that ... my favourite hobbies are skiing, which I've been doing since I was a child, and learning foreign languages. As well as Catalan and Spanish, I'm learning French and English, because of course they're both very important for my job. I think I speak English better. I've been studying it for about nine years, so I should speak good English! I've also been to Britain a couple of times, and also once to the United States ... so it's something I really enjoy.

Recording 5

1 How long have you had your present hairstyle?
2 How long have you been coming to this English class?
3 When did you last go to the cinema?
4 How long have you known your oldest friend?
5 When did you buy the shoes you're wearing?
6 When was your last holiday?
7 How long has the government of your country been in power?
8 When was the last public holiday in your country?
9 How long have you been studying the Present Perfect?
10 How long have you been doing this exercise?

Recording 6

(missing words/phrases only)
a taxi b cold c worse d home e rid of f on okay with
g the message

Recording 7

1 Ah ... she's ... she's not a malicious person, she's ever so good-hearted really, I think she means very well ... and she's always very interested in how I'm getting on at home, always terribly interested in my family and friends and everything. I think she really is interested in people generally. I remember when I started working here, a lot of the others didn't take the trouble to talk to me, you know, as a new person, whereas she was immediately ... she did her best to make me feel welcome, she showed me where everything was, all that kind of thing. It's just that ... oh dear ... I mean, once she starts talking, she just won't leave you alone. I have to say there are times when I just switch off, you know, and stop listening ... I just pretend to listen, but actually I'm thinking about something else. I think with Dorothy, you know ... there's always a problem, she's always telling you about it, in great detail. She's always complaining about something or other, and she just goes on and on about her problems, it's always: 'Oh well, I don't think that's very fair', or 'Have you heard about so and so?' All these pieces of office gossip ... I have to say she really gets on my nerves sometimes.

2 Well, I suppose Jeremy's my oldest friend, really. we were at school together. I still remember the first time I met him ... and he asked if he could borrow some money off me in fact – which was a bit cheeky since he hardly knew me! I said 'no', of course! At school he was always a bit cleverer than me, and he always seemed to have lots of confidence in himself, he's always been a good talker ... he impresses people, I think, although I was better at practical things, maths and sciences. He can be really clever when he wants to be. We always seemed to get on alright, though. I remember we had a holiday together when we were about eighteen – we went hitch-hiking in France ... it was quite an adventure. Then he went to university and I started work. We've stayed friends, though. Obviously we're not as close as we used to be, but we still see each other from time to time ... we still find something to talk about ... he always makes me laugh.

3 I think one reason I really admire her is because she's so positive and enthusiastic about everything. She always sees the good side of things ... you know, if I take the children to see her ... her grandchildren ... and sometimes they're quite naughty and difficult ... but she'll always say, always say: 'Oh, they've been so good. It's been so lovely to see them.' And that really is how she remembers it! When I was younger, she used to really annoy me sometimes ... you know, when I was a depressed, moody teenager, and she would say: 'Depressed! When I was your age, I was always too busy to be depressed!' and I used to think: 'Just go away, you're so insensitive, you don't understand my problems!' But now I'm older, I suppose I realise more that it's not so easy to go through all the things that happen to you in life and still be so cheerful. I suppose I've got a lot more respect for her attitude now ... and I hear about other people's mothers and what a problem they can be, and think: 'I'm really very lucky!'

Consolidation Modules 1–4

Recording 1

a A: Do you speak any other languages?
 B: Yes ... French.
b A: How long have you been here?
 B: Only about a week.
c A: What are you doing at the moment?
 B: I'm working in an advertising agency as a PA, a personal assistant, but what I really want to do is ...
d A: Did you have a good holiday?
 B: Oh yeah, it was great – the scenery, the food, the weather ... fantastic!
e A: So where were you born?
 B: In Caracas. It's the capital of Venezuela.
f A: How often do you go swimming?
 B: Oh, about once a week. I don't swim as often as I'd like to, actually.

Recording 2

Okay, this was about ten years ago ... er ... when I was a student, so of course I wasn't working ... er ... in fact ... er ... I didn't use to do much ... er ... I used to meet my friends in the pub or, or the park, ... erm ... I was also engaged at the time, so I spent a lot of time with my girlfriend ... er ... I'm not engaged anymore, thank God. Erm ... yeah, I was a bit of a hippy. I had long hair, ... erm ... a beard, ... erm ... I was a bit smelly, a bit dirty ... er ... didn't wash much ... erm ... people used to laugh at me quite a lot, but I didn't seem to care. ... erm ... but now that's all changed quite a lot ... erm ... I have to have shorter hair, I've no longer got a beard ... erm ... I'm not exactly smart, I don't wear a suit, but being a teacher I have to wear reasonably clean clothes, be reasonably well presented ... erm ... and I suppose my character has changed a lot. I think ... er ... it changed with the haircut ... erm ... but strangely ... erm ... I'm a lot more relaxed now, a lot more laid-back ... erm ... not as arrogant as I was. I was very self-confident when I was younger and I didn't really care what anybody thought about me. ... erm ... Now I do listen more to people, ... erm ... which I think helps with the job ... erm ... yeah ... erm ... I like myself a lot more now.

Module 5

Recording 1

1 Write down three things that you've already arranged to do this week.
2 Write down two domestic tasks that you intend to do next weekend.
3 Write down either where you're going or where you'd like to go for your next holiday.
4 Write down how you think you'll spend next Sunday morning.
5 Write down what you're going to eat when you get home after class today.
6 Write down one good intention that you have for next week.
7 Write down two items, small or large, that you're planning to buy in the next month or two.
8 Write down where you're due to be after this lesson finishes.
9 Write down what you think your teacher is about to do.

Recording 2

a I really want to go to the gym after work tomorrow night, but I probably won't go. I'll probably go to the pub like I always do!
b I'll probably watch TV and read the newspapers – and my mum'll phone me, almost certainly.
c I'm going to sort out all my college notes this weekend.
d I'm not going to do any domestic tasks this weekend. I'm going to lie in bed, read a book and generally be lazy.
e We're thinking of going to Scotland for our holidays this year, but we haven't really decided.
f I'd like to have a holiday this year, but I can't afford it, unfortunately.

Recording 4

1 I'd been working in a bank for about five years, and actually I wasn't very ambitious or career-minded. Then a new manager came to my branch – he persuaded me to take the job more seriously, so I started studying to become a manager myself. I had to go to evening classes for five years to get the qualifications I needed ... but it's been worth it. I enjoy coming to work much more now. Some people think working in a bank is boring, but for me every day is different. It's all about dealing with people ... and that's always a challenge.

2 I've been doing the job for about eight years now, and I still really enjoy the actual work. There's a lot of job satisfaction, just being with the children and watching them develop, and seeing things the way they see them – that's still great. Mind you, a lot of people have no idea just how tiring and stressful a day with a class of four-year-olds can be. Some people think it's an easy job, because the holidays are quite long, and everything. The thing I find depressing, though, is that there's no real career structure or chance of promotion in education. I could easily still be doing exactly the same thing in twenty years time!

3 I wasn't really that academic at school, but I was always a lot more interested in science subjects than in languages or history or anything ... so at sixteen I applied for apprenticeships with a lot of small companies. I was really shocked to find out that a lot of them only accepted boys! Eventually I was accepted for a course in electrical engineering. I was the only girl out of seventeen students! I'm doing my basic training in the engineering centre here at British Aerospace. The other people who work here are fine to me, it's no problem, but people I meet outside are sometimes very surprised when I tell them what I do, especially older people.

4 About six months ago my wife started saying she couldn't stand it at home any more with the kids, it was driving her mad, so I said: 'Okay then – if you find yourself a job that pays enough, I'll change places with you!' I'm a roofer by trade, mending and building roofs, but I'm self-employed, so I can please myself how much I work. Anyway, to my surprise she found herself a job in less than a week! So here I am – what they call a 'house husband', I suppose, taking the kids to school and doing the shopping and what have you. The wife didn't think I'd be able to do it – but actually I'm really enjoying myself. I never used to see that much of the kids, so it's nice to really spend some time with them, taking them to the park and all that. It's harder work than you imagine, mind you ... I don't think I'd want to do it for ever.

Recording 5

M = Marion   J = Jean-luc Bertrand

J: Hållo, oui.
M: Hello, can I speak to Monsieur Bertrand, please?
J: Yes, speaking.
M: Oh hello, this is Marion O'Neill from Horizons Unlimited. We're recruiting an assistant manager for you.
J: Oh yes. Hello, Marion. How are you?
M: Fine, thanks ... listen, I've just been going through the file, and I've got a couple of questions for you – have you got a moment?
J: Yes, of course.
M: Okay. Obviously the first question is about wanting an assistant manager who can also look after your children ... that's a bit unusual. Can you tell me something more about that?
J: Of course – it would only really be during the time when the hotel is closed. I quite often have to go away on business – perhaps six or seven times a year for perhaps five days or a week at a time ... and as I don't have any relatives nearby, I need someone to look after them ... you know, drive them to school, pick them up, give them their supper, maybe look after them a bit at the weekend.
M: Mmm ... and how old are the children?
J: Olivier, my son is thirteen, and Karine, his sister, is eight. They're very good – they won't be difficult.
M: No, I'm sure, but it's still quite a big responsibility. It's not going to be easy to find someone who can do all the hotel work too ... you say you want someone who can organise reception, so presumably you'll need someone with plenty of experience?
J: Of course, I think experience is necessary.
M: And you mentioned driving a minute ago. How important is that? You say the hotel is quite remote ...
J: Mmm, perhaps it would be possible without driving ... perhaps a neighbour could take the children to school ... but it might be a bit difficult for this person ... they might feel a bit isolated if they can't drive.
M: Okay, so driving is pretty important then. What else? Good French obviously essential ... other languages ... computer skills ... oh, yes ... you say you would prefer someone for two years rather than just one year?
J: Yes, one year is the minimum, but really we'd prefer two ... you know, the children have had a very difficult time since my wife died, and I prefer not to have too many changes. Really, I think more important than anything else is a nice person who we can all get on with.
M: Yes, of course, it must be very difficult for you. As I say, it's not going to be easy to find someone who can do everything you need.
J: Of course not.
M: Really, it's two jobs in one, you know ... still, the salary and conditions are attractive. We'll do our best for you, Monsieur Bertrand.

J: Well, you've found us very nice staff before, so we'll put our trust in you.

M: Okay then – leave it with me. I'll call you when we've got some news. Speak to you soon.

J: Okay, then, bye.

M: Bye.

Recording 6

L = Louisa   T = telephonist   S = secretary

T: Hello, Horizons Unlimited.

L: Hello, I'd like to speak to Marion O'Neill, please.

T: Just a moment, I'll put you through.

S: Hello, how can I help?

L: Err ... could I speak to Marion O'Neill, please?

S: I'll just see if she's available. Can I ask who's calling?

L: Louisa Barry.

S: One moment, please ... hello ... I'm afraid she's in a meeting at the moment. Can I take a message, or would you like her to call you back?

L: Well, I'm just phoning because she interviewed me for a job about two weeks ago, and I haven't heard anything yet. She said she'd let me know last Friday whether or not I'd got it.

S: Okay, well, I'll pass on the message and ask her to call you back. Will you be at home all afternoon?

L: I'll be here until about four o'clock, but anyway, you can leave a message on the answerphone.

S: Fine. Can I just take your number, please?

L: Yes, it's 0165 776 3234.

S: Okay then, thanks for calling.

L: Thank you, bye.

S: Bye.

Recording 8

a I'm just phoning because she interviewed me for a job about two weeks ago.

b I'll pass on the message and ask her to call you back.

c You can leave a message on the answerphone.

d Can I just take your number, please?

e Thanks for calling.

Recording 9

T = telephonist   S = Sharon Elliot

T: Good morning, Bank Direct, Gary speaking. How may I help you?

S: Hello, could you put me through to Sharon Elliot, the personal banker, please?

T: Just a moment. ... I'm afraid she's taking a call on the other line. Would you like to hold, or shall I ask her to call you back?

S: Er ... ask her to call me back. I'm at home.

T: Can I ask what it's about?

S: Yes ... I'm expecting a money transfer from the United States. I know it's been sent, but it's still not in my account. I just wondered what's happening.

T: I see. Can I just take your phone number, please?

S: Yes – 993 4567.

T: Okay, fine. I'll pass on the message. She'll call you back soon.

S: Thanks, then. Bye.

Module 6

Recording 1

Speaker 1

Oh, I just get so annoyed by them ... they never answer the questions the interviewer asks them ... they just come out with these little speeches that they've already prepared, whatever the question is. Sometimes I just want to throw something at the TV ... I mean, why can't they just answer a question properly and just say what they mean?

Speaker 2

Generally, I think they're a very good thing. I think some of them have really made a difference to the way people behave ... you know, like these days far fewer people drink and drive. Some of them are very shocking – like when you see pictures of people who've been in car accidents caused by drink-driving. I suppose they have to be shocking to get their message across.

Speaker 3

My girlfriend loves them, but I get bored after a while. There are so many different characters, and if you miss a little bit, then you lose the whole story completely, so I have to keep asking my girlfriend questions to follow the story – which is very annoying for her ... and I never ever understand who the murderer is!

Speaker 4

Well, I think it's a very interesting question whether children really are influenced by what they see on the television. I know some people are very worried about children seeing all that violence, and maybe copying it. Myself, I think children know that there is a difference between reality and fantasy ... they like all the action, but they know it's not real.

Recording 2

1 The Statue of Liberty, which has stood on Liberty Island in New York Island since 1886, was originally designed and built in Paris by two French architects – Frédéric Auguste Bartholdi and Alexandre Gustave Eiffel, designer of the famous Eiffel Tower. It was transported to the United States by ship in 214 cases, and the parts of the statue were then re-assembled in New York.

2 Ice hockey is widely played in the USA, Canada, Russia, Sweden, Finland and Germany. It was first played by an Englishman on the frozen Kingston Harbour in Ontario, Canada in the 1860s.

3 The largest world producers of gold are Canada (6 per cent), Russia (19.2 per cent) and South Africa (48.8 per cent).

4 *Crime and Punishment*, one of Dostoyevsky's greatest works, was written in 1865 and published in 1866. It tells the story of a murder committed by a young man with desperate financial problems, similar to those that the author was suffering at the time.

5 Hindi and English are the official languages of India, but fourteen languages are spoken throughout the country. Many people, however, speak a local language of their own, and there are well over a thousand such languages spoken in various parts of the country.

6 John Lennon was shot dead on December 8th, 1980 by Mark Chapman, just outside the New York apartment building where he lived with his wife, Yoko Ono, and his young son, Sean.

7 It is estimated that an amazing 100 million bicycles are sold in the world each year – three times the number of cars that are sold!

8 Until 1994, the finals of the football World Cup – held every four years – were held alternately in Europe and South America. The pattern was changed in 1994, when the competition was held in the United States. 2002 sees the first World Cup finals to be held in Asia, the tournament being shared between Japan and South Korea.

Recording 4

Ice hockey was first played in Canada.
Half of the world's gold is produced in South Africa.
Crime and Punishment was written by Dostoyevsky.
More than a thousand languages are spoken in India.
John Lennon was assassinated by Mark Chapman.
A hundred million bicycles are sold in the world each year.
The World Cup finals have never been played in Asia.

Recording 5

a   c = Chris   j = June

c: ... and June Adams is here with us in the studio to let us know
     what's happening around town this week. Hi, June.
j: Hi, Chris.
c: Well, what've you got for us?
j: Right, well, a fairly good week this week for music fans, especially if
     you're into jazz. If you do like jazz, you really must try to see the
     legendary American pianist Mo Davison and his band – they're
     appearing at the Jazz Café in Market Street on Thursday. That
     starts at 10pm, tickets £10 in advance or £12 on the night. If you're
     more into heavy metal, well, the American heavy metal kings
     Megablitz, they're in town, and they're playing at the Queen's Hall
     on Friday of this week as part of their European tour. Tickets on
     sale at the Queen's Hall and through the usual ticket agencies –
     don't forget your earplugs if you're going to that one, should be a
     good night out. And finally for club goers there's a new seventies
     soul night at the Sound Club in Prince's Street – sounds good.
c: Yes, that sounds more like my kind of thing.
j: Well, it certainly is more your era, yes!
c: Well, yes, moving on then, anything new at the theatre this week?
j: Yes, indeed, there's a production of a new play by a young Scottish
     playwright, David Gavin, at the Theatre Royal. The play is called
     Dead End – it stars Charles Lovell and it's directed by Peter Moffatt.
     It's about a young art teacher who suddenly finds ...

b
The city – Washington. The year – 2025. America has a new
President. One man plans to kill her. 'The President dies. Tomorrow.'
Only one man can stop him.
'You have 24 hours. Find him. Kill him!'
Rod Saleno is – the Manhunter. At a cinema near you, from Friday.

c   b = Bob Barrett   k = Kerry

b: ... you can have your say with me, Bob Barrett, here at Radio
     South-West, 630 2525, that's the number to call if you want to air
     your views. We're talking about the huge rock concert at the
     weekend. Were you there? What did you think of it? Our first caller
     is Kerry ... Kerry, you're on Radio South-West. What's on your mind?
k: Hello?
b: Hello, Kerry.
k: Well, yes, about the rock concert, I thought it was ...

d
a: ... and I really wasn't convinced by it, the acting ... well, Donald
     Barlow plays the husband, a man who's faced with the choice of
     either remaining loyal to his best friend or attempting to save his
     marriage. If you think that sounds pretty familiar, the whole film is
     pretty much a cliché from start to finish. I found the whole thing
     very predictable ... the characters and the situation really aren't
     very original. The one person I did like was Elizabeth Bell as the
     wife, I thought she gives a very good performance in her first
     major film ... and the photography is good, the film looks lovely ...
     but frankly, I found the whole thing a bit dull. It's directed by Peter
     Weedon, and I'm sure he's capable of better work than this, not his
     best by any means.
b: So, not recommended, then?
a: I'm afraid this isn't one of the films of the year, no.
b: So, moving on to the next ...

Module 7

Recording 1

a   Can you tell me the time, please?
b   Is it okay if I sit here?
c   Do you mind if I borrow your pen for a second?
d   Would you mind looking after my suitcase for a minute?
e   Is it alright if I put the news on just for a few minutes?
f   Could you possibly change this £5 note for me?
g   Do you think you could pass me the water, please?
h   Excuse me, can I get past, please?

Recording 2

a   a: Can you tell me the time, please?
    b: Certainly, it's quarter past three.
b   a: Is it okay if I sit here?
    b: Sorry, but I think someone's sitting there.
c   a: Do you mind if I borrow your pen for a second?
    b: I'm afraid it isn't working. Sorry!
d   a: Would you mind looking after my suitcase for a minute?
    b: Of course not.
e   a: Is it alright if I put the news on just for a few minutes?
    b: Sure, go ahead!
f   a: Could you possibly change this £5 note for me?
    b: I'm afraid I haven't got any change.
g   a: Do you think you could pass me the water, please?
    b: Sure – here you are.
h   a: Excuse me, can I get past, please?
    b: Yes, of course.

Recording 4

i = interviewer   n = Nikam Nipotam

i: So what kind of things would a visitor to Thailand need to know
     about? Are there any social customs that are very different from a
     European country, say?
n: Well, there are a lot of things that are different ... um ... for
     example, the names, the way you address people is different.
i: How is that?
n: Well, you always call people by the first name ... the polite way to
     address people is by their first name.
i: What, even in a formal situation?
n: Yes, you say 'khun' – it's like 'Mr' or 'Miss' ... or 'Mrs'.
i: Oh ... you mean it's the same for men and women?
n: Yes, 'khun' is for men and women, it's the same. You say 'khun' and
     the first name ... and also, when you meet people, you don't shake
     hands usually ... there's a traditional greeting called a 'wai'.
i: A 'wai'? And what's that exactly?
n: Well, you put your hands together, like when you pray, when you
     say a prayer, and you bow your head forward slightly ... and the
     other person does the same. But it's not usually for friends ... you
     don't need to do it ... you just do it for people older than you.
i: I see. And in public are there any things that you find different? Is
     it true that it's not acceptable for a young couple to hold hands in
     public?
n: Well, nowadays some of them do, maybe because of the influence
     of Western society, but it's not so common. I think twenty years
     ago you couldn't do this, you couldn't hold hands in public, and
     even now, a couple kissing in public ... no, you wouldn't see that.
i: Uh uh.
n: Another thing that people might find very different is that the head
     is very important for Thai people – you can't touch another
     person's head. You have to respect people ... and in the same way
     as the head is the most important part, the feet is the lowest part.
     It's very rude to point at anything with your feet ... if you want to
     open a door with your foot, you can't do it!
i: Right. So if someone invites you to their home, is there anything
     you should know about how to behave?

N: Yes, you have to take off your shoes! Don't forget!

I: You have to?

N: You have to ... and if you're invited to eat in someone's home, it's a little bit different. When we eat a meal, we always put the food in the middle, for sharing – you have a big bowl for the rice and everyone helps themselves to the other dishes with a spoon and fork. We don't have salt and pepper, and we have something, and called 'nam pla' on the table ... it's ... er ... fish sauce. It's got a very strong taste, it's typical of Thailand. For me, Thai food is very good, very delicious!

I: Right. Okay ... anything else, any other 'dos', 'don't forgets!' and 'don'ts'?

N: Mm ... let me see ... erm ... maybe one thing you should know is about the royal family, the Thai royal family – it's not the same as in England. In England you can say anything about the royal family, but in Thailand you can't talk about them like that – you always have to show respect.

I: That is very different from England. Well, thank you very much for your help. I'll try to remember everything you've told me!

N: You're welcome.

Recording 5

R = Roger   L = Laurence

R: Hello?

L: Hello, Roger. It's Laurence.

R: Laurence! I haven't heard from you for ages! How are you?

L: Fine. We've just got back from a few days away with some relatives down on the coast. Anyway, how are things with you and Millie?

R: Great ... fine ... everything's fine. We've got all Millie's sisters round for lunch at the moment.

L: Yes, I can hear you're busy! Listen I won't keep you. I was just phoning to ask if you and Millie are doing anything next Saturday night. If not, would you like to come for a meal? Patrick and Colin are coming over, and we thought it would be nice if you were there too.

R: We can't, I'm afraid. An old mate of mine from college is getting married up in Scotland, and we're going up there for the wedding. What a shame! It'd be nice to see you all again.

L: Yeah, it is a shame ... I know, how about the following Saturday instead? I don't think we've got anything planned that night.

R: Yeah, I think that should be fine. I'll check with Millie and call you back if there's any problem, but ... no ... that'd be great!

L: Great, well we'll look forward to seeing you. I'll let you get back to the family now. Give me a ring in a week or so to arrange a time.

R: Okay, then. Thanks for calling. See you!

L: Yeah, see you!

Module 8

Recording 1

a

A: Okay, so you need to press that button ...

B: What, that one?

A: Yeah, the one that says 'announcement' on it, that's it ... and you need to actually hold it down ... hold the button down ...

B: Okay ...

A: ... and then in a second a light flashes, a red light ... and that means it's ready to record ... and you just record your announcement: 'I'm sorry I can't take your call' ... whatever.

B: Okay, sounds easy ... let's have a go then ...

b

A: ... and it just went 'phutt' ... stopped ...

B: Hmm ... let me see ... did you plug it in properly?

A: What?

B: Is it plugged in at the wall.?

A: Well, of course it is! I'm not that stupid!

B: I'll just check. Sometimes you can unplug it by mistake ... when you're moving around ... hmm, looks okay ... try again ... switch it on ... hmm, nothing.

A: That's what I told you.

B: Well, you'll just have to use a brush then. We can't leave the carpet as it is ...

c

Right, have you got the thing you want to send? You put the document in there, like that ... and then you pick up the handset, and you dial the number. Then you wait for the tone ... and when the tone sounds, it's like a continuous beep ... and when you hear that, it means you can send it off, so you press the start button and it just goes through. Okay?

d

A: So it's perfectly simple, you just follow what it says here.

B: Well, you tell me what it says, and I'll do it,

A: Right, so 'Set TV to video channel' – right we've done that.

B: Right.

A: Load a tape. So put a tape in again ... okay ... right ... and now you just ...

B: But look – it's happened again! The tape gets stuck!

A: Hmm ... well, see if you can get the tape out by pressing the 'eject' button ... that's it ...

B: No, it's not working ... it's still stuck ...

Recording 3

I = interviewer   D = Denise

I: So tell me about your shop, Denise. How long have you owned it?

D: Not that long, I've only been here for a couple of years. It's a small art and crafts shop – I live in the flat above it and work in the shop all day ... so it's kind of my whole life really!

I: And what kind of things do you sell?

D: Anything handmade, basically. A lot of the things are imported from abroad – at the moment I've got some ceramics from Greece and Portugal, they're all very modern designs if you look.

I: Yes, they're lovely. Anyway, tell us more about what you sell.

D: Well, ceramics, plates, bowls, ashtrays ... I sell lots of jewellery – earrings, brooches, that kind of thing ... and generally they're made by local artists.

I: Aha.

D: And then I sell a few clothes ... I've got those Japanese hand-printed dressing gowns at the moment.

I: Oh yes ... they're beautiful, aren't they?

D: Handmade cards ... candles ... picture frames ...

I: And what about the shop itself? I mean, are you happy with the premises or would you like to move somewhere else?

D: Yes and no! I mean the location is actually very good – I'm in quite a busy little high street ... there are plenty of other little shops and cafés nearby, and there are loads of students and young people living around here, you know, the kind of people who buy the stuff I sell.

I: Aha.

D: And I've got several friends who live or work in this area, which is actually quite important for me personally, because I work in here on my own most of the time, so it's really great when they pop in for a chat or whatever.

I: So what are the disadvantages then?

D: Well, there's only one really, but it's a very important one – there just isn't enough space. I've got far too many things in this tiny little shop – people are always knocking things over! Ideally I'd love to have enough space for a little café and a cake shop as well.

I: Yes, that'd be great.

D: Then there would be someone else to work here ... and I wouldn't get lonely!

Recording 4

Emma

E = Emma   I = interviewer

I: So, Emma, what would you most like to have in the world?

E: I think what I'd, I'd really like, and I always have, is a motorbike.

I: Uh uh ...

E: Yeah, I used to have one in Greece, but it was a mixture between a moped and a motorbike. It wasn't very powerful.

I: Uh uh.

E: I have an image of a huge powerful black, its got to be black, motorbike ... erm ... the one where you have two seats, one is raised at the back for the passenger ...

I: Right ...

E: ... yeah, and just the idea of packing my bags, grabbing my passport and ...

I: Just go?

E: Just go. Yes.

I: Where would you go?

E: I'd probably travel down to Spain, France, round there. Just ride off into the sunset, not a care in the world.

I: Sounds lovely.

E: Umm ....

Rodney

I've had a mobile phone for about three and a half years now ... erm ... I first got it because my son was about fifteen at the time and was going out a lot. He'd started a social life, sometimes he was out quite late and, as I like to be out myself seeing friends, then I wanted to know that he could always get in touch with me. Perhaps he'd missed the last bus, that kind of thing, and I could go and fetch him. Erm ... at the moment I'm living in a flat where there isn't a telephone and ... erm ... so it's proving very useful until I get one connected. Erm ... I find it very practical, use it with friends, use it to phone my mother ... er ... I like the design. It's a little bit heavy, new telephones tend to be much lighter, but I like it.

David

What I'd really like is a piano ... erm ... I've had one before, but I had to sell it 'cos I didn't have any money at the time and needed some. This time I'd get a grand, a baby grand. I'd put it in the sitting room and it would have to be black so it went with everything else in the room. I'd put some photographs on it, I think, with maybe a small bust of Beethoven, you know, a small statue of Beethoven, because he's one of my favourite composers. I'd really want this piano because it would help me to relax, and it would help me to maybe get rid of any depression I had ... yes, I think that's why I'd want it.

Daphné

D = Daphné   F = friend

F: I like your ring, Daphné.

D: Do you?

F: Umm.

D: It's my engagement ring.

F: I didn't know you were engaged.

D: Umm, I was, well for a short while, when I was eighteen. Got rid of the boyfriend, though, but I kept the ring.

F: It's a really nice ring.

D: Umm, yes it is quite nice. Look see right here it's got a heart on the front.

F: Was it expensive?

D: Well, he said it was expensive, I'm not sure really ... but, I think it's quite sort of old and he said it was antique silver. I don't know, but I always wear it. It reminds me of my teenage years and ... erm ... well sort of makes me feel nostalgic really.

Consolidation Modules 5–8

Recording 1

a   Singer, actor and political activist Harry Belafonte grew up in New York and Jamaica. He made his first album in 1955, but had his greatest success with his third album 'Calypso', which was released in 1959. It was the first album in history to sell a million copies worldwide. He became politically active in the 1960s, and has made several films.

b   Nadia Comaneci was the first Olympic gymnast to be given a perfect score of ten in an Olympic gymnastic competition. She was voted Heroine of the Year by the Press Association. After retiring from gymnastics, she escaped from Romania and has lived in the United States since 1989.

c   Lakia became the first animal in space on board the Russian Sputnik 2, which was launched in November 1957. Sadly, Lakia could not be brought back to Earth, and she died in space about a week after the launch. The Lakia Foundation in Moscow, one of Russia's most important research institutes, is named after her.

Recording 2

a   D = Dave   J = Jane   F = Fran

D: 761 4503.

J: Hi, Dave. It's Jane here.

D: Oh hi, Jane. How are you?

J: I'm fine. Is Fran there?

D: Yeah, just a minute, I'll get her ... Fran ... Jane on the phone!

F: Okay, I'll pick it up in the other room. ... Hi, Jane!

J: Hi ... listen, this is just a real quick one – I've got a little favour to ask. Have you still got your tent by any chance?

F: Yeah, I think so.

J: It's just that we're going camping next weekend, and I've just opened our tent up and discovered it's got a great big hole in it!

F: Oh no ... that's not good!

J: So I was wondering if we could borrow yours if you're not using it.

F: Sure no problem ... oh, hang on, though. You know what, I think I lent it to my sister.

J: Oh, right.

F: Yeah, she borrowed it last summer, I think. I'm sure she's not using it now, though. I'm just wondering how I can get it back from her before next weekend.

J: Maybe I could go round and pick it up?

F: Yeah ... or she might be coming over this way. I tell you what – I'll just phone her and check she's still got it. I'm sure we can sort something out.

J: Oh well, thanks. Don't ask her to come over specially though, will you? I can easily go round there one evening next week.

F: Okay, well I'll tell her that and I'll call you back in a few minutes, alright?

J: Yeah ... speak to you in a bit. Bye.

b   D = dad   B = Becky

B: Dad?

D: Yeah?

B: You know Sam and I are going to France on Sunday?

D: Yeah.

B: Well, I was just wondering ... it's just that we need to be at the station at seven in the morning.

D: Yes.

B: Well, the thing is – Sam's mum was gonna give us a lift down there, you know with all our stuff, but she's going away herself now, so I was just wondering ...

D: You're not asking me to take you, I hope!

B: Well, it would be a real help ... our rucksacks are going to be ever so heavy and it's going to be really hard to get a bus at that time on a Sunday morning.

D: What time will I have to get up, about half past five? And aren't your mum and I going out somewhere on Saturday night, some dinner or something? I don't suppose we'll be in bed before one in the morning ... I can't be up again at five!

B: Oh please, Dad!

D: Why don't you ask your mother? She's always saying she likes getting up early.

B: I have asked her. She said to ask you!

D: Did she? Well, I'll have to think about it ... but I'm not promising anything.

B: Thanks, Dad. I'll go and ring Sam ...

Module 9

Recording 1

Part 1

a Maybe if it was a very good friend, who had a very good reason for borrowing it ... I don't know ... if he or she needed an urgent operation, or something like that.

b I'd never lend a friend a large amount of money, because I think it would almost certainly be the end of the friendship. It's an awful thing to say, but unfortunately I think it's true.

c I haven't got any money – I never have any money, so it's a completely hypothetical question! But, theoretically, I think I'd probably lend money to any friend ... if I thought they really needed it, and if I was sure they could pay it back!

Part 2

a It's not something I can ever imagine doing ... but I don't know ... perhaps if there was some terrible war, or dangerous political situation, I don't know, I don't know what exactly, but if I was worried about my safety, and the safety of my family, maybe I would leave then.

b Possibly if something really tragic happened to me – some terrible accident or crime or something – I might want to leave the country and start a new life somewhere completely different ... you know, to try and forget.

c Mmm ... perhaps if the police were going to arrest me and send me to prison for years and years – that would be a good reason!

Part 3

a I'm not really a violent person normally, but, erm, maybe if I got really, really angry, if I really lost my temper, I might hit someone. I can't really think of any particular examples, but ...

b Well, obviously if I needed to defend myself for some reason ... I don't know, if there was a burglar in my house in the middle of the night ... if I got the opportunity, I might hit them over the head with a vase, or something like that.

c If someone tried to hurt my family, my children, I would definitely hit them, I wouldn't hesitate.

Recording 2

a I probably won't do anything special.

b I'd move to a big house somewhere by the sea.

c I'll probably buy some new jeans.

d I expect I'll just go to the beach and relax.

e I think I'd be the Prime Minister ... it'd be really interesting.

Recording 3

a A: I can't decide what to wear.
  B: Well, hurry up and make up your mind!

b A: Do you think this car's making a funny noise?

B: It sounds okay to me.

c A: So, what do you want me to do?
  B: If I make the dinner, would you mind tidying up a bit?

d A: Have you locked all the doors?
  B: I think so ... I'll just make sure.

e A: Did you like that book I lent you?
  B: Yes – it was brilliant. It really made me laugh.

f A: What a lovely shirt – what's it made of?
  B: I don't know ... I think it's just cotton.

g A: Sorry, but I don't think that's a very good idea.
  B: Well, can you make a better suggestion then?

h A: There's a hole in my T-shirt.
  B: Well, don't put your finger in it, you'll make it worse!

Recording 4

1 President of the St Ambrosian Hotel and Tourism Association

... and as you know, plans were made last year for a new luxury hotel and golf course just outside the capital at Grand Bay. Unfortunately, the Foundation has not been able to get enough money from our foreign investors for the hotel project to continue. I am sorry to say that this project, which is of the greatest importance for all the people of St Ambrosia, will have to be abandoned if we do not receive money from the Lottery Committee. The benefits of the hotel project continuing are obvious. We believe it will bring an extra 50,000 tourists a year to St Ambrosia – think of how this will help the economy of our island, and the hotel will also create hundreds of jobs for local people. I am sure that your committee will approve our application for SA$4 million so that this very impressive project ...

2 President of the St Ambrosian Sports Association

... we have always encouraged all St Ambrosians to play sport, to make the people of our island healthy in mind and body. But because there are no modern sports facilities on the island, our national athletics and football teams have to train in the public park, and our young people must play sport in the street, and so cannot learn and develop as they should. For SA$6 million, we could build a National Sports Centre for all St Ambrosians, young and old. The Sports Centre would provide a social centre for our island, especially for young people, who often have nothing to do. Our dream is, one day, to send a team to the Olympic Games to represent St Ambrosia. The National Sports Centre is a necessary part of that dream. Please, help the dream become a reality.

3 Vice-Chancellor of the University of St Ambrosia

... we all know that, because of the poor facilities at the University, St Ambrosia is losing its best and most intelligent young people, who are choosing to study abroad, and not returning to the island when they have completed their studies. The young people of this island, the young people who will go on to become engineers, doctors, lawyers, teachers, must have the best possible education here in St Ambrosia, not in some other country. Without education, there is no future for us. We desperately need new equipment in our Computer Science and Technology department. For SA$4.5 million, we could make the necessary improvements to make sure that young St Ambrosians no longer have to go abroad ...

4 Director of the St Ambrosian Children's Hospital

... my message to you is a very simple one. Our hospital, which helps the very poorest children of St Ambrosia, needs money for beds and medical equipment. We cannot continue without your help. We need SA$3.5 million to stay open for another year, and to care for the sick children of our island. Without us, many of these children will have no one to help them. If you care at all about the poor children of St Ambrosia, you must help us.

5 Chief-executive of International Petroleum Incorporated

This is really a simple business proposition. We believe there is a possibility, a good possibility perhaps, that there are large oil deposits under the sea off the north coast of St Ambrosia. Obviously, looking for the oil will take several years, and there is a risk that we will find nothing. Therefore, we feel it is reasonable that the government of St

Tapescripts

Ambrosia shares this risk with International Petroleum Incorporated. SA$8 million seems a small amount if we consider that if we find oil – and I repeat if we find oil – St Ambrosia could become one of the richest islands in the world.

Recording 5

seventy-one per cent
twenty-six thousand
four hundred and eighty-three thousand and eighty square metres
five point seven billion
fifty-five million six hundred and eighty thousand kilometres
three hundred thousand kilometres a second
one hundred and ninety-nine thousand, eight hundred and fifty-nine
ninety-nine point nine, nine, nine, nine per cent
eighty-six million
minus eighty-nine degrees celcius

Recording 6

a   The estimated population of the world in mid-1995 was 5.7 billion.
b   The lowest temperature ever recorded, in Vostok, Antarctica, was −89°C
c   The proportion of the world's surface which is covered in water is 71 per cent.
d   The closest distance between Earth and the planet Mars is 55,680,000 kilometres.
e   The largest crowd ever for a sporting event was 199,859 – at the World Cup Final between Brazil and Uruguay in 1950.
f   The speed of light is 300,000 kilometres a second.
g   There are about 86 million babies born in the world every year.
h   The area of the world's largest shopping mall, in Alberta, Canada is 483,080 square metres.
i   99.999 per cent of the population voted for the Communist party in the elections in Albania in 1982.
j   The average American child has seen 26,000 murders on television by the time he is eighteen years old.

Recording 7

Picture 1

P = passenger   T = taxi driver

P: Taxi! ... Hello, I'd like to go to Onslow Gardens in Kensington, please.
T: Right you are.
P: How much will it cost roughly?
T: Kensington ... I should think that'll be about £7 or £8 from here ... shouldn't be more than eight.
P: Okay, you can stop here – just here on the left. ... How much do I owe you?
T: That's £7.30, please.
P: Right, here you are ... it's okay, you can keep the change.
T: Oh right. Thank you very much.
P: Thank you. Bye!

Picture 2

C = customer   F = friend   S = stall holder

C: Now there's the sort of thing I'm looking for. Look at these ... what do you think?
F: Mmm ... well ...
C: Oh, don't you like them? I think they'd look really good on. Excuse me ... excuse me ... how much do you want for these?
S: Those are £12.50.
C: £12.50? Oh ... I don't know ... what do you think?
F: Well, I prefer these ones.
C: Do you? Well ... they are both nice, aren't they? How much are these, please?
S: Same as the others – £12.50.
C: Mmm ...

S: Tell you what I'll do – you can have them both for £20 – how's that?
C: Well ... I'll give you £18 for both of them.
S: No, sorry, £20, I can't really go any lower than that ...

Picture 3

M = mother   S = son   T = ticket seller

M: Excuse me, how much is the entrance? How much are the tickets?
T: It's £5.50 for adults.
M: £5.50 ... okay ... tell me, is there a reduction for students? My son is a full-time student, you see.
T: Yes, it's £2.75 for full-time students with a student identity card ... and it's free for children under twelve.
M: Okay. Right. Have you got your student card with you, Christopher? I told you to bring it.
S: Yes, Mum. It's here.
M: Right, so that's two adults, one student. Here's the card – oh, my daughter's ten so she goes free.
T: That'll be £13.75 altogether, please. Thank you. And £1.25 change ... thank you.
A: Thanks. Right, come on then, let's see what ...

Picture 4

S = sales assistant   C = customer

S: Right, and how would you like to pay, sir?
C: I'd like to pay by credit card, please.
S: That's fine. If I can just take your card ... right, if you'd just like to sign there, please, on the line.
C: Okay.
S: There's your card ... and your receipt. Thank you very much.
C: Thank you.

Module 10

Recording 1

The man had been out fishing and had caught an unusually large fish. He was so excited that he had phoned his wife to tell her all about it. Unfortunately, as he was describing the fish, he'd flung out his arms to demonstrate how large it was, and had smashed through the glass on either side of the phone box, cutting both of his wrists. As a result, tragically, he'd bled to death.

Recording 2

M = Michael   W = woman   S = secretary
M: Can I speak to Mr Bell ?
W: I'm sorry, but I've only just started working here, and I don't know who Mr Bell is. Can you ring back later when my boss, Mr Findlater, is here?
M: Yes, I will. Is Mr Findlater's first name Harry?
W: Yes, it is.
M: Have you ever noticed a tattoo on the back of Mr Findlater's hand?
W: Yes, I have – a tattoo of an owl.

M: Who gave you my brother's number?
S: It's not a phone number; it's a bank account number for Mr Bell, one of our customers.

Recording 3

The police were desperate to catch the gang and started to question the three men who had been in the bank at the time of the robbery. The crime had been so easy to commit that it seemed to suggest inside help, but they didn't know exactly who to suspect. Meanwhile, business continued as usual. Latif worked day and night, dealing with furious clients who had lost so much. Eventually the police found an important clue: one clear fingerprint on the broken security boxes. Would this help them find the robbers? The British files revealed nothing, but after contacting their colleagues in Interpol, the Italian police soon confirmed that the fingerprint belonged to Valerio Viccei, a well-known bank robber.

The police began to follow anyone who might be associated with Viccei. They noticed that these people often met at the same London hotel – Whites. A black Ferrari was often parked there too, and the police knew of Viccei's love for expensive cars. They watched the hotel day and night, convinced that there was some connection with Viccei.

For several weeks nothing happened. Then, suddenly, Viccei was recognised getting into the Ferrari. The police followed, waiting for their chance. Finally, the Ferrari stopped at some traffic lights, and quickly one of the policemen reached in through the window and tried to grab the ignition key. He was dragged nearly twenty metres before another policeman jumped onto the car and broke the window. Viccei was finally arrested, but when the police searched his flat, they could find nothing to connect Viccei with any of the staff at 'Security Deposits'. They began to check through every phone call Viccei had made in the previous few months, and there, finally, was their evidence – a call to Parvez Latif, the owner of 'Security Deposits'! Latif was arrested and charged. He and his girlfriend, as well as Viccei and his gang, were all eventually tried at the Old Bailey, the most important court in Britain. Viccei was sentenced to twenty-two years, Latif to eighteen. But they could so easily have escaped. Viccei had planned to hide in Columbia with his money, and if he had got away, the police would never have found Latif. However, there had been difficulties arranging the papers needed to export his new car, and Viccei refused to leave without his beloved Ferrari!

Recording 4

The Waratah Omen

Claude Sawyer awoke suddenly from his dream, screaming with panic. He had had the nightmare almost every night since his ship had left Melbourne, three weeks before. The dream was always the same. It was a calm night at sea. He was standing at the ship's rail, looking out at the waves. As he watched, the surface of the sea slowly parted, and out of it rose the figure of a medieval knight, his armour covered with blood. The knight raised his sword and silently mouthed one word: 'Waratah!'

After lying terrified for a few minutes, Sawyer gradually calmed down, but he promised himself that when the ship arrived in Durban a few days later, he would leave and look for another to take him the rest of the way.

It was October 1909, and Sawyer was an engineer on his way from Melbourne in Australia to London, via Durban in South Africa. He was an experienced traveller and had made the same journey several times before, without any such worries. And this time he was travelling on a new ship, launched only a year before in Scotland: her name was the Waratah.

Claude Sawyer told the story of his dream to several of his fellow passengers, but most of them smiled silently to themselves, thinking that he was probably some kind of harmless madman. Nevertheless, when the ship arrived in Durban, Sawyer did as he promised himself. He left the ship, and telegrammed his wife to say that he was going to wait for the next ship to continue his journey.

The Waratah left Durban the next evening, but Claude Sawyer's nightmares did not stop. The very next night, his dream was even more horrific than the ones before: he dreamt that the Waratah was being covered by enormous waves. As he watched, the waves seemed to press her down, and she rolled over and gradually disappeared under the sea.

Sawyer felt that he must do something. The next day, he rushed to the offices of the Union Castle Shipping Line, and told them the full story of his terrifying dreams. The clerk there listened politely and made a careful note of everything he said, but, secretly, he didn't take it too seriously.

Meanwhile, the Waratah was continuing on the next part of her journey towards Cape Town, 600 miles away. Two ships reported seeing the liner on the evening that she left Durban, but on 29th October, the day she was due to arrive in Cape Town, she didn't

appear.

At first no one was very worried: very few ships carried radios in those days, and there were many delays due to bad weather. However, as the days passed, officials at the shipping line became more concerned, and various ships were sent out to look for the Waratah and her 200 passengers.

However, although they searched carefully, nothing was found. Finally, almost a year and a half after the ship disappeared, an official investigation was started, and in February 1911 it was declared that the Waratah had 'capsized in an exceptional gale'. But no evidence had ever actually been found.

All this happened nearly a hundred years ago now, and since then, several people have claimed that they have seen the Waratah: in particular, in 1952, a South African Air Force pilot reported seeing a ship lying on the ocean bed in clear water. However, when the area was searched, once more nothing was found. And so the mystery remains unsolved to this day. What really happened to the Waratah that night in October 1909? And even more extraordinary, what is the explanation for Claude Sawyer's terrible dreams and the strange prophecy they contained? Most probably we shall never know.

Module 11

Recording 1

a Normally you can borrow about four or five books.
b You can't walk around during take-off or landing.
c You must always behave with respect.
d You mustn't jump on and off when it's moving.
e You should give a tip of about ten per cent.
f You shouldn't leave anything valuable in your room.
g You have to leave your room by midday on your last day.
h You don't have to pay for the books you borrow.
i You're allowed to keep the books for about three weeks.
j You're not allowed to smoke in the toilets.

Recording 2

(missing words only)
a weren't allowed to; had to
b couldn't; had to
c weren't allowed to
d couldn't; were allowed to
e weren't allowed to; couldn't; had to; had to

Recording 3

Joan

I = interviewer   J = Joan

I: So do you think your schooldays were very different from children's today then, Joan?
J: Well, of course from the age of seven to twelve I went to a convent school in Belgium, so that was completely different.
I: In Belgium? Really? How come?
J: It was my father's idea. One of his friends was sending his daughter, and my father wanted to impress his friend so he decided to send me too. It was all snobbery really.
I: Fancy sending your seven-year-old daughter all the way to Belgium just to impress one of your friends. It's hard to believe!
J: I know.
I: So what was it like? Was it very strict?
J: Oh, terribly!
I: What sort of thing?
J: Well, a lot of the things were religious, you know. We had to get up early and go to church before lessons.
I: Uh uh ...
J: And at mealtimes we weren't allowed to talk ... we just had to sit silently with our hands folded in our laps.
I: Really?

J: And I wasn't allowed to speak English at all – if you couldn't speak French you ... well, I mean you just had to learn ... nobody taught me ... I just had to sit in the lessons and try to understand. I was so lonely the first year – it was terrible!

I: Yes ... it's awful ... for a child of seven!

J: And they were terribly strict about manners! I suppose that was one good thing. I had the most beautiful manners when I left, everyone used to think I was the most perfectly behaved child!

Gareth

I = interviewer   G = Gareth

I: So, Gareth, you've been at your school for about three years now.

G: Yeah, that's right.

I: And would you describe your school as strict or fairly relaxed?

G: No, not really strict ... not compared to what grandma was saying. Then it was really strict, but nowadays I think there aren't nearly so many rules. I think children are treated much more fairly. They have a lot more rights.

I: So are there any rules you have to follow, things you really have to do?

G: Well, you have to wear school uniform – you know the school jumper, shirt and trousers ... you have to do that ... and you're supposed to wear what they call 'proper shoes' – which means not trainers.

I: You're supposed to?

G: I mean the rule is that you mustn't wear trainers, but in fact everyone does ... well, not everyone, but a lot of people do, and the teachers never do anything. I think it's a bit stupid actually. I'd prefer it if we didn't have to wear uniform.

I: Are there any other things you mustn't do?

G: Well, obviously there are certain things – you're not allowed to go into the teachers' room without permission, and you're not allowed to go into certain places with dangerous equipment like the chemistry lab.

I: So what happens if you break the rules?

G: Well it depends really. If it was something not very serious, like not wearing a tie, they just tell you a couple of times and after that you might get a detention, you know – stay at school after class. If it's something really serious, they give you a warning, and you're given first a yellow report and, if it's really, really serious, you get a red warning.

I: Bit like football, really?

G: Yeah, except that I've never known anyone actually get a red warning ... it doesn't happen really.

Recording 4

1 Who usually does the shopping in your house?
2 Who usually does the washing up?
3 How often do you do the ironing?
4 How often do you do an exercise class?
5 Do you have to do military service in your country?
6 How many years do people normally do at university in your country?
7 Are you planning to do any studying tonight?
8 Do you usually do your homework with the radio on or off?
9 Did you do any languages at primary school?
10 What about at secondary school?
11 When did you last do an exam?
12 Do you usually do well in exams or badly?

Recording 6

a Actually, I think men are often better cooks than women.
b I personally believe that you should never hit children.
c In my opinion, all forms of gambling should be banned!
d I really believe that men are better drivers than women – it's just a fact!
e If you ask me, the government needs to spend a lot more money on schools and hospitals, and less money on things like building roads.
f I think teachers should earn more money – they do a very difficult job!

Recording 7

a A: Actually, I think men are often better cooks than women.
   B: Mmm ... I'm not really sure ... I suppose a lot of famous chefs are men ... but then think of all the men who can't cook at all!

b A: I personally believe that you should never hit children.
   B: Yes, I agree in theory ... completely ... sometimes it can be difficult though. If you lose your temper, ...

c A: In my opinion, all forms of gambling should be banned!
   B: Mmm ... I don't really agree. I think if people want to spend their money like that, it's up to them really.

d A: I really believe that men are better drivers than women – it's just a fact!
   B: What! That's absolute rubbish! Men are the ones who drive too fast and cause all the accidents. No, I'm sorry, I completely disagree with you about that!

e A: If you ask me, the government needs to spend a lot more money on schools and hospitals, and less money on things like building roads.
   B: Yes, but where's the money going to come from? More taxes, higher this ...

f A: I think teachers should earn more money – they do a very difficult job!
   B: Yes, you're absolutely right! Their salaries should be doubled at least!

Module 12

Recording 1

a They should have taken more water.
b They shouldn't have gone without a good map.
c They could have built a fire and waited.
d I wouldn't have moved out of the volcano – he could have fallen again.
e They were lucky, both of them could have died.
f Personally, I'd never have gone on a trip like that.

Recording 2

Luke

I = interviewer   L = Luke

I: Luke, you made a big decision four or five years ago – what was it?

L: Yeah ... basically, I gave up my business studies course, and decided to try acting as a career instead.

I: Uh uh ... so how did it all happen?

L: I'd completed about two years of my university course ... I'd done pretty well in all my exams and everything, and I was planning a career as a manager in some kind of big company. I think I had a fairly good chance of doing it ... anyway, it was during the summer holidays ... it's quite hard to describe really ... I suddenly had this terrible depressed feeling that I just didn't want to do this ... it was almost as if I panicked ... and, anyway, I wrote to my college and said that I wasn't going back.

I: What did your parents think?

L: Oh, I think they were probably horrified, but they didn't actually say anything ... they were very good, I suppose. They just said it was my life and I had to make up my own mind.

I: So what did you do?

L: Well, I didn't do anything much for a while, then I travelled for a bit in India and the Far East, with some money I'd inherited, and while I was there ... obviously I thought a lot about what I was going to do with my life, and in the end I decided that I just had to try acting as a career ... it had always been something that I loved doing, and I wanted to find out if I was good enough to do it professionally.

I: Uh uh ...

L: So I applied to drama school, and luckily they accepted me.

I: You finished that course a couple of years ago – have you been able to find work as an actor since then?

L: Yeah ... to some extent ... I get some bits of work, but I'm certainly not rich and famous yet. I also spend a lot of time working in bars or restaurants ... you know temporary jobs, when I haven't got any acting work.

I: And do you ever regret the decision you made?

L: Oh no – never, never.

I: Why not?

L: Well I ...

Sandra

I = interviewer   S = Sandra

I: Sandra, you've made a different sort of decision – you've given up a very successful career to become a full-time mother. Can you tell us about that?

S: Yes ... it all happened about twelve months ago, when I had my second baby. I was going back to work, you know, six months after the baby was born, and I slowly began to realise that I simply couldn't do it ... do my job properly and be a good mother of two children. I thought about it for weeks and weeks, and talked it over with my husband ... and in the end I decided to resign.

I: Tell us a bit more about your job. Why did you feel it was so difficult to do it and to bring up children at the same time?

S: Well, I was director of a large travel company, so it was a very, very pressurised job, and to do it properly I obviously needed to travel myself a lot ... and of course the hours were very long ... and I just realised I didn't want to be away from my children that much ... I didn't want to leave them with somebody else all the time and just see them for half an hour at bed-time.

I: It must have been a very difficult decision, though. I mean it was a very good job ... well-paid, glamorous, lots of travelling ...

S: Yes ... before the children were born, I loved all that ... you know, one week I was in India, and the next week I was in South America ... it was wonderful. But I think the most difficult thing was that I'd just worked so hard to get that position – you know, I became a director at the age of thirty, which was the result of a lot of work, I mean, you can't imagine ...

I: No, I'm sure. Do you think you'll be able to go back to your job one day?

S: No, I can't really imagine it. The travel business will have changed too much, and I think I'll have changed too much, too ... but who knows what the future will be like. I never thought I'd be perfectly happy to spend all day at home with a one-year-old and a three-year-old ... but here I am!

Recording 3

(missing words only)

Luke

a 'd done; would have made; wouldn't have met

b 'd have stayed; hadn't decided

Sandra

c 'd stayed; would have suffered   d was; wouldn't be; would really miss   e 'd be; hadn't left

Consolidation Modules 9–12

Recording 1

1 Well, of course, looking back it's all too easy to see the mistakes you made. At the time it seemed like a great idea – the city's first Brazilian music club, fantastic ... and we thought: 'Yeah, let's go for it!' So Dino – that's my ex-partner, my ex-business partner – we borrowed money from the bank ... too much really, I think I borrowed far too much money, we owed so much, you know were always in debt, I couldn't pay the staff some weeks ... never mind

myself. And, well, after we opened we didn't get as many people in the club as we'd hoped. The place was empty a lot of nights, the atmosphere wasn't right, and the club just didn't take off ... and of course it didn't help when my dear friend Dino disappeared one day with most of what money we did have ... and we never saw him again! So we had all kinds of problems, really. We closed about six months later, and I lost everything – my house, everything! So here I am, still looking for a job ... you know ... but maybe if I'd thought about it a bit more, ...

2 Tennis now, and Florida-born teenager Patsy Kapinski has reached the final of her first major pro-tournament, the Australian Open Championships, by beating South African Lotte de Kuyper 6-1, 6-1 in the semi final. It's Kapinski's first season on the pro-circuit, and she'll be the youngest player ever to play in the finals of the Australian Open. Victory in the final would bring Ms Kapinski approximately $800,000 in prize money. The beaten finalist will receive approximately $200,000. In the final, she is due to play fellow American Carine Mendel, the number one seed, who beat the French woman Beatrice Garros 6-4, 4-6, 6-2 in the other semi-final. Mendel has already played Kapinski twice this season, winning both matches comfortably. If Kapinski wins this final, ...

3 I find it so hard to imagine, really ... I'm the kind of person who likes to be outside, you know, to be active. Here, where I live now, I have the beach very close, I can go to the beach every day, I can see my friends there, go swimming – you know, it's very nice, very sociable. But I think in Britain you can't do this, I think maybe you don't have the beaches like we have in my country, people live in another way, the weather is cloudy, often raining ... I suppose, I don't know, but I can imagine. Also, someone like me, I'm the kind of person really I need the sun every day. I really miss the sunshine, the warm weather ... I don't like dark, winter ... and of course, all of my friends are here. My friends are very important to me. Maybe I could find new friends, I don't know. I think if I lived in Britain, ...

Recording 2

a Personally, I think *(bleep)* is better in every possible way than *(bleep)*. I mean, who wants to walk around looking at cows and sheep all day? It's okay for a few hours, a weekend possibly, but that's enough. Basically, life in the country is completely boring – I'd die of boredom in a week if I had to live in the countryside. In the city there's always something to do, somewhere to go – bars or theatres or whatever. It's interesting just walking around seeing all the different types of people and you can get lost in the crowd. No one worries about who you are and what you are doing. In the countryside everyone wants to know what you're doing and where you're going. People are far too nosy, they don't have enough to think about ...

b I don't think *(bleep)* should be allowed anywhere in public, not in offices, not in shops, not in restaurants, not even in the street. If people want to indulge in this disgusting habit, then they should do it in the privacy of their own home and absolutely nowhere else. Why should they pollute the air that I and my children breathe? Why should I risk my health by breathing in their disgusting smoke? I shouldn't have to tolerate it even on the other side of a restaurant. Personally, I don't think the rest of the public should have to pay for smokers' bad habits. I mean why should we have to pay for them to be looked after in hospital, when it's their own disgusting habit that has made them ill? I think they should be strung up ...

c My dream is to work with horses again, so that would definitely be *(bleep)*. I used to be in the army and my job was to look after horses, training them mostly and giving riding lessons to other people. I've always been really keen on horses ever since I was a kid, so yes, ideally I'd buy a house in the country with some land and get some horses, and maybe open a riding school, or else look after other people's horses for them, you know, train them. The problem is that it would need a lot more money than I've got at the moment ... still maybe one day. You can always dream, can't you?

Addison Wesley Longman Limited
Edinburgh Gate, Harlow
Essex CM20 2JE, England
and Associated Companies throughout the world

First published 1998

Set in 9/12.5pt ITC Stone Informal
and 10/13pt Congress Sans

Printed in Spain by Mateu Cromo, S.A. Pinto (Madrid)

ISBN 0582 302072

Author acknowledgements

We would like to thank the following people for their help
and contribution: Helen Barker, Rodney Blakestone, David
Carr, Anna Groome, Martin Johnson, Tim Perry, Daphné
Vallas, Emma Walton, Caroline Zyc; in addition all the
teachers and students at International House, London for
their inspiration, and in particular Suzanna Harsányi
(Editorial Director), Lizzie Warren (Senior Publisher),
Frances Woodward (Senior Development Editor), and
Liz Smith (Senior Designer) for their invaluable input,
support and encouragement.

The publishers and authors are very grateful to the
following people and institutions for piloting and/or
reporting on the manuscript:
Raffaela Bergonzi, Sally Burgess, Daniela Burtet, John Clark,
Sarah Ellis, Barbara Garside, Fiorenza Gorian, Jane Hudson,
Cathy Mitchell, Jacky Newbrook, Jane Willis; Julia Adamson,
British Institute, Florence; Anna Bogobovich, Stefan Batory
High School, Warsaw; Casa Branca School, Santos; Tom
Bradbury, London School of English; Margaret Curtis, EOI
Alcorcon, Madrid; Sonia Cury, Centro Britânico, São Paulo;
David Folkers, The Lincoln Centre, Madrid; Caroline Hollway,
Eurocentre, Cambridge; Mark Jones, Hilderstone College,
Broadstairs; Anna Kolbuszweska, Intersection, Poznan;
David Maule , Stevenson College, Edinburgh; Anne McKee,
Chambre de Commerce, Pontoise; Barbara Morris,
Fontainebleau Langues et Communication; Will Moreton,
Chester Formacion, Madrid; John Poole, Language Forum,
Courbevoie; Augusta Rabinovich, BAE Centre, Buenos Aires;
Marta Rosinta/Magdalena Woszczynsta, British Council
Studium, Lodz.

We are grateful to the following for permission to reproduce
copyright material:

Carlton Books for adapted extracts from *Fantastic Facts* by
John May; Headline Book Publishing Ltd for an adapted
extract from *The Lucky Generation* by William Davis
(Headline, 1996); News International Syndication for the
article 'Job Creation' from *The Times* 16.7.97 © Times
Newspapers Ltd, 1996; the author's agent on behalf of the
author for adaptations of 'The Most Unsuccessful Prison
Escape' and 'The Worst Tourist' from *The Book of Heroic
Failures* by Stephen Pile. Copyright © Stephen Pile 1979;
Reuters Ltd for the extracts 'Monsoon Flooding Kills 200' in
The Times 17.7.96 and 'Preacher, 136, meets his maker' in
The Times 22.7.96; Solo Syndication Ltd for the extracts
'Love-lorn man begs Tiger to eat him' in *The Evening
Standard* 6.8.96, 'Thunder saves girl from crash' in *The
Evening Standard* 12.8.96, and 'One Sneeze and You'll die!'
in *The Evening Standard* 2.8.96.

We have unfortunately been unable to trace the copyright
holder of *Encounters with the Unknown* and would
appreciate any information which would enable us to do so.

Illustrated by: David Atkinson, Melanie Barnes,
Kathy Baxendale, Stanley Chow (The London Art Collection),
Mickey Finn (The Organisation), Kevin Jones Associates,
Renee Mansfield and Sandy Nichols (3 in-a-box),
Ian Mitchell, Michael Ogden, Stuart Robertson (The Inkshed),
Peter Richardson, Nicky Taylor, Ron Tiner.

Photo acknowledgements

We are grateful to the following for permission to reproduce
copyright photographs:

AWL/Gareth Boden for 6, 12 top right, 12 bottom left, 12
bottom right, 44 top, 44 bottom, 44 left, 50, 52 top, 52
centre top, 52 centre bottom, 80 centre top, 84 bottom
centre, 99 top, 114 top, 123 top and 123 bottom;
AWL/Digital Vision for 26; AWL/Maggy Milner for 84 top left,
84 top centre left, 84 bottom centre left, 84 bottom left, 98,
99 bottom left and 99 bottom right; AWL for 80 centre
bottom; Bruce Coleman Ltd for 81 bottom (Jane Burton) and
81 centre top (Kim Taylor); Colorific for 42/43 centre, 43 top
middle (Alon Reininger) and 117 centre bottom (Alon
Reininger/Contact); Getty Images for 7 bottom (Timothy
Shonnard), 15 (James Darell), 29 top (Marc Dolphin), 29
bottom (Gavin Hellier), 31 top (Robert Frerck), 31 bottom
(Hugh Sitton), 33 top left (Oliver Benn), 33 top right (Paul
McKelvey), 33 bottom (Paul Harris), 40 (Gerard Loucel), 52
bottom (Kevin Horan), 53 (Bruce Ayres), 55 centre left (Ken
Fisher), 55 centre right (Dale Durfee), 63 top right (David
Madison), 64 bottom left (Christopher Bissell), 74 bottom
right (Ed Pritchard), 80 top (Greg Pease), 84 top right, 84
centre top right (Laurance Monneret), 84 centre bottom right
(Joe Polollio), 84 bottom (Frank Orel), 104 left (Andrew
Sacks), 114 bottom right (Paul Rees) and cover (Brett
Baunton); Ronald Grant Archive for 64 bottom right and 89
top (Richi Howell); Robert Harding Picture Library for 63 left
and 76 top; Hulton Getty for 20 right, 21, 80 bottom and 81
top; Images Colour Library for 63 bottom right and 78;
Panos Pictures/Morris Carpenter for 117 centre top;
Performing Arts Library/Henrietta Butler for 64 top left;
Pictor International for 7 top, 31 centre, 74 top left, 75 and
117 top; Popperfoto for 43 right and 89 centre; Retna/Steve
Double for 42 top left; Rex Features for 42 top centre, 42 top
right, 42 bottom left (Moryan), 43 top left, 43 bottom left
(Tim Rookt), 96, 104 top left and 104 top right; San Diego
Childrens Hospital for 36; Superstock for 9 top, 9 bottom, 12
top left, 20 left, 55 top, 55 top centre, 55 bottom and 64 top
right; Sygma for 42 bottom right and 89 bottom (Keystone);
Telegraph Colour Library for 45 (Masterfile), 56 (Robert
Brimson), 74 top right (FPG/R Gage), 74 bottom left (B.
Tanaka), 76 bottom (FPG/Barbara Peacock), 114 bottom left
(FPG/J Whitmer) and 117 bottom (Bavaria-Bildagentur).